Communications in Computer and Information Science **1144**

Commenced Publication in 2007
Founding and Former Series Editors:
Phoebe Chen, Alfredo Cuzzocrea, Xiaoyong Du, Orhun Kara, Ting Liu,
Krishna M. Sivalingam, Dominik Ślęzak, Takashi Washio, Xiaokang Yang,
and Junsong Yuan

More information about this series at http://www.springer.com/series/7899

Chawki Djeddi · Akhtar Jamil ·
Imran Siddiqi (Eds.)

Pattern Recognition and Artificial Intelligence

Third Mediterranean Conference, MedPRAI 2019
Istanbul, Turkey, December 22–23, 2019
Proceedings

 Springer

Editors
Chawki Djeddi ⓘ
Larbi Tebessi University
Tebessa, Algeria

Akhtar Jamil
Istanbul Sabahattin Zaim University
Istanbul, Turkey

Imran Siddiqi
Bahria University
Islamabad, Pakistan

ISSN 1865-0929   ISSN 1865-0937   (electronic)
Communications in Computer and Information Science
ISBN 978-3-030-37547-8   ISBN 978-3-030-37548-5   (eBook)
https://doi.org/10.1007/978-3-030-37548-5

This Springer imprint is published by the registered company Springer Nature Switzerland AG
The registered company address is: Gewerbestrasse 11, 6330 Cham, Switzerland

Preface

It gives us immense pleasure to introduce this volume of proceedings for The Third Mediterranean Conference on Pattern Recognition and Artificial Intelligence (MedPRAI 2019). The conference is organized by the Department of Computer Engineering, Istanbul Sabahattin Zaim University, Istanbul, Turkey, during December 22–23, 2019. The conference aims to provide an interdisciplinary forum for discussions on recent advancements in different areas of pattern recognition and artificial intelligence.

We are pleased to share that the response to the Call for Papers for MedPRAI 2019 was very encouraging. A total of 63 papers covering different themes in pattern recognition and artificial intelligence were submitted to the conference. Among these, 54 papers qualified for the peer review process and were reviewed by renowned researchers in the respective fields from all over the world. After a thorough and competitive paper review and selection process, 19 high quality papers were accepted for presentation at the conference yielding an acceptance rate of 35%. This volume is comprised of 16 papers which eventually qualified for presentation in the conference.

We would like to take this opportunity to thank the reviewers for their time and efforts in reviewing the papers and providing constructive feedback to the authors. We are also thankful to the keynote speakers, the authors, and the participants of the conference. We would also like to extend our cordial appreciation to all members of the Organizing Committees for their untiring efforts in making this event a success.

We thank all the attendees for participation in the conference and hope that the event provided valuable knowledge sharing and networking opportunities.

November 2019

Chawki Djeddi
Akhtar Jamil
Imran Siddiqi

Organization

General Chairs

Ismail Kucuk	Istanbul Sabahattin Zaim University, Turkey
Akhtar Jamil	Istanbul Sabahattin Zaim University, Turkey

Program Chairs

Imran Siddiqi	Bahria University, Pakistan
Chawki Djeddi	Larbi Tebessi University, Algeria

Steering Committee

Javad Sadri	Concordia University, Canada
Mohammed El Youssfi El Kettani	Ibn Tofail University, Morocco
Arcangelo Castiglione	University of Salerno, Italy
Chang Choi	Chosun University, South Korea
Zeeshan Bhatti	University of Sindh, Pakistan

Publicity Committee

Moises Diaz	Universidad de Las Palmas de Gran Canaria, Spain
Mohamed Ben Halima	University of Sfax, Tunisia
Mustafa Ali Abuzaraida	University of Utara Malaysia, Malaysia

Publication Chairs

Haoxiang Wang	Cornell University, USA
Fernand Cohen	Drexel University, USA

Sponsors and Exhibitions Chairs

Amani Yahiaoui	Istanbul Sabahattin Zaim University, Turkey
Kevser Nur Cogalmis	Istanbul Sabahattin Zaim University, Turkey

Invited Speakers Chair

Akhtar Jamil	Istanbul Sabahattin Zaim University, Turkey

Web Chair

Chawki Djeddi   Larbi Tebessi University, Algeria

Registration Committee

Aydın Tarık Zengin   Istanbul Sabahattin Zaim University, Turkey
Ahmed Sheikh Abdullahi   Istanbul Sabahattin Zaim University, Turkey
  Madey
Jawad Rasheed   Istanbul Sabahattin Zaim University, Turkey

Local Arrangements Committee

Alaa Hameed   Istanbul Sabahattin Zaim University, Turkey
Ayşenur Gençdoğmuş   Istanbul Sabahattin Zaim University, Turkey
Sahra Tilki   Istanbul Sabahattin Zaim University, Turkey
Hasibe Büşra Doğru   Istanbul Sabahattin Zaim University, Turkey

Technical Program Committee

Abbas Cheddad
Abdelhakim Hannousse
Abdeljalil Gattal
Abdelmalek Metrouh
Akthar Jamil
Ameur Bensefia
Arzucan Ozgur
Babahenini Mohamed Chaouki
Bart Lamiroy
Bennour Akram
Cemal Okan Sakar
Chawki Djeddi
Chayan Halder
Faisal Shafait
Francesco Fontanella
Georgios Louloudis
Gokhan Bilgin
Hammad Afzal
Hassiba Nemmour
Imran Siddiqi
Javad Sadri
Jean-Marc Ogier
Jocelyn Chanussot
Josep Llados
Khurram Khurshid
Laimeche Lakhdar
M. Erdem İsenkul
Malek Mouhoub
Mekhaznia Tahar
Menassel Rafik
Meraoumia Abdallah
Mohamed El Bachir Menai
Momina Moetesum
Muhammad Shehzad Hanif
Muhammad Usman Akram
Muhammed Cinsdikici
Murat Gezer
Mustafa Dagtekin
Nabin Sharma
Najoua Essoukri Ben Amara
Nicolas Sidère
Nicole Vincent
Nikolaos Stamatopoulos
Oğuz Altun Altun
Paulo Batista
Pinar Kirci

Rachid Hedjam
Ranju Mandal
Said Ghoul
Sankar Pal
Selcuk Sevgen
Sibel Senan
Somaya Al-Maadeed

Tolga Berber
Toufik Sari
Vincent Christlein
Volker Märgner
Yaâcoub Hannad
Youcef Chibani
Yousri Kessentini

Contents

Room-Level Indoor Localization with Artificial Neural Networks

Ahmet Serdar Karadeniz$^{(\boxtimes)}$ and Mehmet Önder Efe

Hacettepe University, Ankara, Turkey
{ahmet.karadeniz,onderefe}@hacettepe.edu.tr

Abstract. Indoor localization system determines the location of the users or some assets in indoor environments. There are important applications of indoor localization including smart home systems, indoor navigation and tracking systems. In this work, a reliable neural network model is developed for localizing users in room level. Model is based on Wi-Fi signals received by the users' devices at different rooms from various Wi-Fi access points. A neural network with two hidden layers with sigmoid activation functions is trained with back-propagation optimizing collected signal data. Some of the signals are set to 0 during the training process, which gives significant stability to the model under the conditions where some of the data required for prediction are not available. An additional dataset is collected for the evaluation in addition to the existing datasets. Performance of the model on the existing datasets as well as the new collected dataset is discussed and evaluated. Results are promising in terms of reliability and accuracy.

1 Introduction

As Global Positioning System (GPS) has plenty of applications that can easily be developed, determining the location of a user in an indoor environment is still a challenging problem as it requires a system with high accuracy and reliability with cost-effective technology. Proposed systems generally require different technologies such as GPS, Bluetooth beacons, RFID tags and Wi-Fi signals. There are some disadvantages of some of these technologies in terms of accessibility, cost and accuracy. GPS is only reliable in outdoor environments and may not give the desired accuracies [1]. Bluetooth beacons can only be used for short ranges [2]. RFID tags require users to carry an additional tag and may be expensive in terms of price [3]. Using the received signal strength (RSS) values of Wi-Fi access points (AP) makes use of the existing infrastructures by using smartphones and Wi-Fi APs which are highly available these days. Smartphones can be used to collect RSS values of the near Wi-Fi sources. Initially, a machine learning algorithm can be used to train with the RSS data and location of the users can be determined later with the trained algorithm. If a well-generalizing machine learning model can be developed, Wi-Fi RSS values can remove the need of additional cost and technology. Therefore, using RSS of Wi-Fi access points

© Springer Nature Switzerland AG 2020
C. Djeddi et al. (Eds.): MedPRAI 2019, CCIS 1144, pp. 1–8, 2020.
https://doi.org/10.1007/978-3-030-37548-5_1

can be considered as a feasible solution to this problem and an accurate, stable machine learning model needs to be developed for indoor localization systems.

Indoor localization as a machine learning problem have been considered as both supervised and unsupervised problem. For example, Chen et al. proposed a subarea localization scheme based on unsupervised clustering and subarea matching [4]. Indoor localization can also be described as a supervised classification or regression problem. Most of the existing solutions for solving indoor localization problem with RSSI try to find the 2D coordinate locations of the users [5,6]. However, such precise localization may not be needed for some applications. For instance, an indoor navigation system can be developed by using only room-level position of the user by calculating the paths between different rooms. Another example is a smart home system where the room-level location of the users may improve efficiency and intelligence.

Room-level classification of indoor locations have been studied by various scholars and different solutions are proposed. Rezgui et al. have used SVM for room-level classification and introduced normalized rank transformation to reduce the effect of signal fluctuations [7]. Buchman et al. have used overlapping rings method which is based on the location of the access points [8]. Rohra et al. have used fuzzy hybrid of particle swarm optimization and gravitational search algorithm with Artificial Neural Networks (ANN) for room level indoor localization [2]. Their model has high classification accuracy and also includes fuzzy branch for dealing with uncertainties [2]. Furthermore, dataset used by Rohra et al. have been used in other works as well. For instance, Gomes et al. obtained a high accuracy with the dataset used in [2] by training a Random Forest classifier [9]. Altay et al. also obtained high classification accuracy with Linear Discriminant Analysis (LDA) classification [10]. Sabanci et al. compared different classifiers on the same dataset and obtained that k-Nearest Neighbors (k-NN) was the most successful classifier. Most of the works for room-level indoor localization give decent accuracies but few of them give stable performances of the proposed solutions under disturbances such as lack of a signal from an AP on which the model was trained. In this paper, a simple yet efficient solution to this problem is proposed and the performance of the model under different conditions is provided [11].

In the following sections, implementation details, behavior and the performance of the model is explained. In Sect. 2, the datasets used in the experiments are described. In Sect. 3, ANN implementation details and its behavior with respect to different parameters are discussed. Moreover, an algorithm for robustness is proposed. Finally, the model is evaluated on different datasets with classification accuracies and confusion matrices. Results show that proposed model is accurate and reliable which can be used for an indoor localization system.

2   Datasets

For training and evaluation, two different datasets are used which will be called
Dataset1 and Dataset2. Both datasets include RSS values of the APs and the
corresponding room labels. Dataset1 is collected by Rohra *et al.* where the indoor
environment is located in an office in United States [2]. In this dataset, there
are seven APs and the data is collected in four different rooms with 1 second
intervals [2]. Dataset2 is collected in a in a house located in Ankara, Turkey. In
the collection process for Dataset2, a simple Python script, which calls `iwconfig`
command from an Ubuntu terminal, for receiving RSS values of the routers
is executed every 500 ms in different rooms. In Dataset2, there are two APs
and four different rooms. This can be seen as a more challenging dataset when
compared to Dataset1 as four rooms are covered by only two APs. Wi-Fi RSS
signals have values changing from -30 to -90. There are two thousand samples
in each dataset. For preprocessing, we scaled the data to have zero mean and
unit variance.

In Fig. 1, distribution of the training data is plotted for Dataset1. Note that
Principal Component Analysis (PCA) for dimensionality reduction is applied as
there are seven APs for Dataset1 and the explained variance ratio of PCA is
94.45%. x_1 and x_2 are input signals in the projected feature space. Different
shapes correspond to the four rooms in Dataset1.

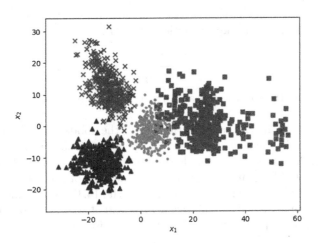

Fig. 1. Distribution for Dataset1

3   Proposed Method

ANNs have been powerful tools in solving many tasks. These tasks include identification of nonlinear systems, medical diagnosis, financial applications and many
others. A neural network with 2 hidden layers is implemented in this work. In

all layers, sigmoid function is used as it is one of the mostly chosen for classifying nonlinear data. 20% of the Dataset1 is used for parameter optimization.
Furthermore, to validate the convergence of the model, all the tuning process is
made only for Dataset1 and the model is tested on Dataset2 without changing
any parameters.

There are four layers including the input and output layers. Let w^k be the
weight matrix between the layers k and $k+1$, o^k be the output of the k-th layer
and o^0 represent the input layer. w^k is initialized to random small numbers and
o^0 corresponds to the input data. Then, the feedforward operation used can be
represented as

$$s^{k+1} = w^k o^k \qquad (1)$$

$$o^{k+1} = f(s^{k+1}) \qquad (2)$$

where f is the sigmoid function $f: \mathbb{R} \to [0,1]$ which is defined as $f(x) = \frac{1}{1+e^{-x}}$.
We used mean squared error $J: \mathbb{R}^n \times \mathbb{R}^n \to \mathbb{R}$ defined as $J(y, \hat{y}) = \frac{1}{n} \sum_{i=1}^{n} (y_i - \hat{y}_i)^2$ where $\hat{y}$ is the output vector, y is the true labels vector and n is the number
of samples. To prevent overfitting, L_2 regularization is used. After L_2 regular-
ization, loss function becomes

$$\frac{1}{n} \sum_{i=1}^{n} (y_i - \hat{y}_i)^2 + R(W) \qquad (3)$$

where $R(W) = \frac{\lambda}{2} \sum_k \sum_l (W_{k,l}^2)$. Thus, we add λw to the gradients in the
backpropagation. Then, backpropagation with the gradient descent algorithm
becomes

$$\Delta w_t^k = -\eta \frac{\partial J}{\partial w_{t-1}^k} + \lambda w_{t-1}^k \qquad (4)$$

where t represents the iteration, λ and η are the regularization and the learning
rate terms.

As we discussed in the introduction part, the model has to be stable in
situations where the device is not able to receive the signals from some routers.
We simulated this situation by randomly setting the RSS values from random
access points to 0. Thus, an average of 519 signals out of 3500 signals are set to
zero in the validation set, which corresponds to the 14.1% of all validation data.
In practice, when a device cannot receive the signal, the same 0 value can be
used instead of the expected RSS value. To be precise, the simulation algorithm
is illustrated in Algorithm 1.

An intuitive solution to this problem is to set some of the features in the
input vector to zero randomly during the training. At each iteration, we set
different signals to zero with probability $p = 0.20$. In this way, the network learns
the cases where some signals are missing in the input data. Thus, feedforward
equation is changed as initial o^0 is replaced by the disturbed input vector $\tilde{o}^0$.
Note that $\tilde{o}^0$ changes at each iteration due to the randomness in the disturbance
algorithm. While this operation can decrease the overall accuracy slightly, it may
be tolerated when the stability is important.

Algorithm 1. RSS Disturbance Simulation

1: $p \leftarrow 0.2$ ▷ Disturbance probability
2: **for** $i = 0 \ldots n_{samples}$ **do**
3:     **for** $j = 0 \ldots n_{features}$ **do**
        $r \leftarrow random(0, 1, p)$ ▷ Choose 0 or 1 with probability p
4:         **if** r == 0 **then**
            $\hat{X}[i, j] \leftarrow 0$
5:         **end if**
6:     **end for**
7: **end for**

A proper initialization and tuning of the parameters is essential for training neural networks. Therefore, we optimized the parameters of the network such as learning rate, number of epochs, regularization parameter and disturbance probability parameter. Results of the learning rate experiments are shown in Fig. 2 where loss graphs with different learning rates are plotted. $\eta = 0.01$ gives a fast and smooth drop on the training loss curve. All the other chosen parameters are shown in Table 1.

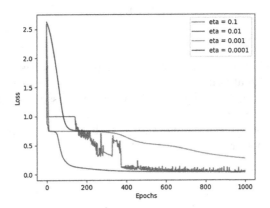

Fig. 2. Training loss with different learning rates

Table 1. Parameters of the ANN and training algorithm

Parameter	Value
Learning rate	0.01
Regularization	0.001
Number of epochs	500
Number of neurons in the 1st hidden layer	7
Number of neurons in the 2nd hidden layer	7
Disturbance probability	20%

4   Performance Evaluation

In this section, performance of the model is evaluated. First, we tested the model
for Dataset1 and Dataset2. We used 10-fold cross validation in the reported
accuracies. Then, impact of the proposed algorithm is discussed. Moreover, we
compared our model with other classifiers where around 20% of the signals in
the test sets of Dataset1 were set to zero. Finally, confusion matrices for both
datasets are provided.

As shown in Table 2, 96.44% and 91.45% classification accuracies were
obtained on Dataset1 and Dataset2, respectively. Although all the parameter
optimization process was made on the validation set of Dataset1, the model
was also able to perform well for the Dataset2 with the same parameters. This
shows that our model can be used in different indoor environments without any
modification.

Table 2. Classification accuracies

Dataset	Accuracy
Dataset1	96.44%
Dataset2	91.45%

In Fig. 3, training and validation accuracies were plotted to illustrate the
effect of the proposed algorithm. In this figure, blue and orange curves are training and validation accuracies of ANN without the proposed modification, red and
green curves represent the training and validation accuracies of ANN with the
proposed modification. From the figure, it is deduced that the proposed method
makes the model more robust against disturbances.

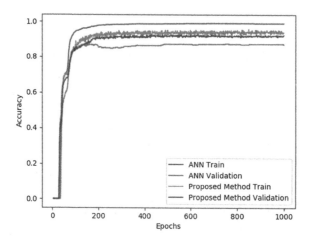

Fig. 3. Impact of proposed method (Color figure online)

In Table 3, classification accuracies are compared with various classifiers. Classifiers used in other works were chosen to compare our model [9–11]. k-NN was used in [11], Random Forest was used in [9] and LDA was used in [10]. Although reported accuracies were high in [9–11], it is observed that they can significantly drop when some of the data are missing if there is no proper modification. Table 3 shows that our method yielded the highest accuracy under the condition that 20% of the test data were missing.

Table 3. Classification accuracies

Model	Accuracy
k-NN [11]	90.70%
Random forest [9]	84.35%
LDA [10]	87.35%
Proposed method	**93.05%**

In Fig. 4, average confusion matrices with 10-fold cross validation are illustrated. Diagonal elements in the confusion matrices correspond to per class accuracy. Note that test sets were not disturbed in the reported confusion matrices. In Fig. 4a, confusion matrix for Dataset1 is illustrated. We have above 98% accuracy for room 0, room 1 and room 3. For room 2, we have 89% accuracy. In Fig. 4b, class accuracies are around 90% except room 1 which have 98% classification accuracy.

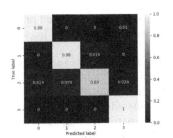
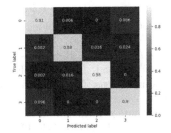

(a) Confusion matrix for Dataset1   (b) Confusion matix for Dataset2

Fig. 4. Confusion matrices

5 Conclusion

Room-level indoor localization problem is challenging especially when there is a lack of data at test time. Furthermore, the number of Wi-Fi access points is another important factor obtaining high accuracies. Main concentration in this work was to develop a room-level indoor localization algorithm which is resistant to lack of signals and generalizable into different indoor environments. An accuracy of 96.44% and 91.45% was obtained in two different datasets. Moreover, 93.05% classification accuracy was obtained where around 20% of the collected data were assumed to be missing at prediction time, which is around 3% higher than the closest classifier. In the future, more advanced architectures can be used to improve the overall performance of the proposed algorithm.

References

1. Martin, E., Vinyals, O., Friedland, G., Bajcsy, R.: Precise indoor localization using smart phones. In: Proceedings of the 18th ACM International Conference on Multimedia, pp. 787–790. ACM (2010)
2. Rohra, J.G., Perumal, B., Narayanan, S.J., Thakur, P., Bhatt, R.B.: User localization in an indoor environment using fuzzy hybrid of particle swarm optimization & gravitational search algorithm with neural networks. In: Deep, K., et al. (eds.) Proceedings of Sixth International Conference on Soft Computing for Problem Solving. Advances in Intelligent Systems and Computing, vol. 546, pp. 787–790. Springer, Singapore (2010). https://doi.org/10.1007/978-981-10-3322-3_27
3. Pratama, A.R., Widyawan, W., Lazovik, A., Aiello, M.: Indoor self-localization via bluetooth low energy beacons. IDRBT J. Bank. Technol. 1, 1–15 (2017)
4. Chen, Q., Wang, B.: FinCCM: fingerprint crowdsourcing, clustering and matching for indoor subarea localization. IEEE Wirel. Commun. Lett. 4(6), 677–680 (2015)
5. Chintalapudi, K., Padmanabha Iyer, A., Padmanabhan, V.N.: Indoor localization without the pain. In: Proceedings of the Sixteenth Annual International Conference on Mobile Computing and Networking, pp. 173–184. ACM (2010)
6. Lim, C.-H., Wan, Y., Ng, B.-P., See, C.-M.S.: A real-time indoor wifi localization system utilizing smart antennas. IEEE Trans. Consum. Electron. 53(2), 618–622 (2007)
7. Rezgui, Y., Pei, L., Chen, X., Wen, F., Han, C.: An efficient normalized rank based SVM for room level indoor wifilocalization with diverse devices. Mob. Inform. Syst. (2017)
8. Buchman, A., Lung, C.: Received signal strength based room level accuracy indoor localisation method. In: 2013 IEEE 4th International Conference on Cognitive Infocommunications (CogInfoCom), pp. 103–108. IEEE (2013)
9. Gomes, R., Ahsan, M., Denton, A.: Random forest classifier in SDN framework for user-based indoor localization. In: 2018 IEEE International Conference on Electro/Information Technology (EIT), pp. 0537–0542. IEEE (2018)
10. Altay, O., Ulas, M.: Location determination by processing signal strength of Wi-Fi routers in the indoor environment with linear discriminant classifier. In: 2018 6th International Symposium on Digital Forensic and Security (ISDFS), pp. 1–4. IEEE (2018)
11. Sabanci, K., Yigit, E., Ustun, D., Toktas, A., Aslan, M.F.: Wifi based indoor localization: application and comparison of machine learning algorithms. In: 2018 XXIIIrd International Seminar/Workshop on Direct and Inverse Problems of Electromagnetic and Acoustic Wave Theory (DIPED), pp. 246–251. IEEE (2018)

A Simple Authentication Method with Multilayer Feedforward Neural Network Using Keystroke Dynamics

Ahmet Melih Gedikli$^{(\boxtimes)}$ and Mehmet Önder Efe

Department of Computer Engineering of Hacettepe University, Ankara, Turkey
{ahmet.gedikli, onderefe}@hacettepe.edu.tr

Abstract. Keystroke dynamics is a widely accepted user recognition and verification behavioral biometric, which has been studied nearly for a century. Intrinsically, this biometric is used together with id/password authentication forming multi-factor authentication. There are several anomaly detection algorithms that have been proposed for this task. While some proposals handle this problem with measuring data distance by taking correlation and dependence into account, some models use complex and time-consuming models deep neural networks to train to reach the right approximation. Our paper addresses a simple, accurate and lightweight method for user authentication. We show the effectiveness of our approach through comparisons with existing methods, which have also used the CMU keystroke dynamics benchmark dataset used here too. Using feed forward multilayer neural network with resilient backpropagation, we obtained an Equal Error Rate (ERR) equal to 0.049 for authentication with overall identification accuracy of 94.7%.

Keywords: Feed forward multilayer neural networks · Keystroke dynamics · User recognition and authentication · Biometrics · Resilient backpropagation

1 Introduction

Today's world requires fast, reliable, secure and easy to use/access to information. Security concerns paved the way for many different techniques uses user information such as passwords and user details. However, such information brings the threat together if they are not used combined with other techniques. A well-discussed, foolproof, automated and proven technique is biometrics, which uses personal characteristics and unique individual behaviors such as voice, fingerprint patterns [1]. Combining password security with biometrics forms a multi-factor authentication [2]. Physiology based and behavior based systems together forms the biometrics systems. While fingerprint, 2D face and voice authentication systems are physiology based ones, on the other hand, behavior based approach is comprised of keystroke dynamics on keyboard, touch screens and mouse click patterns. A behavioral biometric method used in user verification and identification is keystroke dynamics, which analyses typing rhythms of users and classifying them according to their keystroke behaviors. Each individual has unique keystroke timing patterns which can form a user protective

C. Djeddi et al. (Eds.): MedPRAI 2019, CCIS 1144, pp. 9–23, 2020.
https://doi.org/10.1007/978-3-030-37548-5_2

evaluation. Using this protective evaluation to authenticate using a compromised password could be detected and rejected immediately because evaluation consists an undoubtedly different pattern from genuine one. Typing behavior subject is firstly touched on as idiosyncratic behavioral characteristics in 1936 [3]. Back in the 19th century, telegraph operators could recognize each other based on their typing rhythms [4]. Also comparing other biometric systems, keystroke dynamics has more advantages like being user-friendly and non-intrusive. Continuous authentication is possible with no need of user awareness and additional required hardware equipment. There are numerous research that physiology based authentications like fingerprints, 2D face and voice can be imitated easily [5–9]. Also, it is proven that a weak password with keystroke dynamics supported authentication too can be attacked by imitators [10]. However, the attacker has to know the whole typing behavior of the subject to intrude. On the other hand, a strong password can't be imitated easily with keystroke dynamics [10]. In most cases the username and password are leaked, but the typing behavior information is not easy to be captured. Therefore, keystroke dynamics is one of the most secure biometric which can't be imitated if a strong password is used along with it. In summary, keystroke dynamics biometrics is cut out mechanism for user authentication since it is software based, easy, cheap and online [2].

Keystroke dynamics of an individual shows inconstancy due to external factors like input keyboards, different keyboard layouts etc. and transient internal factors such as emotion, stress, drowsiness [11]. These results basically show that a genuine individual will be eliminated when s/he is under a threat and forced to be authenticated due to affected neurophysiological pathway.

Keystroke dynamics features are extracted using timing information of key up, key down and key hold events. These features forms digraphs, which are the time latencies between two successive keystrokes, trigraphs, which are the time latencies between every three consecutive keys and n-graphs which are time latencies between every n consecutive keys. Digraphs, trigraphs and n-graphs are discriminative at word-specific level. These extracted features especially used in user classification. In this paper, we use a static text for verification and authentication.

Neural network based models are frequently used in the field of computer vision, speech signal processing, text representation and automatic control systems. They are also widely used and adopted to computer security domains. Being different from classical methods, which rely on complex distance metrics or manual feature engineering, neural network models have some advantages like simplification of the whole process and getting a scalable problem definition with property of high performance. With motivation of superior performance of neural network models in some problem sets, in this paper, we used a multilayer simple feedforward neural network for user authentication. We have trained three different neural network structure with CMU keystroke dynamics benchmark dataset, each of which has different number of hidden layers and activation functions between hidden layers.

This paper is organized as follows. In Sect. 2, we give the background. In Sect. 3, we described CMU Keystroke Dynamics Benchmark Dataset. In Sect. 4, we introduced our neural network model. In the fifth section, we explained the training mechanism and evaluation of the neural network structures. In the sixth part of the paper, we discussed the results and the conclusions are given at the end of the paper.

2 Related Works

Distinguishing users via keystroke patterns was first discovered in 1970s [12, 13]. These works were focused on static type of text. The long passage text identification by keystroke dynamics was also considered in [14]. Later digraph and trigraphs' mean and variances were used first to extract the keystroke features by Monrose and Rubin [15]. They used the Euclidean distance metric with Bayesian-like classifiers and observed quite successful results. A number of detailed survey papers were published from 2009 to 2015 each of which takes different perspective of keystroke dynamics [2, 16–22]. To extract keystroke features, relative order of duration times for different n-graphs is proven to be stronger to intra-class differences than absolute timing [23].

2.1 Distance Based Classification

In this approach, feature vectors are extracted from typing behavior. These vectors are then classified for authentication and verification procedures. Euclidean distance is used in early days due to its simplicity, but it has drawbacks. It was highly sensitive to scale differences in the extracted features and it cannot deal with correlation between the vectors. Mahalanobis distance, however, takes covariances of data to reduce heterogeneity in real data. Mahalanobis distance is widely used for comparing features via disconnecting the interactions between features based on their covariance matrix [24]. Another method which is the Manhattan distance have become prominent with simple computation and easy breakdown into contributions made by each variable. From this perspective, it is hard to be influenced by outliers when compared to higher order distance metrics including Euclidean distance and Mahalanobis distance. A performance comparison study showed that the Manhattan distance pointed out that the top performers are classifiers using scaled Manhattan distance with an equal error rate of 0.096, and the nearest neighbor classifier using the Mahalanobis distance with an equal error rate of 0.10 [25].

2.2 Advanced Machine Learning Based Classification

Over the years, keystroke biometrics research has taken advantage of many existing classification techniques including K-means methods, K-nearest neighbor classifiers, Bayesian classifiers, fuzzy logic, boost learning and random forests. Support vector machines are used to accommodate non-linear decision boundaries for complicated classification issues. The persistent features of keystroke dynamics are extracted using SVMs and used in classifying user typing [26]. Deep learning techniques has also been used in classification and reported that it outperforms before mentioned techniques [31, 33, 34]. In these models, Deep Learning structure is fed with timing features of keystroke dynamics, since the training procedure can take quite a long time, ADAM optimization and Leaky Rectified Linear Unit are used for faster learning process [33]. Besides faster convergence, the most valuable EER is obtained in [33]. Another research used Deep Belief Nets to extract hidden feature detectors and those feature detectors were used building a pretrained Artificial Neural Network for real training process instead of starting to the training with a random model [31]. More complex Deep

Learning models were also used recently in this research area. For example, Recurrent Neural Network (RNN) with Convolutional Neural Network (CNN) was used in a research in whose model 5 different sequence length of texts from 10 to 100 (10, 30, 50, 70, 100) and 3 keystroke time characteristics were used for evaluation [35]. The CNN was used for extracting high level timing features, later, these features were provided as inputs to the RNN. It is stated that using 30 sequence length of texts and 3 keystroke time characteristics results better than other cases. In addition to Deep Learning techniques, a recent research used NeuroEvolution of Augmenting Topologies (NEAT), which is a type of Genetic Algorithm, resulted highest identification accuracy, however, they have built their own dataset and tested their models with that [36].

3   CMU Keystroke Dynamics Benchmark Dataset [25]

The dataset provided in CMU Keystroke Dynamics Benchmark consists of three types of timing information named the hold time, key down-key down time and key up-key down time. This timing information was collected for one static password, which is .tie5Roan1 with keystroke timing information of 51 users. Whole data for one user is collected in 8 different sessions with 50 repetitions on each one of them. Figure 1 illustrates keystroke timing types. Hold time or dwell time in Fig. 1 represent the duration of time during pressing a key, concisely it is calculated as the difference time between release and press of a single key. In Fig. 1, Hold Time represents this type. Key-down key-down time is the time from pressing a key to pressing a consecutive key which is represented Down-Down Time in Fig. 1. Finally, key-up key-down time is the time from releasing a key to pressing a consecutive key. This type of time can be negative because user might have not released the former pressed key while pressing last consecutive key. In Fig. 1, Up-Down Time demonstrates this type of timing. There are 31 features for each trial of user with 11 of them are hold time ending with introducing enter key, 10 of them are key-down key-down time, finally 10 of them are key-up key-down time.

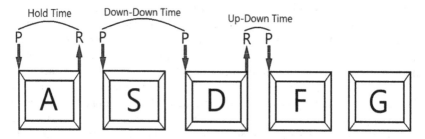

Fig. 1. Demonstration of features in keystroke dynamics benchmark data set

4   Neural Network Model

CMU Keystroke Dynamics Benchmark Dataset is used as input to our neural network layout. We start with a subject considering as genuine user. We took other 50 subjects as impostors to that user's authentication. The first 200 timing features of genuine user and the impostors' features are used as training data for a genuine user. This anomaly detection process has been repeated for each user taking that specific user as genuine and the others as impostors. Using impostors' data in training process leverages capability of differentiating features extracted by the neural network model. The other 200 timing features of genuine user is used as validation and randomly selected 5 timing features for each impostor, in total 250, are used as test data. These evaluation criteria for CMU Keystroke Dynamics Benchmark Dataset are mentioned in [25]. For each user, there exists a trained neural network model produces output between 0 and 1 as response to timing features. We designed three different neural network models. We started by designating one of our 51 subjects as the genuine user, and the rest as impostors. We train an anomaly detector by extracting 200 initial timing feature vectors for a genuine user from the dataset. We repeat this process, designating each of the other subjects as the genuine user and the remainders are as impostors. Thus, number of

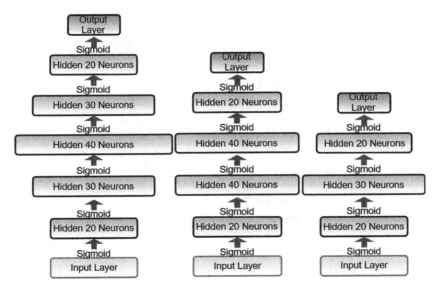

Fig. 2. Illustration of three neural network models

created models equal to number of distinct subjects. Three different neural network models are represented in Fig. 2. Training process were done in each model for every user for 10 times. We used resilient backpropagation (Rprop) method changing the weights with using momentum factor to diminish the fluctuations in weight changes over consecutive iterations. Equation (1) describes this procedure where $E(\omega)$ is the loss function, ω is the weight vector and η is the learning rate.

$$\Delta\omega_i(t+1) = -\eta\frac{\partial E}{\partial \omega_{i,j}} + \alpha\Delta\omega_i(t) \tag{1}$$

There are numerous research outcomes that prove resilient backpropagation is more successful than plain error backpropagation [27, 28]. Also, we decreased the learning rate parameter in each epoch towards a predefined minimum value. The algorithm in Fig. 3 states Rprop backpropagation process with weight momentum factor and decreasing learning rate. While Δ denotes Rprop weight changes, E denotes mean square error in one epoch and $\omega_{i,j}$ denotes a weight between neurons. Neural network hyperparameters used in algorithm shown in Fig. 3 are listed in Table 1 with the corresponding initial values. All three neural network models in Fig. 2 were initialized to the values listed in Table 1.

Table 1. Hyper parameters used in neural network model with their initial values

Hyperparameter name	Value
Learning Rate (η)	0.15
Minimum Learning Rate (η_m)	0.05
Learning Rate Decrease Value (η_d)	0.0001
Momentum Alpha (α)	0.05
Rprop Learning Rate Plus (η^+)	1.2
Rprop Learning Rate Minus (η^-)	0.5
Rprop Minimum Delta Weight (Δ_{min})	10^{-6}
Rprop Maximum Delta Weight (Δ_{max})	10
Initial Rprop Delta Weight (Δ_0)	0.9

$$\forall i,j : \Delta_{i,j}(t) = \Delta_0$$

$$\forall i,j : \frac{\partial E}{\partial \omega_{i,j}}(t-1) = 0$$

Repeat

Compute Gradient $\frac{\partial E}{\partial \omega}(t)$:

For all weights and biases:

$$\text{IF } \frac{\partial E}{\partial \omega_{i,j}}(t-1)\frac{\partial E}{\partial \omega_{i,j}}(t) > 0$$

$$\Delta_{i,j}(t) = \min(\Delta_{i,j}(t-1)\eta^+, \Delta_{max})$$

$$\text{ELSE IF } \frac{\partial E}{\partial \omega_{i,j}}(t-1)\frac{\partial E}{\partial \omega_{i,j}}(t) < 0$$

$$\Delta_{i,j}(t) = \max(\Delta_{i,j}(t-1)\eta^-, \Delta_{min})$$

$$\Delta\omega_{i,j}(t) = -sign\left(\frac{\partial E}{\partial \omega_{i,j}}(t)\right)\Delta_{i,j}(t)$$

$$\omega_{i,j}(t+1) = \Delta\omega_{i,j}(t) + \left(\eta\Delta\omega_{i,j}(t)\right) + \alpha\Delta\omega_{i,j}(t-1)$$

$\eta = \max(\eta - \eta_d, \eta_m)$

$t = t + 1$

Until Convergence

Fig. 3. A mathematical notation of Rprop backpropagation algorithm

5 Training and Evaluation

5.1 Evaluation Methodology

To measure model performance in biometrics some rates are used to measure performance. Table 2 shows the confusion matrix of any binary classifier.

Then we can express all rates used in the evaluations as given in below.

$$True\,Positive\,Rate\,(TPR) = \frac{TP}{TP+FN} \tag{2}$$

$$True\,Negative\,Rate\,(TNR) = \frac{TN}{TN+FP} \tag{3}$$

$$False\ Positive\ Rate\ (FPR) = \frac{FP}{TP+FN} \tag{4}$$

$$False\ Negative\ Rate\ (FNR) = \frac{FN}{TP+FN} \tag{5}$$

$$Accuracy = \frac{TP+TN}{TP+FP+TN+FN} \tag{6}$$

Table 2. Confusion matrix of binary classifier

		Predicted Class	
		Positive	Negative
Actual class	Positive	True Positives (TP)	False Negatives (FN)
	Negative	False Positives (FP)	True Negatives (TN)

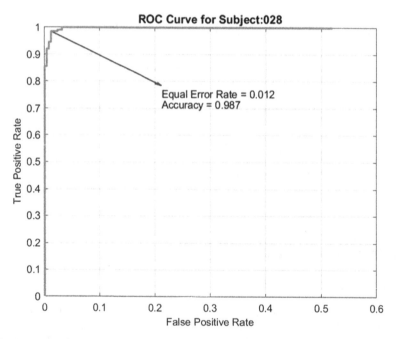

Fig. 4. An example Receiver Operating Characteristics (ROC) curve of a subject which visualizes the performance of the neural network model. The curve demonstrates the trade-off between the true positive rate (hit rate) and the false positive rate (false-alarm rate). The performance can be calculated with proximity to the top-left corner of the graph visually.

False Positive Rate (FPR) also called False Acceptance Rate (FAR) and False Negative Rate (FNR) also called False Rejection Rate (FRR) are used for calculating

Equal Error Rate [29]. A Receiver Operating Characteristics (ROC) curve example in Fig. 4 depicts the performance of the model with FPR and TPR graph.

Equal Error Rate is seen in a clear way in Fig. 5. Basically, ERR is cross point of the FAR and FRR curves when they are plotted to the same graph with similarity threshold in x-axis and error rate in y-axis. Figures 4 and 5 show the performance of model on same subject from different perspectives. Figure 5 also shows accuracy of the model for the current subject. Mean Accuracy and Mean Equal Error Rate represents the mean values of sum of accuracies and sum of equal error rates up to current subject. In this manner, the graph of the last subject will show whole model's average accuracy and average equal error rate in the end.

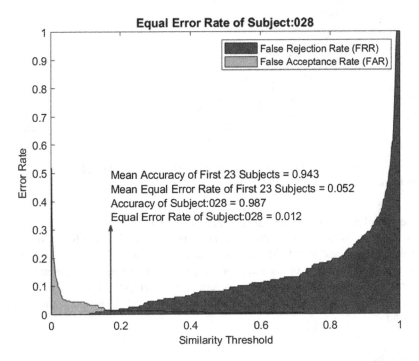

Fig. 5. An example of False Acceptance Rate (FAR) and False Rejection Rate (FRR) versus Similarity Threshold. The equal error rate (EER) is shown as cross point between False Acceptance Rate (FAR) and False Rejection Rate (FRR).

5.2 Training and Stopping Criteria

We trained the three neural network models for each subject for 10 times and plotted ROC Curve graph, Similarity Threshold vs. Error Rate and Mean Squared Error (MSE) vs Epochs graphs. Figure 6 shows MSE vs number of epochs graph of all subjects.

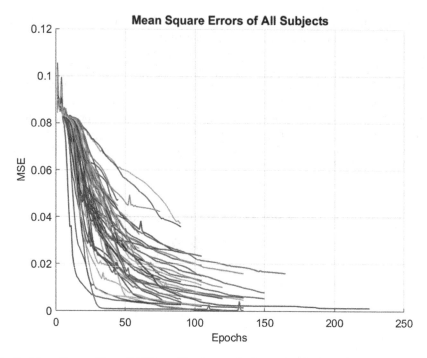

Fig. 6. Mean Square Error (MSE) vs. Epochs graph shows the decline of loss function with respect to increasing epochs

The neural network training convergence is decided with respect to the validation timing features. At each epoch, the cross point between FAR and FRR is found and using the cross points' threshold value accuracy of the model is calculated. For each 15-epochs set, the average of accuracy for the current 15-epochs is compared with that of the previous 15-epochs, and training is resumed if average is increased and stopped if average is decreased. Here, we aimed to prevent neural network model from overfitting.

6 Results

The used evaluation approach was explained in the previous section. There are 51 subjects in CMU Keystroke Dynamics Benchmark Dataset, however, enumeration of them is not in sequential order. This sequencing starts with 2 and ends with 57 having missing sequences in the range [25]. To keep the relation same, we used the same subject enumeration. In Fig. 7, all ROC Curves of these subjects are plotted together to visualize the success of the model easily.

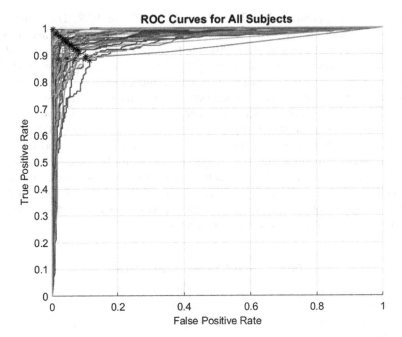

Fig. 7. ROC curves of all users after ending training.

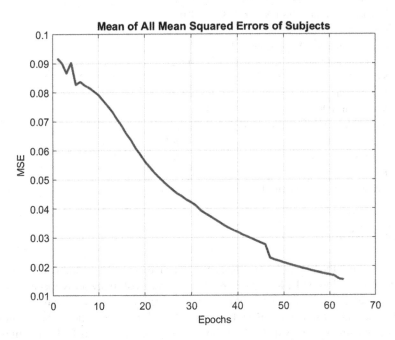

Fig. 8. Average of the MSE levels vs. the epoch number

The star marked points in Fig. 7 denote TPR and FPR on EER. The accuracy of model for a subject can be found by using (6) on EER point [30]. Then average accuracy is found from all these values. Starting from the first subject to the last subject we obtained the average EER and accuracy by incremental averaging method. The results are quite impressive compared to other techniques seen in Table 3, the best results are achieved with 20-30-20 neural network configuration. The neural network having 3 hidden layers produces slightly better results than those having more than 3 hidden layers. 20-30-20 model managed average Equal Error Rate of 0.049 with the average identification accuracy of 94.7%. Also, the average number of epochs needed for the convergence, considering all the models of users, is 70 as seen in Fig. 8.

Table 3 shows comparisons of models which uses CMU Keystroke Dynamics Benchmark Dataset. Our model is positioned in the third place with respect to Average EER, and positioned in the first place with respect to user identification accuracy, which has not been considered in some research reports.

Table 3. Model/Algorithm comparisons

Model/algorithm	Average EER	Average accuracy
Deep Secure	**0.030**	93.59% [33]
Deep Belief Nets (DBN) [31]	0.035	65.60% [33]
Our Model	**0.049**	**94.7%**
Median Vector Proximity [32]	0.080	–
Manhattan-Mahalanobis (No Outlier) [23]	0.084	–
Manhattan-Mahalanobis (Outlier) [23]	0.087	–
Manhattan (scaled) [25]	0.0962	81.20% [33]
Nearest Neighbor (Mahalanobis) [25]	0.0996	–
Outlier Count (z-score) [25]	0.1022	–
SVM (one-class) [25]	0.1025	66.40% [33]
Mahalanobis [25]	0.1101	–
Manhattan (Filter) [25]	0.1360	–
Neural Network (Auto-associated) [25]	0.1614	–
Euclidean [25]	0.1706	–
Fuzzy Logic [25]	0.2213	–
K Means [25]	0.3722	–
Neural Network (Standard) [25]	0.8283	–

7   Conclusions

The studies about the keystroke dynamics and improvements don't claim that keystroke dynamics has the lowest EER, as well as, it is not the most trustworthy mechanism for the user authentication. As a matter of fact, there are retina methods that have much low EERs than keystroke dynamics like 0.01 or even 0 [37]. However, the studies show that keystroke dynamics can rival these methods even with respect to EER although the performance is lower when compared. Above all, there are mainspring motives behind the preferability of keystroke dynamics. First, it doesn't require any additional expensive cumbersome hardware setup, and maintenance. Also, keystroke dynamics doesn't claim that it is the primary authentication mechanism, rather, by nature of the method, it is a supportive mechanism used with universally accepted username/ password authentication. In addition, it is proven that imitating a user using the keystroke dynamics is barely possible. Combining whole above, keystroke dynamics is still an under-research area. On the one hand the advantages of keystroke dynamics make it a plausible option, on the other hand, improvements helps keystroke dynamics compete with other methods.

In this work, we have introduced a successful feedforward neural network scheme with resilient backpropagation based user identification approach. Our model was used for CMU Keystroke Dynamics dataset and the goals were identification and recognition with static text type. The results and the comparisons have shown that the proposed method is able to yield promising values for identifying subjects from keystroke information. We plan extending our models to other long text provided datasets to check if the model is also successful in other datasets.

References

1. Kim, H.-J.: Biometrics, is it a viable proposition for identity authentication and access control? Comput. Secur. **14**, 205–214 (1995)
2. Zhong, Y., Deng, Y.: A survey on keystroke dynamics biometrics: approaches, advances, and evaluations. Gate to Computer Science and Research Recent Advances in User Authentication Using Keystroke Dynamics Biometrics, pp. 1–22 (2015)
3. Dealey, W., Dvorak, A., Merrick, N., Ford, G.: Typewriting behavior (1936)
4. Leggett, J., Williams, G.: Verifying identity via keystroke characteristics. Int. J. Man Mach. Stud. **28**, 67–76 (1988)
5. Goicoechea-Telleria, I., Sanchez-Reillo, R., Liu-Jimenez, J., Blanco-Gonzalo, R.: Attack potential evaluation in desktop and smartphone fingerprint sensors: can they be attacked by anyone? Wirel. Commun. Mob. Comput. **2018**, 1–16 (2018)
6. Ramachandra, R., Busch, C.: Presentation attack detection methods for face recognition systems. ACM Comput. Surv. **50**, 1–37 (2017)
7. Garofalo, G., Rimmer, V., Hamme, T., Preuveneers, D., Joosen, W.: Fishy faces: crafting adversarial images to poison face authentication (2018)
8. Albakri, G., Alghowinem, S.: The effectiveness of depth data in liveness face authentication using 3D sensor cameras. Sensors **19**, 1928 (2019)
9. Zhou, Z., Tang, D., Wang, X., Han, W., Xiangyu, L., Zhang, K.: Invisible mask: practical attacks on face recognition with infrared (2018)
10. Meng, T.C., Gupta, P., Gao, D.: I can be you: questioning the use of keystroke dynamics as biometrics. In: Proceedings of the 20th Network and Distributed System Security Symposium (2013)
11. Epp, C., Lippold, M., Mandryk, R.L.: Identifying emotional states using keystroke dynamics. In: Proceedings of the 2011 Annual Conference on Human Factors in Computing Systems - CHI (2011)
12. Forsen, G., Nelson, M., Staron Jr, R.: Personal attributes authentication techniques. Technical report RADC-TR-77-333, Rome Air Development Center (1977)

13. Spillane, R.: Keyboard apparatus for personal identification. IBM Tech. Disclosure Bull. **17** (3346), 3346 (1975)
14. Gaines, R., Lisowski, W., Press, S., Shapiro, N.: Authentication by keystroke timing: some preliminary results. Technical Report Rand Rep. R-2560-NSF, RAND Corporation (1980)
15. Monrose, F., Rubin, A.D.: Keystroke dynamics as a biometric for authentication. Future Gener. Comput. Syst. **16**, 351–359 (2000)
16. Alsultan, A., Warwick, K.: Keystroke dynamics authentication: a survey of free-text methods. Int. J. Comput. Sci. Issues **10**, 1–10 (2013)
17. Banerjee, S.P., Woodard, D.: Biometric authentication and identification using keystroke dynamics: a survey. J. Pattern Recogn. Res. **7**, 116–139 (2012)
18. Bhatt, S., Santhanam, T.: Keystroke dynamics for biometric authentication—a survey. In: 2013 International Conference on Pattern Recognition, Informatics and Mobile Engineering (2013)
19. Crawford, H.: Keystroke dynamics: characteristics and opportunities. In: 2010 Eighth International Conference on Privacy, Security and Trust (2010)
20. Karnan, M., Akila, M., Krishnaraj, N.: Biometric personal authentication using keystroke dynamics: a review. Appl. Soft Comput. **11**, 1565–1573 (2011)
21. Shanmugapriya, D., Padmavathi, G.: A survey of biometric keystroke dynamics: approaches, security and challenges. Int. J. Comput. Sci. Inform. Secur. **5**, 115–119 (2009)
22. Teh, P.S., Teoh, A.B.J., Yue, S.: A survey of keystroke dynamics biometrics. Sci. World J. **2013**, 1–24 (2013)
23. Zhong, Y., Deng, Y., Jain, A.K.: Keystroke dynamics for user authentication. In: 2012 IEEE Computer Society Conference on Computer Vision and Pattern Recognition Workshops (2012)
24. Bleha, S., Slivinsky, C., Hussien, B.: Computer-access security systems using keystroke dynamics. IEEE Trans. Pattern Anal. Mach. Intell. **12**, 1217–1222 (1990)
25. Killourhy, K.S., Maxion, R.A.: Comparing anomaly-detection algorithms for keystroke dynamics. In: 2009 IEEE/IFIP International Conference on Dependable Systems and Networks (2009)
26. Yu, E., Cho, S.: GA-SVM wrapper approach for feature subset selection in keystroke dynamics identity verification. In: Proceedings of the International Joint Conference on Neural Networks (2003)
27. Souza, B., Brito, N., Neves, W., Silva, K., Lima, R., Silva, S.D.: Comparison between backpropagation and RPROP algorithms applied to fault classification in transmission lines. In: 2004 IEEE International Joint Conference on Neural Networks (IEEE Cat. No.04CH37541) (2004)
28. Prasad, N., Singh, R., Lal, S.P.: Comparison of back propagation and resilient propagation algorithm for spam classification. In: 2013 Fifth International Conference on Computational Intelligence, Modelling and Simulation (2013)
29. Swets, J.A., Pickett, R.M.: Evaluation of Diagnostic Systems: Methods from Signal Detection Theory. Academic Press, New York (1982)
30. Fawcett, T.: An introduction to ROC analysis. Pattern Recogn. Lett. **27**, 861–874 (2006)
31. Deng, Y., Zhong, Y.: Keystroke dynamics user authentication based on gaussian mixture model and deep belief nets. ISRN Signal Process. **2013**, 1–7 (2013)
32. Al-Jarrah, M.: An anomaly detector for keystroke dynamics based on medians vector proximity. J. Emerg. Trends Comput. Inform. Sci. **3**, 988–993 (2012)
33. Maheshwary, S., Ganguly, S., Pudi, V.: Deep secure: a fast and simple neural network based approach for user authentication and identification via keystroke dynamics (2017)

34. Muliono, Y., Ham, H., Darmawan, D.: Keystroke dynamic classification using machine learning for password authorization. Proc. Comput. Sci. **135**, 564–569 (2018)
35. Xiaofeng, L., Shengfei, Z., Shengwei, Y.: Continuous authentication by free-text keystroke based on CNN plus RNN. Proc. Comput. Sci. **147**, 314–318 (2019)
36. Baynath, P., Soyjaudah, K.M.S., Khan, M.H.-M.: Machine learning algorithm on keystroke dynamics pattern. In: 2018 IEEE Conference on Systems, Process and Control (ICSPC) (2018)
37. Chihaoui, T., Jlassi, H., Kachouri, R., Hamrouni, K., Akil, M.: Personal verification system based on retina and SURF descriptors. In: 2016 13th International Multi-Conference on Systems, Signals and Devices (SSD) (2016)

A Comparative Study of ANN Tuning Methods for Multiclass Daily Activity and Fall Recognition

Tevfik Aktay[1(✉)] and Mehmet Önder Efe[2]

[1] Department of Industrial Engineering, Hacettepe University,
Beytepe, Ankara, Turkey
`tevfik.aktay12@hacettepe.edu.tr`
[2] Department of Computer Engineering, Hacettepe University,
Beytepe, Ankara, Turkey
`onderefe@hacettepe.edu.tr`

Abstract. Smart phones and other sensor-enabled devices are very frequently used daily life devices. Movement data obtained by sensors from these devices can be interpreted by artificial intelligence algorithms and this may be critically helpful in some daily life issues. Such a daily activity and fall classification mechanism is particularly important for rapid and accurate medical intervention to the elderly people who live alone. In addition, the real time human activity recognition (HAR) is important for healthcare solutions and better assistance of intelligent personal assistants (IPAs). In this study, the dataset is obtained from 6 different wearable sensors. It contains 20 daily activities and 16 fall motions on the 3060 observations. To classify these movements separately, 3 different Artificial Neural Network (ANN) training algorithms were chosen as the basis. These are gradient descent, momentum with gradient descent and Adam algorithms. Dropout and L2 regularization techniques are used to obtain better results for the test data. The results have shown that the ANN based approach correctly recognizes the daily activities and falls with 94.58% accuracy score on the test set.

Keywords: Multiclass classification · Human activity recognition · Fall detection · Artificial neural networks · Optimization · Regularization

1 Introduction

In recent years, development of hardware technology on sensors, GPS-enabled devices and miniaturized accelerometers have enabled the data collection and analysis of different kinds of data [1]. This has led to enormous amounts of real-time data, which allows for a variety of analytical insights [2]. With the development of these technologies and the rise in the living standards, human activity recognition and fall detection have gained more interest in applications,

© Springer Nature Switzerland AG 2020
C. Djeddi et al. (Eds.): MedPRAI 2019, CCIS 1144, pp. 24–38, 2020.
https://doi.org/10.1007/978-3-030-37548-5_3

such as health, entertainment services and technology. Today, most smart phones and wearable devices like smart watches have sensitive embedded sensors. These sensors include pedometer, accelerometer, gyroscope and magnetometer, thus they continuously gather movement data. Because of the growing volume of this data and easy to access to it, many research studies are devoted to recognize daily activity as well as falls using machine learning solutions.

Fall detection and classification are getting more important especially for elderly people for early and accurately treatment. According to [3], every one-third of elderly people who are 65 or older falls at least one time in a year. 20% of people who fall need medical treatment [4]. Therefore, fall detection and early alert systems are critical to prevent permanent injuries or saving people's lives. In these systems, false negative alarm is another noteworthy fact. In this case, a fall occurs but the learning algorithm does not label it as a fall. This means that the model does not perform one of the most critical tasks. This is an issue handled in this paper. Also, identification of the 16 different fall types can be helpful to manage accurate first aid.

Human daily activity recognition is a popular research area in machine learning. Some research studies have focused on the energy expenditure during the daily exercises [5]. Recognition of daily activities opens the data driven analysis for personalized health care programs. Also, it improves the quality of physical rehabilitation that is applied to elderly people [6]. Calculating daily activity type and their iteration counts provide information to doctors for patient-based care plans [7]. They can use the data as a feedback mechanism to follow their treatment effects. Another approach is to exploit the internet and mobile technologies for IPAs. Next generation smart assistants could merge the human activity recognition and daily routines for serving specific recommendation and reminder systems. This systems collects the user/patient location, heart rate, and sensor data [8]. Furthermore, collected information is forwarded to a caretaker IPA, in real time, that will manage a set of human activity recognition (HAR) and alarms appropriately. In this case, accuracy and reliability expectations on the daily activity classifiers get higher.

During the last two decades, the computational capacities of computing platforms have increased dramatically while the size and cost have been decreasing. These platforms have also provided an increasing number of different sensor data at increasing rates of sampling. Typically, the movement data is gathered by the wearable sensors, mobile-based sensors and recorded visual data [9]. However, personal privacy could be an issue in visual system solutions. Therefore, sensor based researches and developments have less security and privacy risks for the users. Machine learning and especially ANN algorithms are preferred to build models to improve the daily activity recognition and fall detection. A HAR study is considered in University of California Irvine (UCI) HAR dataset to classify 6 different daily activities [10]. Authors examined three models, namely, single layer neural networks, multi layer neural networks and reservoir computing with multi layer neural networks. The last model achieved to 96.2% accuracy rate on the test set. Another study uses video data to recognize totally 6 falls and daily activities and accuracy of approximately 98% is reported in [11]. However, the experiments in [11] consider only indoor recordings. Lack of outdoor recordings is a major issue, further, video based recordings have several drawbacks, such as the motion of the other persons may result in incorrect decisions. Another study and its dataset, which we used in this paper is Simulated Falls and Daily Living Activities Dataset. It is acquired and considered by Özdemir et al. [12]. The dataset is available at UCI Repository and [12] covers 6 machine learning algorithms to improve binary classifier in between falls and daily activities. The work in [12] achieves the best results with the k-nearest neighbor (k-NN) classifier and least squares method (LSM). These two algorithms have scores above 99% in sensitivity, specificity, and accuracy measurements. A recent study [13], a convolutional neural network model is proposed to detect fall from accelerometer data. They achieved significant results on binary classification over 99% accuracy score and precision.

When the current studies are examined, it is seen that a small number of daily activities and fall movements are generally classified. However, a broad spectrum of daily activity and fall recognition is likely to bring more focused healthcare services and personal products. For example, a accurate prediction of the fall type can be provide a specific first aid for the elderly peoples. On the other hand, a successful classification of the personalized daily activities increase the recommendation performance of the IPAs in calculating the burned calories according to the activity type. In this context, the aim of the proposed article is to serve both groups that have been noted above by classifying more daily life activities and falls with high accuracy. To do that, we used different optimization and regularization techniques on ANN to achieve best classification results. Our motivation in using neural networks is to be successful in learning the patterns in the time series sensor data and the network-based approaches are suitable for classification problems.

The rest of the paper is organized as follows. In Sect. 2, we provide details of the dataset and also data preprocessing techniques to prepare it for the learning algorithms. Then, in Sect. 3, we describe the generic classification algorithm and its dependencies for our research. Also, the section includes details of 3 optimization algorithms and 2 regularization techniques. Section 4 provides a technical description about tests and analysis. Afterwards, Sect. 5 discusses the similarities and differences between the proposed model and the reference studies. Finally, Last section explains the conclusion and the remarks for future work.

2   Dataset and Preprocessing

In this section, we explain the dataset and its structure. The preprocessing steps as well as the feature extraction and regularization issues on the raw dataset are discussed in the sequel.

2.1 Dataset

In the laboratory environment, 20 falls and 16 daily living activities are examined by 17 volunteers. Each volunteer suits 6 wearable sensors and then repeats the 36 simulated movements 5 times. The experiments are foldered for 17 volunteers separately to the raw data folder. At the end of the data collection procedure, folder stores totally 18360 instance .txt files (17 volunteers × 36 movements × 5 trials × 6 sensors). All of the trials, which are realized by volunteers are collected by 6 wearable sensors, which are located at different points of the subjects' body. These wireless sensor units fit to the subjects' heads, chests, waists, right wrists, right thighs and right ankles. Recording of the data has been accomplished by using 6 Xsens MTw Motion Tracking Kit sensors and its MTw Software Development Kit made by Xsens Technologies [14]. With the recording capacity of the sensor unit, any trial data is tracked with 6 sensor units simultaneously with sampling frequency of 25 Hz [12]. This also means that data is received every 40 ms. There are approximately 375 rows of record, which corresponds to a sequence of sensory information that lasts 15 s for any sensor instance. Each sensor unit collects 22-columns recorded features, however 9 of them are used for the next steps. These features are the 3 perpendicular axes (x, y, z) of accelerometer, gyroscope and magnetometer. These axes are called as $A_x, A_y, A_z, G_x, G_y, G_z, M_x, M_y, M_z$. A, G, and M stand for the linear acceleration data from accelerometer, rotational acceleration from the gyros and the magnetometer data, respectively.

To preserve the reference dataset file structure, it is preferred to enumerate the motions same as in [12]. According to Table 1, fall motions are enumerated between 1 and 20, and also daily human activities are enumerated between 21 to 36.

2.2 Data Preprocessing

According to the dataset described above, a total of 6 different sensor-instances were collected simultaneously for each trial. Each instance consists 9 column features and 375 rows data. To decrease the computational burden and extracting the persistent information from the raw data, firstly, feature extraction and then dimensional reduction techniques are used. Furthermore, some daily activities and falls can be easily misclassified because they share similar motion patterns. Therefore, extraction of the new features is considered from the instance groups. The total acceleration of the waist accelerometer is selected for the further feature extraction steps as a reference. The magnitude of the measured acceleration is given in (1).

$$A_T = \sqrt{A_x^2 + A_y^2 + A_z^2} \tag{1}$$

The expression above is used to identify the peak acceleration value of the waist accelerometer instance in each trial. After that, the data is separated into 2-seconds (50 samples) blocks centering the peak instant. Thus, waist sensor file is reduced to the 101 rows which are placed before and after the peak value

Table 1. Fall and daily activities according to the dataset.

Motion ID	Label	Detailed description
1	Front-lying	From vertical falling forward to the floor
2	Front-protecting-lying	From vertical falling forward to the floor with arm protection
3	Front-knees	From vertical falling down on the knees
4	Front-knees-lying	From vertical falling down on the knees and then lying on the floor
5	Front-quick-recovery	From vertical falling on the floor and quick recovery
6	Front-slow-recovery	From vertical falling on the floor and quick recovery
7	Front-right	From vertical falling down on the floor, ending in right lateral position
8	Front-left	From vertical falling down on the floor, ending in left lateral position
9	Back-sitting	From vertical falling on the floor, ending sitting
10	Back-lying	From vertical falling on the floor, ending lying
11	Back-right	From vertical falling on the floor, ending lying in right lateral position
12	Back-left	From vertical falling on the floor, ending lying in left lateral position
13	Right-sideway	From vertical falling on the floor, ending lying
14	Right-recovery	From vertical falling on the floor with subsequent recovery
15	Left-sideway	From vertical falling on the floor, ending lying
16	Left-recovery	From vertical falling on the floor with subsequent recovery
17	Rolling-out-bed	From lying, rolling out of bed and going on the floor
18	Podium	From vertical standing on a podium going on the floor
19	Syncope	From standing falling on the floor following a vertical trajectory
20	Syncope-wall	From standing falling down slowly slipping on a wall
21	Walking-fw	Walking forward
22	Walking-bw	Walking backward
23	Jogging	Running
24	Squatting-down	Squatting, then standing up
25	Bending	Bending about 90 degrees
26	Bending-pick-up	Bending to pick up an object on the floor
27	Limp	Walking with a limp
28	Stumble	Stumbling with recovery
29	Trip-over	Bending while walking and then continuing walking
30	Coughing-sneezing	Coughing or sneezing
31	Sit-chair from vertical	To sitting with a certain acceleration onto a chair (hard surface)
32	Sit-sofa from vertical	To sitting with a certain acceleration onto a sofa (soft surface)
33	Sit-air from vertical	To sitting in the air exploiting the muscles of legs
34	Sit-bed from vertical	To sitting with a certain acceleration onto a bed (soft surface)
35	Lying-bed	From vertical lying on the bed
36	Rising-bed	From lying to sitting

generated by (1). Data from the remaining axes of each sensor unit are reduced according to the time index of the waist sensor used as a reference for the related trial. Each movement file collected by six sensors are reduced six 101 × 9 array data. Then, new features are extracted from 9 measured signals by using minimum, maximum, mean, skewness, kurtosis, the first 11 values of the autocorrelation sequence and the first 5 frequencies and 5 amplitudes with maximum magnitude of the Discrete Fourier Transform (DFT) for every column vectors (10 DFTs features × 9 columns + 11 autocorrelation features × 9 columns + first 5 statistical metrics × 9 columns). In this way, 234 features are extracted from each sensor unit. After that, remaining 5 sensors' data are processed same way and all six are merged as a feature vector of dimension 1404 × 1 (234 features × 6 sensors) for each trial.

There are totally 3060 trials in the dataset. Each trial is labeled according to the its movement type from 1 to 36. So our extracted dataset dimension is 1440 × 3060 array of data. Firstly, the dataset is normalized to the interval [0, 1] for reducing the computational complexity. Also, we reduced the number of features from 1440 to 60 components using Principal Component Analysis (PCA). PCA is an approach for deriving a low-dimensional set of features from a large set of variables [15]. After the implementation of PCA, 60 components represent 90% of the total variance. Their cumulative explained variance distributions are illustrated with all features and principal components in Figs. 1 and 2 respectively.

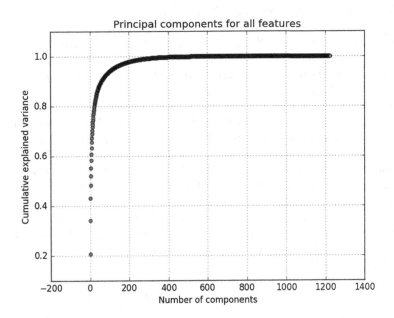

Fig. 1. The illustration of the all features with their cumulative explained variance.

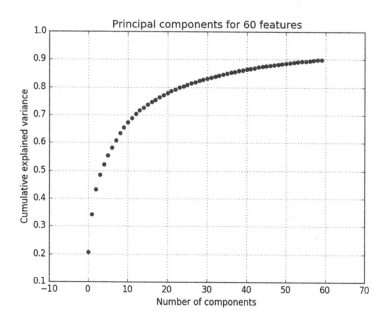

Fig. 2. The illustration of the 60 principal components after PCA with their cumulative explained variance.

3   Architecture of Neural Networks

In this study, a two-layer ANN structure is used in all experiments and it is outlined in Fig. 3. Firstly, hidden layer and output layer weights are initialized using the initialization approach discussed in He et al. [16] to improve of the performance of the model. This method remembers the previous layer size and that helps to reach minimum of the cost function quickly and efficiently. Afterwards, inputs x_j are multiplied by the weights W_{ij}^L in hidden layer and bias B_i^L values are added as shown in (2)–(3). Next, new values y_i are processed by the hyperbolic tangent activation function in (4) and the evaluated values are sent to the output layer weights W_{ij}^R and bias B_i^R in (5). Then, sigmoid activation function is used at the output layer. Output layer produces a matrix that contains probabilities between 0 and 1. According to (6)'s output matrix, a value larger than 0.5 is equal to the predicted class for the movement. At the end of the forward propagation using equations (2)–(7), the Mean Squared Error (MSE) is computed by using the output matrix of the network and desired output values of the dataset (See (7)).

$$\tau = \text{sigmoid}\left(W^R \text{tanh}(W^L x + B^L) + B^R\right) \tag{2}$$

where W^L is the leftmost weight matrix, W^R is the rightmost weight matrix, B^L and B^R are the corresponding bias vectors respectively. The neural network has m inputs and n outputs, and there are M_1 hidden neurons. With these

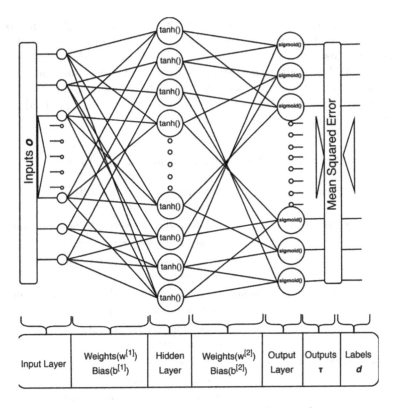

Fig. 3. A generic form of the two-layer neural network structure.

definitions, in the above input/output relation, $W_L \in \Re^{M_1 \times m}$, $B_L \in \Re^{M_1 \times 1}$, $W_R \in \Re^{n \times M_1}$ and $B_R \in \Re^{n \times 1}$.

The above equation can be written explicitly as follows

$$y_i^L = \sum_{j=1}^{m} W_{ij}^L x_j + B_i^L, \quad i = 1, 2, \ldots, M_1 \tag{3}$$

$$o_i^L = \tanh\left(y_i^L\right) \text{ where } i = 1, 2, 3, \ldots, M_1 \tag{4}$$

$$y_i^R = \sum_{j=1}^{M_1} W_{ij}^R o_j^L + B_i^R \text{ where } i = 1, 2, 3, \ldots, n \tag{5}$$

$$o_i^R = \text{sigmoid}(y_i^R) = \frac{1}{1 + e^{-y_i^R}} \text{ where } i = 1, 2, 3, \ldots, n \tag{6}$$

$$E := \frac{1}{2n} \sum_{i=1}^{n} (d_i - \tau_i)^2, \quad \tau_i = o_i^R \tag{7}$$

To decrease the training time and computational burden, number of neurons in hidden layers and input batch size are determined on the entire dataset. Then,

3 different optimization algorithms are used to compare classification models' performances on test set using 10-fold cross validation technique. The optimization algorithms used in this study are gradient descent, gradient descent with momentum and Adam algorithm. In order to prevent overtraining and memorization, all training algorithms are regularized by using dropout and L2 cost regularization techniques. A total of 9 different models are examined in this study and these models are shown in Table 2.

Table 2. 9 Models which are examined in this study.

Optimization algorithm	Optimization algorithm with regularization technique
Gradient descent	Gradient descent without regularization
	Gradient descent with dropout
	Gradient descent with L2 cost regularization
Gradient descent with momentum	G.D. Momentum without regularization
	G.D. Momentum with dropout
	G.D. Momentum with L2 cost regularization
Adam optimization algorithm	Adam without regularization
	Adam with dropout
	Adam with L2 cost regularization

As given in (2)–(7), forward propagation step is followed by gradient descent algorithm. This is given in (8)–(11).

$$W_{ij}^L(k+1) = W_{ij}^L(k) - \alpha \frac{\partial E}{\partial W_{ij}^L(k)} \tag{8}$$

$$W_{ij}^R(k+1) = W_{ij}^R(k) - \alpha \frac{\partial E}{\partial W_{ij}^R(k)} \tag{9}$$

$$B_i^L(k+1) = B_i^L(k) - \alpha \frac{\partial E}{\partial B_i^L(k)} \tag{10}$$

$$B_i^R(k+1) = B_i^R(k) - \alpha \frac{\partial E}{\partial B_i^R(k)} \tag{11}$$

Second optimization algorithm used in this work is gradient descent algorithm with momentum. Gradient descent with momentum is an algorithm that increases the gradient descent velocity in the related direction and reduces oscillations [17]. According to (12), a scaled value of the last update amount is used in the current update equation. The momentum term β is generally used as

0.9 or close values. After the calculation, standard weight update procedure is implemented, (See (13)).

$$v(k+1) = \beta v(k) + (1-\beta) \left.\frac{\partial E(W)}{\partial W}\right|_k, \quad W \in \{W^L, W^R, B^L, B^R\} \qquad (12)$$

$$W(k+1) = W(k) - \alpha v(k+1) \qquad (13)$$

Adaptive Moment Estimation (Adam) [18] is an optimization algorithm that computes adaptive learning rates for each parameter. It stores the previous gradients v_t, like momentum. Also it keeps exponentially decaying average of the previously squared gradients as m_t. At the beginning, v_t and m_t are initialized to zero vectors of appropriate dimensions. In (14) and (15), the mean moment and the uncentered variance moment of the gradients are defined respectively. Also the algorithm includes bias correction steps, which are given in (16) and (17). Then, these variables are used for updating the parameters (See (18)). Default Adam configuration parameters are 0.9 for β_1, 0.999 for β_2, and 10^{-8} for ϵ selected for the training [18].

$$v(k+1) = \beta_1 v(k) + (1-\beta_1) \left.\frac{\partial E(W)}{\partial W}\right|_k, \quad W \in \{W^L, W^R, B^L, B^R\} \qquad (14)$$

$$m(k+1) = \beta_2 m(k) + (1-\beta_2) \left.\frac{\partial E(W)}{\partial W}^2\right|_k, \quad W \in \{W^L, W^R, B^L, B^R\} \qquad (15)$$

$$v(k+1) = \frac{v(k+1)}{1-\beta_1} \qquad (16)$$

$$m(k+1) = \frac{m(k+1)}{1-\beta_2} \qquad (17)$$

$$W(k+1) = W(k) - \alpha \frac{v(k+1)}{\sqrt{m(k+1)} + \epsilon} \qquad (18)$$

Neural network models can memorize the training data. This causes a high variance problem. To overcome this problem, a remedy is to try regularization techniques. Adding regularization generally helps to prevent overfitting. In this study, we applied two different regularization techniques to each one of three different training algorithms. In addition, all 3 major models are trained without any regularization too.

Dropout [19] is a technique that prevents the model from overfitting. Basically, the dropout technique randomly closes the nodes in the hidden layer according to a specified rate, which prevents to overfitting to the training dataset.

L2 regularization is another approach to prevent the model from overtraining. It affects weights and cost function at the same time. L2 regularization method uses lambda parameter to penalize the weights and the cost function.

4   Test and Analysis

During the tests, an ANN with 2 hidden layers is used in 9 different classification models. As a result of the PCA implementation in data preprocessing step, the number of the features are reduced to the 60 principal components. Therefore, the weight matrix dimension in the hidden layer is in a generic form size (N × 60). The number of neurons in hidden layer is expressed by the N parameter in the general notation because its optimal values are found in the further tests. Lastly, in the output layer, 36 neurons are used for the recognition for 20 falls and 16 daily activities, so their generic weight matrix size is (36 × N).

All dataset contains 3060 observations. Each of the 36 movements is homogeneously distributed on the dataset and they are iterated 85 times. In order to obtain a good performance for the test set, the training steps are started directly with 10-fold cross validation. This means that the model is trained with 2754 observations and tested with 306 observations in every cycle. Also, each major algorithm is executed without regularization as well.

Firstly, we try to define optimal number of hidden layer units in major learning algorithms. Each trial is worked with 10-fold cross validation approach. Basically, the whole dataset is divided into 10 units and 9 of them are used for training and 1 of them used for testing the model. This scheme is continuously repeated for changing the test dataset.

Table 3. Mean accuracy score for the selections of optimization algorithm and number of hidden layer neurons.

Number of hidden layer neurons								
Optimization algorithm	10	20	40	60	100	150	200	250
Gradient descent	67.7%	87.7%	**90.5%**	91.0%	91.1%	91.1%	91.2%	91.3%
G.D. with momentum	71.8%	88.2%	90.4%	**91.7%**	91.6%	91.9%	91.7%	91.6%
Adam	89.4%	93.2%	**94.1%**	94.2%	94.1%	94.3%	94.4%	94.6%

As shown in the Table 3, number of neurons in the hidden layer is defined for three cases. For the gradient descent algorithm, gradient descent with momentum and Adam optimization algorithm, the number of neurons are selected 40, 60 and 40 respectively. The data listed in the table suggests better accuracy scores yet those cases come up with unaffordable computational burden.

In order to find the optimal batch sizes for the feedforward and backpropagation steps, we try 2754, 2048, 1024, 512, 256, 128, 64 batch sizes for the optimization algorithms. During these attempts, 10-fold cross validation is used and Table 4 shows the optimal learning rates and their batch sizes for each one of the algorithms considered. 3000 iterations are found to be sufficient in both parameter searches.

After the determining of the hidden layer units and optimal batch sizes for the three major models, they are analyzed for improving the test set accuracy score. In order to accomplish that, dropout and L2 cost regularization techniques are

Table 4. Mean accuracy scores for selections of optimization algorithms, learning rates and optimal batch sizes.

Optimization algorithm	Learning rate	Batch size	Accuracy score of test set
Gradient descent	0.7	2754	90.56%
G.D. with momentum	0.7	2754	91.83%
Adam	0.07	2754	**93.63%**

used for all discrete models. The selected hyperparameters of the regularization are defined during the experiments. Thus, λ is set 0.0009 for the L2 regularization and ratio for dropout is selected 0.85.

According to the result given Table 5, all models' mean accuracy performances on the test set are improved after the regularization techniques.

Table 5. Performance comparison of the nine models.

Optimization algorithm with regularization technique	Mean accuracy score of test set
Gradient descent without regularization	90.56%
Gradient descent with dropout	92.29%
Gradient descent with L2 cost regularization	90.70%
G.D. momentum without regularization	91.83%
G.D. momentum with dropout	92.16%
G.D. momentum with L2 cost regularization	93.46%
Adam without regularization	93.63%
Adam with dropout	**94.58%**
Adam with L2 cost regularization	94.25%

To visualize and analyze the performance of the classified daily activities and falls separately, a normalized confusion matrix is illustrated in Fig. 4. The matrix is created by using the model that executed with Adam optimizer with dropout via optimized hyperparameters. The vast majority of activity misclassifications take place in the front-lying fall which is numbered by 1st. Additionally, except for 7 and 9 fall types, other falls are classified correctly. Therefore, it can be said that the false negative alarm is kept at the minimum level.

The proposed model classified some daily activities as front-lying fall as seen in Fig. 4. When the definitions of the 18th, 21th, 22nd, 24th and 29th movements are examined according to the Table 1, these have similar action patterns with falling forward. Moreover, the rate of these misclassifications does not exceed 30%.

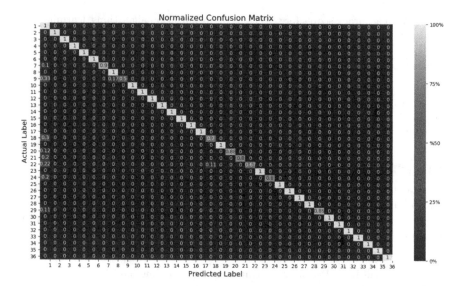

Fig. 4. The normalized confusion matrix is formed using the samples of the test set. The rows in the matrix show the actual class of the sample and the columns represent the class assigned by the classifier. The main diagonal shows the percentage of the movement types are predicted correctly. The numbers on the edges represent the falls and daily activities as explained in Table 1

To enable early intervention of IPAs, the real-time classification is very important. Proposed model is capable to predict a movement approximately at 0,000006 s. Time can be maximum 1 s on embedded platforms with data acquiring from sensors, data preprocessing and classification steps.

All training experiments are deployed on a Ubuntu 16.04 LTS linux-based computer with 64-bit Intel Core i7-3630QM processor, CPU @ 2.40 GHz × 4 for the CPU measurements and 8 GB of RAM.

5   Discussion

When we evaluate the results of our model with reference articles, we can say that the developed model is resulted in a slightly lower accuracy. One of the main reasons for that the proposed model aims to classify more falls and daily activities than other studies. When the number of classification capabilities of the model increases, a decreasing on the overall accuracy is also expected. For instance, while the studies [12] and [13] only perform binary fall recognition, thus they achieved highly accurate results. However, [10] and [11] classify 6 different movements with 96.2% and 98% accuracy scores on the test set respectively. As a result, When the model is evaluated according to these results, it has 6-times wider movement classification spectrum than the existing studies with 94.58% accuracy score.

6 Conclusion

In this paper, we focus on classification of 36 different movement types in the domain of falls and daily activities. Three different learning algorithms and two different regularization techniques are compared and all of the 10-fold cross validation mean accuracy scores are observed above 90%. The most successful classifier obtained at the end of the study is the Adam optimization technique with dropout, which produced 94.58% mean test accuracy. When the result is compared with exist studies, the fact that 16 daily human activities and 20 falls can accurately be defined at such a rate is remarkable for sensory data and the scheme it is obtained. ANN based classifiers are found versatile in processing the information considered here and in generating useful outputs. In the future, smart phones are aimed to be used for data acquisition and classification.

References

1. Sankarasubramaniam, Y., Akyildiz, I.F., Su, W., Cayirci, E.: A survey on sensor networks. IEEE Commun. Mag. **40**(8), 102–114 (2002)
2. Aggarwal, C.C.: Managing and Mining Sensor Data. Springer, New York (2009)
3. Sherrington, C., Menz, H.B., Close, J.C., Lord, S.R.: Falls in Older People: Risk Factors and Strategies for Prevention. Cambridge University Press, Cambridge (2007)
4. Gillespie, L.D., et al.: Interventions for preventing falls in older people living in the community. Cochrane Database Syst. Rev. (9) (2012). ISSN 1465-1858. https://doi.org/10.1002/14651858.CD007146.pub3
5. Crouter, S., Bassett, D., Freedson, P., Staudenmayer, J., Pober, D.: An artificial neural network to estimate physical activity energy expenditure and identify physical activity type from an accelerometer. J. Appl. Physiol. **107**(8), 1300–1307 (2009)
6. King, R., Yang, G.Z., Atallah, L., Lo, B.: Sensor placement for activity detection using wearable accelerometers. In: Proceedings of International Conference on Body Sensor Networks, pp. 24–29 (2010)
7. Oliveira, N.H., et al.: Relationship between pulmonary function and physical activity in daily life in patients with COPD. Respir. Med. **102**(8), 1203–1207 (2008)
8. Rodrigues, J., Silva, B., Casal, J., Saleem, K., Denisov, V., Santos, J.: An iot-based mobile gateway for intelligent personal assistants on mobile health environments. J. Netw. Comput. Appl. **71**(8), 1203–1207 (2016)
9. Labrador, M., Delahoz, Y.: Survey on fall detection and fall prevention using wearable and external sensors. Sensors **14**, 19806–19842 (2014)
10. Morgül, Ö., Çatalbaş, B., Çatalbaş, B.: Human activity recognition with different artificial neural network based classifiers. In: 25th Signal Processing and Communications Applications Conference, pp. 1–4 (2017)
11. Conde, I.G., Sobrino, X.A.V., Olivieri, D.N.: Eigenspace-based fall detection and activity recognition from motion templates and machine learning. Expert Syst. Appl. **39**(5), 5935–5945 (2012)
12. Barshan, B., Özdemir, A.T.: Detecting falls with wearable sensors using machine learning techniques. Sensors (Basel, Switzerland) **14**, 10691–10708 (2014)

13. Monteiro, K., Rocha, E., Silva, I., Lynn, T., Leoni, G., Endo, P.: Accelerometer-based human fall detection using convolutional neural networks. Sensors **19**, 1644 (2019)
14. Xsens Technologies B.V.: MTw Awinda User Manual and Technical Documentation (2019). http://www.xsens.com/. Accessed 2 Mar 2019
15. Hastie, T., Tibshirani, R., James, G., Witten, D.: An Introduction to Statistical Learning: With Applications in R. Springer, Heidelberg (2014). https://doi.org/10.1007/978-1-4614-7138-7
16. Ren, S., Sun, J., He, K., Zhang, X.: Delving deep into rectifiers: surpassing human-level performance on imagenet classification. In: Proceedings of the 2015 IEEE International Conference on Computer Vision (ICCV), Washington, DC, USA, pp. 1026–1034. IEEE Computer Society (2015)
17. Qian, N.: On the momentum term in gradient descent learning algorithms. Neural Netw.: Off. J. Int. Neural Netw. Soc. **12**, 145–151 (1999)
18. Ba, J., Kingma, P.: Adam: a method for stochastic optimization. In: International Conference in Learning Representations (2015)
19. Krizhevsky, A., Sutskever, I., Salakhutdinov, R., Srivastava, N., Hinton, G.E.: Dropout: a simple way to prevent neural networks from overfitting. J. Mach. Learn. Res. **15**(1), 1929–1958 (2014)

Exploring Model Transfer Potential
for Airborne LiDAR Point Cloud Classification

Yuzhun Lin, Chuan Zhao[⊠], Daoji Li, Junfeng Xu,
and Baoming Zhang

Information Engineering University, Zhengzhou 450001, China
hehe549124@outlook.com

Abstract. The deep learning paradigm has been shown to be an effective framework in many applications, including airborne light detection and ranging point cloud classification. However, even a simple deep neural network has large quantities of parameters, and the optimal parameters generally need several hours to be learned. In this paper, we propose a framework to take full advantage of existing deep neural networks in image processing domains and to reduce the training time for classification. The framework is composed of four key steps: (1) calculate low-level features; (2) transform three-dimensional point clouds into multi-scale feature images by the proposed feature image generation strategy; (3) extract multi-scale deep features from the feature images by introducing transfer learning, i.e., a pre-trained neural network; and (4) learn higher-level features via a fully connected network and fuse higher-level features using a convolutional neural network. Our framework has been evaluated using a benchmark dataset provided by the International Society for Photogrammetry and Remote Sensing, and experimental results show that the proposed framework can reduce the time needed for obtaining an optimal classification model and effectively classify nine objects, such as buildings, the ground, and cars, with an overall accuracy of 90.1%, which is beneficial for providing reliable information for further applications.

Keywords: Transfer learning · Classification · Feature image · Airborne LiDAR point cloud · Multi-scale · High-level features

1 Introduction

Airborne laser scanning (ALS) is a spatial information acquisition technology that can directly and rapidly acquire large-scale, high-precision, and high-density point clouds, and it has made great progress in recent years. The point cloud data obtained by ALS have been widely used in many applications, such as urban three-dimensional modeling [1], power line patrol and reconstruction [2], ocean soundings, and biomass estimation [3]. Despite recent advances, since the airborne light detection and ranging (LiDAR) point cloud data only represent a discrete set of points in space, it is difficult to directly obtain semantic information about the object surface; thus, there are still many problems to be solved in airborne LiDAR point cloud data post-processing. Airborne LiDAR point cloud classification, as one of the key steps in airborne LiDAR point

© Springer Nature Switzerland AG 2020
C. Djeddi et al. (Eds.): MedPRAI 2019, CCIS 1144, pp. 39–51, 2020.
https://doi.org/10.1007/978-3-030-37548-5_4

cloud data post-processing, has received extensive attention. However, due to the inherent characteristics of point cloud data (such as irregular distribution and uneven density) and the complexity of real-world scenarios, it is still a great challenge to achieve automatic and high-precision point cloud classification.

1.1 Related Work

To date, airborne LiDAR point cloud classification has been extensively studied, and researchers have developed a large number of classification methods to improve the classification accuracy from different aspects. Based on the type of point cloud features used in the classification, existing airborne LiDAR point cloud classification methods can be generally divided into two categories, i.e., low-level feature-based and deep feature-based.

As there are many elaborate hand-crafted features, most studies focus on low-level feature-based classification methods, which utilize strategies like unsupervised or supervised learning or a combination of both to classify the point clouds. The unsupervised point cloud classification methods usually design specific rules to classify point clouds into a few object categories according to their characteristics, such as point cloud filtering [4] and specific object extraction (e.g., buildings and trees). Although training samples are not required, these methods normally depend on many thresholds that may lower their adaptability to some extent; in addition, their performance is greatly affected by scenario complexity. On the other hand, supervised point cloud classification methods make use of prior information in training samples, which potentially improves their adaptability; the core of these methods is the use of single or multiple traditional machine learning algorithms, such as SVM (support vector machine) [5], AdaBoost [6], JointBoost [7], RF (random forest) [8], and CRF (conditional random fields) [8, 9], to learn hyperplane parameters from training samples; then, the point cloud feature space is divided into multiple subspaces via the learned hyperplane parameters. However, as these methods still use low-level features of point clouds without learning their high-level features, it is difficult for them to further improve the classification accuracy, especially in multi-class classification tasks (more than five classes). Point cloud classification methods that combine unsupervised and supervised strategies usually apply specific rules to pre-process point clouds in an unsupervised way (e.g., region growing and voxel segmentation) [10] and then use traditional machine learning algorithms to achieve classification in a supervised way. Although the classification accuracy of the methods largely depends on the unsupervised strategies used, their efficiency could be significantly improved.

In recent years, with the development of deep learning and its wide application in computer vision, image processing, and other fields [11], point cloud classification methods based on deep learning have gradually attracted the attention of researchers. Since the density of point clouds acquired by ALS systems is relatively lower than that acquired by mobile laser scanning systems, it is more difficult to extract detailed information from the ALS point clouds, and few studies have attempted to apply deep learning to classify ALS point clouds. As deep learning can automatically extract deep features with strong representation ability in the process of classification, ALS point cloud classification methods based on deep learning can not only reduce the tedious work of manually designing and extracting low-level features of point clouds but can also further improve the classification accuracy [12]. However, the deep neural networks used for point cloud classification usually contain a large number of hyperparameters that require more training samples and time to obtain optimal classification models, which, to some extent, limits the further application of deep learning in airborne LiDAR point cloud classification.

1.2 Contribution

We propose an airborne LiDAR point cloud data classification framework by designing a feature image generation strategy and exploring the potential of directly applying a neural network pre-trained on ImageNet. The main contributions of our work are as follow: firstly, we build up a bridge between a three-dimensional (3D) point cloud and transfer learning by employing geometric features (i.e., normalized height, normal vector and intensity) to generate feature images; secondly, we explore the potential of different pre-trained neural networks for point cloud classification and conclude that a pre-trained residual network is more suitable to transfer for this task; thirdly, by designing a simple classification neural network to learn and fuse high-level features, we could efficiently train and ensure preferable classification accuracy within the framework.

2 Methodology

In this paper, we are interested in classifying airborne LiDAR point clouds into multi-type object classes (i.e., nine different classes) rather than into some easily distinguishable classes, such as buildings, vegetation, and the ground. Figure 1 shows the overall flow chart of our framework; there are four key steps in the framework, which will be described in detail in the following section.

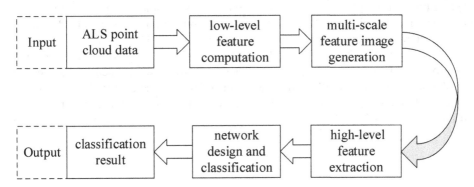

Fig. 1. Overall flow chart of the proposed framework.

2.1   Low-Level Feature Computation

As we intend to apply a pre-trained neural network in the next step, it is necessary to extract a few low-level point cloud features with high discrimination to generate point cloud feature images.

According to the characteristics of airborne LiDAR point clouds and the attributes of different objects, researchers have designed a variety of point cloud features [8, 9]. Although the features are designed to reflect the attributes of objects from different aspects to improve the classification accuracy, it is not beneficial to use all the features since they are not entirely irrelevant, and the correlation between them is averse to improving the classification accuracy. On the other hand, using more features in the classification process means more time is needed.

To decrease the correlation and classification time without sacrificing accuracy, many scholars have applied feature selection algorithms to reduce the dimensions of the feature space. For example, some researchers have first extracted several different features then used RF to select important features according to their scores [8, 13, 14]. Based on the analysis and results of these studies, we selected normalized height, the z component of the normal vector, intensity, and the normalized difference vegetation index (NDVI) to generate feature images. To extract the normalized height, we generated digital terrain model by using cloth simulation filtering [15], which is implemented in the open source software CloudCompare. As the point cloud normal vector based on covariance analysis is not accurate for points near transition areas, we utilized a robust normal vector estimation algorithm [16] that can accurately estimate the normal component of the points, even if they are at the border of different objects.

2.2   Multi-scale Feature Image Generation

In general, converting point clouds into images for point cloud classification reduces the accuracy of classification, as this projection method will lead to information loss. However, since the feature image contains information about the point and its neighboring points, each point image increases some redundant information, which may be beneficial for classification. Thus, in this paper, we propose a new point cloud feature image generation strategy, whose main process is shown in Fig. 2.

As shown in Fig. 2(a), for point P, points in its cube neighborhood are selected to be projected onto an x-y plane; the neighborhood size is determined by the image resolution, length, and width of the feature image to be generated (unless otherwise noted, both the length and width in this paper are set to $l_{wh} = 33$); and the projection result is shown in Fig. 2(b).

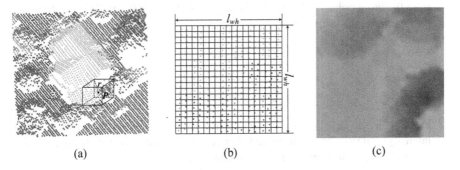

(a)   (b)   (c)

Fig. 2. The point cloud feature image generation process. From left to right: (a) cube neighborhood selection, (b) cube neighborhood projection, and (c) generated feature image.

Since a point cloud is usually non-uniformly distributed and has uneven density, not all grids contain points, so it is necessary to interpolate values for those containing no points. In order to maintain the spatial information of a neighborhood, we firstly interpolate height for each pixel grid by searching a neighborhood point in two dimensions and then interpolate the pixel value by searching the grid points in three dimensions. The detailed steps are described as follows.

(1) Assume P is the point used to generate a feature image, according to its coordinates (X_P, Y_P), image resolution, length, and width; the coordinates $(X_{P_{i,j}}, Y_{P_{i,j}})$ of pixel grid point $P_{i,j}$ are then calculated by:

$$\begin{cases} X_{p_{i,j}} = X_P + (j - [0.5 * l_{wh}]) * \omega \\ Y_{p_{i,j}} = Y_P + (i - [0.5 * l_{wh}]) * \omega \end{cases} \tag{1}$$

In Eq. (1), i, j are the row and column number of pixel grid point $P_{i,j}$ in the feature image, respectively.

(2) Search the nearest n neighboring points for point $P_{i,j}$ in the two-dimensional neighborhood of point P (unless otherwise stated, n is set to 3). Interpolate the height $Z_{P_{i,j}}$ of the current pixel grid point $P_{i,j}$ by using the inverse distance weighted (IDW) algorithm:

$$Z_S^{p_{i,j}} = \sum_{k=1}^{n} w_k * Z_S^{p_k}$$
$$w_k = \frac{1/d_k}{\sum_{k=1}^{n} 1/d_k} \tag{2}$$

In Eq. (2), Z_S denotes height; P_k is the nearest k point of $P_{i,j}$; and d_k is the distance between point P_k and pixel grid point $P_{i,j}$ in two dimensions.

(3) Through the above two steps, the spatial coordinates of pixel grid point $P_{i,j}$ $(X_{P_{i,j}}, Y_{P_{i,j}}, Z_{P_{i,j}})$ are obtained. Then, we search the nearest n neighboring points of $P_{i,j}$

from the input point cloud and interpolate the features of $P_{i,j}$ by applying IDW and using Eq. (3) to determine its RGB value:

$$\begin{cases} R=\lfloor 255 * f_{zv} \rfloor \\ G=\lfloor 255 * f_{in} * f_{ndvi} \rfloor \\ B=\lfloor 255 * f_{ht} \rfloor \end{cases} \tag{3}$$

In Eq. (3), f_{zv}, f_{in}, f_{ndvi}, and f_{ht} denote the z component of the normal vector, intensity, NDVI, and normalized height of the interpolated feature of $P_{i,j}$, respectively; $\lfloor \rfloor$ denotes the rounding-down function.

By setting a certain image resolution and utilizing the point cloud feature image generation strategy in this section, a point cloud feature image of a single scale can be obtained, as shown in Fig. 2(c). Generally, using multi-scale point cloud features can achieve higher classification accuracy [8]; however, point cloud features obtained at different scales are correlated, which makes it difficult to improve the classification accuracy by only increasing the number of scales. Thus, we only set three different image resolutions, i.e., 0.1, 0.2 and 0.3 m, to obtain the multi-scale point cloud feature images in this paper.

2.3 High-Level Feature Extraction

Deep learning can automatically extract high-level features from data by combining low-level features, which can approximate the intrinsic attributes of objects. Therefore, compared with low-level features, the generalization of high-level features is stronger. However, constructing and training a complete deep neural network generally requires a large number of training samples and a lot of training time. Furthermore, deep neural networks usually involve a lot of parameters that must be set manually, e.g., the number of hidden layer neurons and initial learning rate. Unfortunately, as there is no standard principle of how to set these parameters, they can be determined only by many experiments, leading to a lot of cumbersome work.

To solve the above problems, researchers have proposed the idea of transfer learning, which can reduce the number of training samples needed, training time, and model complexity of deep neural networks by transferring knowledge from source tasks to target tasks. Tan et al. [17] divided deep transfer learning into four categories, i.e., instances-based, mapping-based, network-based, and adversarial-based. The network-based methods transfer knowledge from source tasks to target tasks by reusing the structure and parameters of networks pre-trained in the source domain [17], which avoids the tedious work of designing the network structure and reduces the training time. In addition, Tan et al. [17] indicated that LeNet, AlexNet, VGG (Visual Geometry Group), Inception, and ResNet (Residual Networks) are better network models for deep transfer learning. Thus, we extracted high-level features by applying a pre-trained neural network on ImageNet, i.e., VGG (including VGG16, VGG19), Inception V4, or ResNet50, to explore the potential of model transfer.

2.4   Network Design and Classification

Although multi-scale high-level features extracted by a pre-trained neural network have preferable generalization in theory, the difference between the source (image) and target (airborne LiDAR point cloud) domains is large, so we follow the conclusion of Zhang et al. [18] to design a basic fully connected (FC) network to learn higher-level features, as the FC layer plays an important role in achieving high accuracy. Then, we design a convolutional neural network (CNN) to fuse the higher-level features. Considering that the deeper the network model, the more complex the model and that the training time is usually increased, both the FC network and the CNN involve only two layers. The detailed architecture of our designed neural network is shown in Fig. 3 (the number under the FC layer denotes the number of neurons).

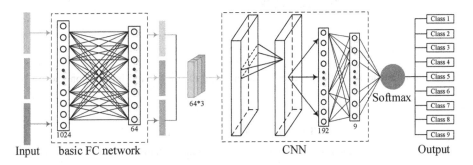

Fig. 3. The architecture of the designed network.

3   Experiments

In this section, we present experiments to evaluate the performance of our proposed framework. Firstly, we describe the dataset and experimental configuration. Then, we explore the potential of different pre-trained networks and present the experimental results and analysis.

3.1   Dataset Description

We evaluated our method using an airborne LiDAR point cloud dataset from Vaihingen, Germany, which was acquired in August 2008 by ALS50 with an average flying height of 500 meters and a field view of 45°; the point density is about 4–8 points/m². The dataset is manually labeled into nine classes, i.e., powerline, low vegetation, impervious surfaces, car, fence/hedge, roof, facade, shrub, and tree. Both the airborne LiDAR point cloud and the classified benchmark are provided by the International Society for Photogrammetry and Remote Sensing. Figure 4 shows the dataset color-coded by spectral information (IR, R, G) and by height. Detailed information on the dataset is shown in Table 1.

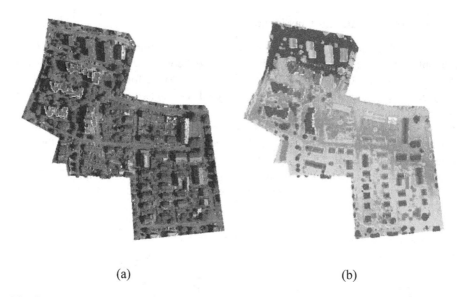

(a)   (b)

Fig. 4. From left to right: the point cloud color-coded (a) by spectral information and (b) by height.

Table 1. Details of the dataset.

Class	Original dataset (number)	Training set (number)	Test set (number)
Power line	546	346	200
Low vegetation	180,850	15,005	165,845
Impervious surfaces	193,723	15,516	178,207
Car	4614	2614	2,000
Fence/Hedge	12,070	10,070	2,000
Roof	152,045	15,045	137,000
Facade	27,250	12,250	15,000
Shrub	47,605	11,605	36,000
Tree	135,173	13,173	122,000
Total	753,876	95,624	658,252

3.2 Experimental Configuration

Our algorithms are implemented by using C++ (for image generation), Python 3.6, TensorFlow, and Keras (for the neural network) on a laptop with an Intel Core i7-7700HK processor, 64 GB RAM, and a NVIDIA GTX 1080 TI 11 GB GPU. We trained the network by utilizing the Adam optimizer with an initial learning rate (lr) of 0.001 and a batch size of 128 for a total of 120 epochs. The lr is changed based on the number of current epochs and the value itself, according to:

$$lr = \begin{cases} 0.1 * lr \ \ if \ epoch\%2 = 0 \\ 10^{-5} \ \ if \ lr < 10^{-7} \end{cases} \tag{4}$$

The numbers of each class used for the training set and test set are shown in Table 1. We employed some common quantitative performance metrics, i.e., precision, recall, F1-score, and overall accuracy, to evaluate the classification results of the test set.

3.3 Results and Analysis

We applied the four pre-trained neural networks described in Sect. 2.3 to extract high-level features and then trained the designed neural network to compare their classification capabilities. Figure 5 shows the visual comparison of the classification results of the test set between the different neural networks.

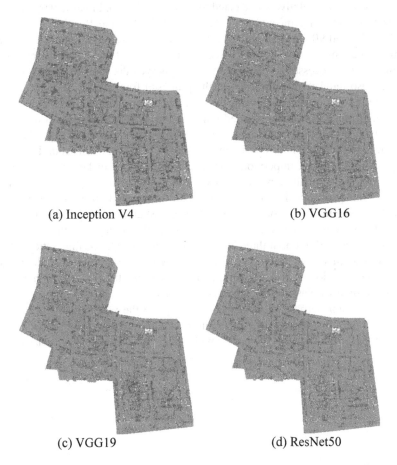

(a) Inception V4   (b) VGG16

(c) VGG19   (d) ResNet50

Fig. 5. Visual comparison of the classification results of the test set between different neural networks. Green and red denote true and false classifications, respectively. (Color figure online)

As can be seen from Fig. 5, most points—especially those of impervious surfaces and roof—can be labeled correctly by the framework, while shrub and hedge/fence points are not well classified regardless of which pre-trained neural network is used. This is possible because the selected low-level features are already of high discrimination in labeling objects such as roof, the ground, and tree, and their discrimination is further improved through abstracting via the framework. However, as the low-level features have large similarities between shrub and hedge/fence, even after abstraction, their discrimination is still not sufficient for correct labeling, which results in poor classification. Furthermore, we find that using the pre-trained Inception V4 to extract high-level features for classification obtains the worst result, especially for shrub and hedge/fence, and there is almost no difference in the results acquired by using VGG16 and VGG19. In contrast, the classification result of applying ResNet50 to extract high-level features is fairly well. This demonstrates that ResNet50 is more suitable for model transfer in our framework compared with the other networks.

To better illustrate the classification performance of employing the four networks for each class, we quantitatively evaluated the results in Fig. 6. In particular, the overall accuracy levels utilizing Inception V4, VGG16, VGG19, and ResNet50 are 83.7%, 87.9%, 87.4%, and 90.1%, respectively. In addition, as training and high-level feature extraction take almost the entire classification time in this framework, we present the times of the two processes to compare the efficiency of the four networks (Table 2), which can also indicate the efficiency of the proposed framework.

As noted in Fig. 6, our framework has high recall for all objects except powerline, whereas high precision can be reached only for low vegetation, impervious surfaces, roof, and tree. In addition to the aforementioned reasons, unbalanced data distribution is also an important factor in this issue. Moreover, it can be seen from Table 1 that points of low vegetation, impervious surfaces, roof, and tree make up the majority of the dataset; thus, a small number of misclassified points in these objects has little impact on their precision. From Fig. 6, we can also conclude that ResNet50 is more suitable for model transfer in our framework, as almost all of its metrics are higher than those of the other three networks. In terms of algorithm efficiency, the classification time of our framework is about three hours, which demonstrates its high efficiency. It is also noteworthy that the training time of the framework is less than half an hour, as the designed classification neural network is fairly simple; this is very beneficial for obtaining an optimal classifier in a shorter amount of time.

Since our main purpose in the paper is to explore the potential of directly transferring pre-trained models in image domain to classify airborne LiDAR data, experiments are not performed to compare with other good point cloud classification methods.

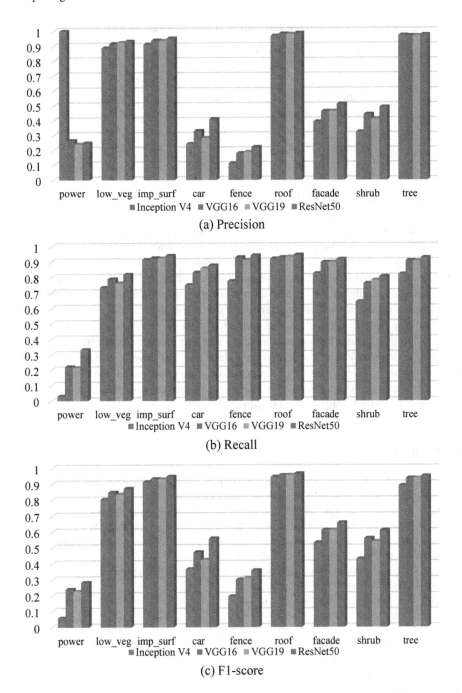

(a) Precision

(b) Recall

(c) F1-score

Fig. 6. Quantitative comparison of the classification results of the test set among different neural networks.

Table 2. Training time and high-level feature extraction (in hours).

Networks	Training time	High-level feature extraction time		Total
		Training set	Test set	
Inception V4	0.359	0.493	2.083	2.935
VGG16	0.422	0.361	1.626	2.409
VGG19	0.417	0.406	1.806	2.629
ResNet50	0.382	0.412	1.837	2.631

4 Conclusions and Outlook

In this paper, we have proposed a framework to take full advantage of existing deep neural networks in the image processing field for airborne LiDAR point cloud classification. By exploring the potential of different pre-trained neural networks, we were able to conclude that ResNet50 is more suitable to transfer for this task compared with other networks, although it needs more time to extract high-level features. Our experimental results show that the framework needs less than half an hour for training, which is very beneficial for obtaining optimal classifiers. Additionally, the framework can provide good classification results in the labeling of nine objects with an overall accuracy of 90.1%. Future work will consider more low-level features, such as the normal variance, covariance, and density, into consideration in the feature image generation strategy. Moreover, we are going to consider contextual information in the framework to further improve the classification accuracy.

References

1. Zhang, L., Li, Z., Li, A., et al.: Large-scale urban point cloud labeling and reconstruction. ISPRS J. Photogr. Remote Sens. **138**, 86–100 (2018)
2. Jwa, Y., Sohn, G., Kim, H.B.: Automatic 3D powerline reconstruction using airborne LiDAR data. Int. Arch. Photogr. Remote Sens. Spat. Inform. Sci. **38**(3), W8 (2009)
3. Wang, C., Nie, S., Xi, X.H., et al.: Estimating the biomass of maize with hyperspectral and LiDAR data. Remote Sens. **9**(1), 11 (2017)
4. Hu, X., Yuan, Y.: Deep-learning-based classification for DTM extraction from ALS point cloud. Remote Sens. **8**(9), 1–16 (2016)
5. Huo, L.Z., Silva, C.A., Klauberg, C., et al.: Supervised spatial classification of multispectral LiDAR data in urban areas. PLoS One **13**(10), 1–17 (2018)
6. Zhang, Z., Zhang, L., Tong, X., et al.: Discriminative-dictionary-learning-based multilevel point-cluster features for ALS point cloud classification. IEEE Trans. Geosci. Remote Sens. **54**(12), 7309–7322 (2016)
7. Guo, B., Huang, X., Zhang, F., et al.: Classification of airborne laser scanning data using JointBoost. ISPRS J. Photogr. Remote Sens. **100**, 71–83 (2015)
8. Niemeyer, J., Rottensteiner, F., Soergel, U.: Contextual classification of LiDAR data and building object detection in urban areas. ISPRS J. Photogr. Remote Sens. **87**(1), 152–165 (2014)

9. Niemeyer, J., Wegner, J.D., Mallet, C., Rottensteiner, F., Soergel, U.: Conditional random fields for urban scene classification with full waveform LiDAR data. In: Stilla, U., Rottensteiner, F., Mayer, H., Jutzi, B., Butenuth, M. (eds.) PIA 2011. LNCS, vol. 6952, pp. 233–244. Springer, Heidelberg (2011). https://doi.org/10.1007/978-3-642-24393-6_20

10. Xu, S., Vosselman, G., Elberink, S.O.: Multiple-entity based classification of airborne laser scanning data in urban areas. ISPRS J. Photogr. Remote Sens. **88**(2), 1–15 (2014)

11. Lecun, Y., Bengio, Y., Hinton, G.: Deep learning. Nature **521**(7553), 436 (2015)

12. ISPRS Test Project on Urban Classification and 3D Building Reconstruction. http://www2.isprs.org/commissions/comm2/wg4/vaihingen-3d-semantic-labeling.html. Accessed 19 May 2019

13. Chehata, N., Guo, L., Mallet, C.: Airborne lidar feature selection for urban classification using random forests. In: International Archives of Photogrammetry, Remote Sensing and Spatial Information Sciences, Paris, France, pp. 207–212 (2009)

14. Weinmann, M., Jutzi, B., Hinz, S., et al.: Semantic point cloud interpretation based on optimal neighborhoods, relevant features and efficient classifiers. ISPRS J. Photogr. Remote Sens. **105**, 286–304 (2015)

15. Zhang, W., Qi, J., Wan, P., Wang, H., Xie, D., Wang, X., Yan, G.: an easy-to-use airborne LiDAR data filtering method based on cloth simulation. Remote Sens. **8**(6), 501 (2016)

16. Boulch, A., Marlet, R.: Fast and robust normal estimation for point clouds with sharp features. In: Computer graphics forum, pp. 1765–1774, Blackwell Publishing Ltd., Oxford (2012)

17. Tan, C., Sun, F., Kong, T., Zhang, W., Yang, C., Liu, C.: A survey on deep transfer learning. In: Kůrková, V., Manolopoulos, Y., Hammer, B., Iliadis, L., Maglogiannis, I. (eds.) ICANN 2018. LNCS, vol. 11141, pp. 270–279. Springer, Cham (2018). https://doi.org/10.1007/978-3-030-01424-7_27

18. Zhang, C.-L., Luo, J.-H., Wei, X.-S., Wu, J.: in defense of fully connected layers in visual representation transfer. In: Zeng, B., Huang, Q., El Saddik, A., Li, H., Jiang, S., Fan, X. (eds.) PCM 2017. LNCS, vol. 10736, pp. 807–817. Springer, Cham (2018). https://doi.org/10.1007/978-3-319-77383-4_79

Haralick Feature Guided Network for the Improvement of Generalization in Landcover Classification

Yuzhun Lin, Daoji Li[(✉)] [iD], Chuan Zhao, Junfeng Xu,
and Baoming Zhang

Information Engineering University, Zhengzhou, Henan, China
wanglll@alumni.sjtu.edu.cn

Abstract. This study examined the application of semantic segmentation in landcover classification, a recently popular task in the field of remote sensing. Most semantic segmentation methods exhibit strong sample dependence. This tends to have high prediction accuracy in similar areas, but low accuracy in other areas or the same area at different time phases. Our approach utilizes three Haralick features to enhance the generalization ability. In addition, several variants were also implemented for comparison. We found that these features can effectively improve generalization of landcover classification.

Keywords: Landcover classification · Generalization · Haralick feature · Remote sensing

1 Introduction

Landcover refers to the pattern of ecological resources and human activities dominating different areas of the Earth's surface. Improving the accuracy of landcover classification is of great significance to the various environmental science and land management applications at global, regional, and local scales [1].

Landcover classification has been studied for decades in the field of remote sensing, and lots of traditional methods have been proposed. Most of these methods focus on features that are extracted by hand [2]. However, the accuracy of the classification depends on the features extracted from remote sensing images. For example, Mahmoud et al. confirmed that integrated landcover classification using the textural information of TerraSAR-X has a high potential for landcover mapping [3]. Applying a texture-based analysis, they achieved an overall accuracy of 95% with a kappa coefficient of 93% with the TerraSAR-X image. With the increasing number of remote sensing data being acquired and the corresponding number of annotated samples, supervised classification methods are being widely applied for landcover classification, such as random forests (RFs) and support vector machines (SVMs) [4, 5]. These methods can achieve better classification accuracy compared with the aforementioned. Nevertheless, these methods can only extract the shallow features, in other words, they still rely on artificial designed features.

© Springer Nature Switzerland AG 2020
C. Djeddi et al. (Eds.): MedPRAI 2019, CCIS 1144, pp. 52–64, 2020.
https://doi.org/10.1007/978-3-030-37548-5_5

With the rapid development of deep learning and computer vision, lots of methods including deep neural networks are being applied to landcover classification [6–9]. In fact, landcover classification is the process of pixel-wise classification, which is also called semantic segmentation in natural image classification. The landmark fully convolutional network (FCN) first adopted a novel end-to-end segmentation learning method, which greatly promotes the development of a semantic segmentation network [10]. After that, Badrinarayanan et al. proposed a typical case of using an alternative decoder variant, SegNet [11]. This network has two main structures, the encoder and decoder structures, which are regarded as the standard structures in other semantic segmentation structures. Ronneberger et al. proposed the U-Net that concatenates feature maps from different levels through skipped connections, which combines low-level detail information and high-level semantic information [12]. The U-Net is mainly used to handle binary classification problems, which has achieved promising performance on biomedical image segmentation. The deep residual U-Net, which is an improvement on the U-Net, has also achieved an excellent classification effect on road extraction from remote sensing imagery [13]. Based on the design concept of the preceding excellent network, Chen et al. proposed the deeplabv3+, which has attained the state-of-the-art level on PASCAL VOC 2012 and Cityscapes datasets [14]. This network takes the Xception model as its backbone and applies the depthwise separable convolution to both Atrous Spatial Pyramid Pooling and decoder modules, resulting in a faster and stronger encoder-decoder network.

Most semantic segmentation networks can have high accuracy on the specified database, but the strong dependence on the sample limits the generalization. As for the field of remote sensing, the images from different time phases often show different spectral characteristics. For example, the vegetation is green in summer, but brown in autumn. This will greatly diminish the model identification accuracy and practicability.

The major contribution of this research is to present a sample framework, which is based on the deeplabv3+. The difference is that some Haralick features are added into the input channels, such that combined with the spectral channels, the generalization is greatly enhanced.

The remainder of this paper is organized as follows. Section 2 elaborates the proposed method, including three variants. Some preliminary work is introduced in Sect. 3. The experiments are shown in Sect. 4, we conclude this work in Sect. 5.

2 Proposed Methodology

2.1 Selection of Haralick Features

The spectral radiation characteristics of ground objects are quite different from each other at different time phases, so it is essential to select some robust features by hand, instead of training on spectral features alone.

Texture features are important characteristics for the analysis of many types of images, especially for multispectral scanner images or remote sensing images. Therefore, the Haralick texture features were selected as the features to improve the generalization [15]. There are a total of 13 texture features from which to select. In order to improve the practicability of landcover classification, three representative landcover categories were annotated: vegetation, water, and built-up. Then, it is important to choose the appropriate features that can highlight the differences of these areas.

However, not all Haralick features are useful for classification. Five Haralick features are candidates for selection, namely, variance, homogeneity, contrast, dissimilarity and angular second moment (ASM). In order to explore the feasibility of the method, the features of the red channels were used for the experiments. Some simple experiments were imployed to select three favorable features.

The precision of Haralick feature combination is shown in Fig. 1. It is obvious that the combination of variance, contrast and ASM achieves the best performance.

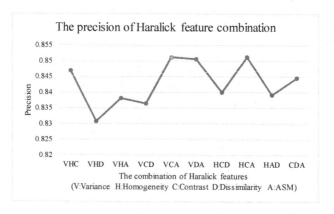

Fig. 1. The precision of Haralick feature combination

The specific calculation formulas of these texture features are as follows:

$$contrast = \sum_{i=0}^{quant_k} \sum_{j=0}^{quant_k} p(i,j) * (i-j)^2 \tag{1}$$

$$variance = \sum_{i=0}^{quant_k} \sum_{j=0}^{quant_k} p(i,j) * (i - Mean)^2 \tag{2}$$

$$ASM = \sum_{i=0}^{quant_k} \sum_{j=0}^{quant_k} p(i,j)^2 \tag{3}$$

where $p(i, j)$ represents the pixel value in the image, and $quant_k$ represents the number of the pixel in the convolution window. In this paper, the size of the window is 3×3.

2.2 Approach Framework

In Sect. 1, we have already mentioned that deeplabv3+ is by far the most capable network for semantic segmentation. This network was adopted here as the main inference network. The whole approach framework is shown in image 2.

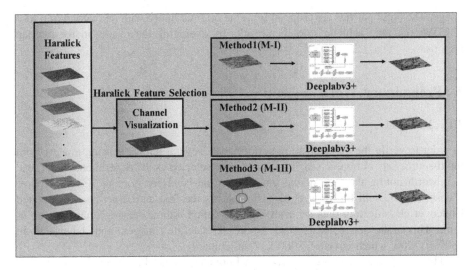

Fig. 2. The framework of the approach

In order to prove the effectiveness of the proposed method, three experimental schemes were implemented, which are presented in the framework. As for the first one, the RGB channels were fed into the network for training. This is the conventional way. In the second method, three Haralick features were normalized and displayed in the three channels. In the last, the RGB channels and Haralick features were concatenated and fed into the network, increasing the input channels to six.

2.3 Loss Function

To calculate the loss function, $w \times w$ was set to the size of the probability matrix predicted by the deeplabv3+, c represents the number of the classes, xi denotes the *i-th* pixel in the probability matrix, $\tilde{p}_{ik}$ and $\hat{p}_{ik}$ denote the true label and the probability of the *i-th* pixel belonging to class k, respectively. In this paper, we used categorical crossentropy as the loss function. The loss function may then be expressed as (4):

$$L = -\frac{1}{w^2} \sum_{i=1}^{w^2} \sum_{k=0}^{c} [\tilde{p}_{ik} ln \hat{p}_{ik}] \tag{4}$$

2.4 Refinement of Result

Given the resolution of the objects in remote sensing images, the size of the input patch first needs to be re-determined for a better classification accuracy. Experimentation proved that the accuracy was best when the size of the input patch is 128×128. In addition, we used an overlap strategy to produce the segmentation results for a large image. The input patches are cropped from the original image with an overlap of o (o = 32). We can then achieve smoother results by averaging the results in the overlap regions.

3 Preliminary Work

3.1 Data Set

In order to verify the generalization performance, several remote sensing images from multi-source sets of remote sensing images were selected as the experimental data sets. It is worth noting that one of the images and the label are from the Gaofen Image Dataset (GID), built by Tong et al. [16]. GID is the first and largest well-annotated landcover classification data set with high-resolution remote sensing images of up to 4 m. This data set consists 150 Gaofen-2 satellite images and labels, sized 6800 × 7200, which covers 50,000 km^2 in China

The study area we chose is located in Luoyang, Henan Province. The image and label are shown in Fig. 3. The image acquisition time was on October 12, 2015. It can be seen that three land-use categories: vegetation, water, and built-up are labeled with three different colors: green, red, and blue, respectively. Areas that do not belong to the above three categories or cannot be artificially recognized are labeled as unknown and are labeled with black color.

vegetation   built-up   water   background

Fig. 3. The image and label from the GID data set (located in Luoyang, Henan Province) (Color figure online)

In addition, four images of the same area are shown in Fig. 4. The difference is that these images come from different satellite platforms and from different times. They are used to test the generalization of our method. Assisted by the platform of ENVI, these images are strictly registered by hand. The images in the first line and second line are from GF1 and ZY3, respectively. The image acquisition time is shown in the legend of Fig. 4. It can be seen that the spectral characteristics of the same area are quite different

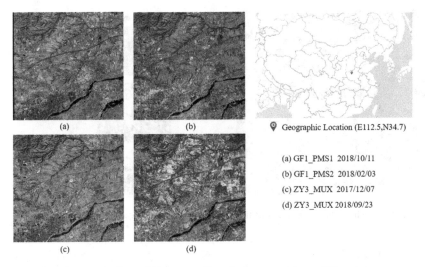

Geographic Location (E112.5,N34.7)

(a) GF1_PMS1 2018/10/11

(b) GF1_PMS2 2018/02/03

(c) ZY3_MUX 2017/12/07

(d) ZY3_MUX 2018/09/23

Fig. 4. Images from different satellite platforms and from different times

because of the seasonal differences. For example, the vegetation is always green in summer, but brown in autumn or winter; the water is always dark and uniform most of the time, but it is white and complex in winter due to freezing and snow. These differences will pose a big challenge to the generalization.

3.2 Implementation Details

The proposed method was implemented using Keras. The test area and the validation area are shown in Fig. 5, covered by translucent red and translucent blue, respectively. The size of the test area and the validation area are 2200 × 2800 and 550 × 5440, respectively. The rest of the image is used for training.

In order to balance the number of categories, 2000 samples were randomly sampled from the training area for each class. Finally, 6000 samples were generated and fed into deeplabv3+ to learn the parameters. Beyond that, the augmentation operation including rotation, gamma correction, and salt and pepper noise were randomly implemented on the training samples.

We began training the model on a Titan 1080-Ti GPU with 11 GB of onboard memory (Nvidia Corp., USA). The loss function was minimized by using the Adam optimizer with mini-batches (n = 12), and an initial learning rate of 0.001. The learning rate declined by 0.5 every 10 epochs.

There were 500 steps in each epoch. The model converged in 80 epochs. In order to compare the effects of each approach fairly, the checkpoint generated by the last epoch, is used to inference the test area, instead of the checkpoint with the highest verification accuracy. Then, we can judge the validity of the method according to the verification accuracy after stabilization. It is simply more logical.

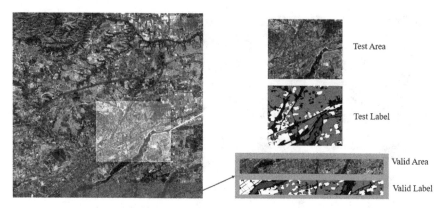

Fig. 5. The validation area and the test area in the image. (Color figure online)

3.3   Evaluation Metrics

In order to fully evaluate the effectiveness and the generalization of the proposed method, precision and recall are shown in the next section. In the field of landcover classification, precision and recall are called correctness and completeness, which are also the most common metrics for classification. In addition, the overall accuracy, intersection over union (IoU), and mean intersection over union (mIoU) are also calculated for comparison. Importantly, IoU is a more appropriate criterion to evaluate the prediction results, which is essentially a method to quantify the percent overlap between the target mask and our prediction output. And this evaluation metric is always used in object detection challenges or semantic segmentation challenges. It reflects the overlap between predicted detections and the ground truth. The formula of IoU and mIoU are as follows:

$$IoU = \frac{target \cap prediction}{target \cup prediction} \qquad (5)$$

$$mIoU = \frac{1}{c}\sum\nolimits_{i=1}^{c} IoU_i \qquad (6)$$

4   Experiments and Discussion

4.1   Training Results

The training curves are presented in Fig. 6. We can see that the curves on the verification data set are oscillating within the initial 20 epochs. After that, the curves converge gradually. The validation loss of M-III is lower than the others, which are shown in Fig. 6c. This indicates that the generalization is improved with the aid of Haralick features. Due to the loss of the spectral information, it is only poor using the Haralick features to train the parameters. However, the validation accuracy is only five points lower than that of M-I, which utilizes the whole of the spectral characteristics. The accuracy of the former is 83.43%, and the latter is 88.12%. This indicates that the Haralick features selected contain most of the information. In other words, the Haralick features can effectively improve the generalization due to the lack of redundant and interfering information. Figure 7 is the image of the Haralick feature visualization, displayed through the RGB channels. Parts of the ground objects can already be easily outlined in Fig. 7, such as built-up.

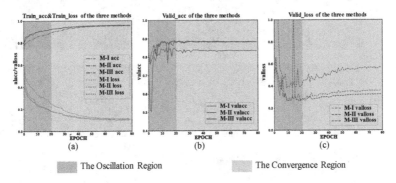

Fig. 6. The training curves of the three methods: (a) accuracy and loss on the training data set; (b) accuracy on the validation data set; (c) loss on the validation data set.

Fig. 7. The Haralick feature visualization. (Color figure online)

4.2 Generalization Comparison

In order to study the generalization of different features, the results obtained after training in Fig. 3 were used to predict other images. The results are shown in Fig. 8. The original images are shown in the first column. The predictive maps for the three methods are shown in the next three columns. Either way, the prediction effect for the first image was the best, which can be seen in the first row. After all, the same area has similar textural and spectral characteristics in the same time phase. As a result, all three

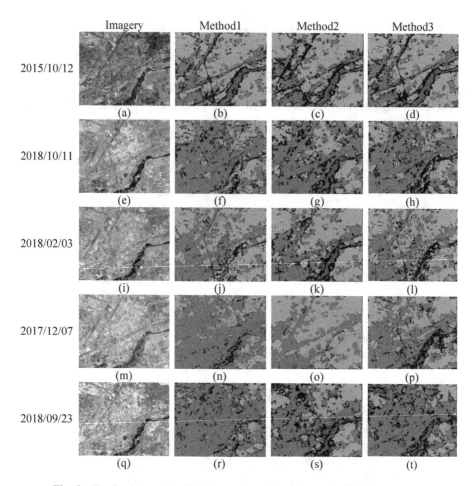

Fig. 8. The landcover classification results of the images from different times.

methods have performed well, even if M-II only used the Haralick features to infer the object classes.

The first and second images were taken almost in the same season of different years. However, due to light conditions and human factors, the features show obvious distinction in spectral properties. Of course, the variability of the sensors (one is from GF2, the other is from GF1) can make a difference. To our surprise, M-I almost completely failed in the second image (in Fig. 8f), whereas the M-II achieved the best result (in Fig. 8g). Theoretically, the first method, which utilizes the spectral features should get more information than M-II. Nevertheless, the generalization performance was inferior to that of M-II. For example, the water in the second image could still be, for the most part, extracted by M-II, but none was extracted by M-I and M-III. This indicates that some certain features in the spectrum seriously affect the generalization. The Haralick features chosen from the spectrum, can significantly improve generalization, because Haralick features contain more general information highly relevant to

Table 1. The evaluation metrics of image 3.

Method	M-I			M-II			M-III		
Class	Veg.	Water	Built	Veg.	Water	Built	Veg.	Water	Built
Prec.	0.7901	0.0514	0.4738	**0.8765**	**0.9354**	0.5196	0.8131	0.6714	**0.5294**
Recall	0.8213	0.0016	0.9797	**0.8587**	**0.5833**	0.9615	0.8283	0.1141	**0.9660**
IoU	0.6742	0.0015	0.4692	**0.7661**	**0.5607**	0.5091	0.6958	0.1081	**0.5197**
Acc.	0.8100	0.9631	0.8092	**0.8744**	**0.9836**	0.8404	0.8266	0.9662	**0.8463**
mIoU	0.3348			**0.5337**			0.3962		
Acc.	0.6365			**0.7135**			0.6716		

Table 2. The evaluation metrics of image 5.

Method	M-I			M-II			M-III		
Class	Veg.	Water	Built	Veg.	Water	Built	Veg.	Water	Built
Prec.	0.8458	0.0003	0.2489	**0.9249**	**0.8287**	**0.4174**	0.9132	0.8111	0.3025
Recall	0.2329	0	0.9970	**0.6095**	**0.5483**	0.9807	0.2944	0.2252	**0.9915**
IoU	0.2234	0	0.2487	**0.5808**	**0.4925**	**0.4140**	0.2864	0.2140	0.3017
Acc.	0.6124	0.9594	0.4815	**0.7894**	**0.9797**	**0.7610**	0.6488	0.9703	0.6049
mIoU	0.1448			**0.4261**			0.2425		
Acc.	0.3302			**0.5820**			0.4038		

specific objects. Surprisingly, M-III did not achieve a better result than M-II, even though spectral and Haralick features were both utilized.

As for the built-up in the third image (in Fig. 8i), all three methods worked well. However, M-I and M-III still have some difficulties with water extraction. We can see that there is a lot of noise in Fig. 8j and l. The last two images present a significant challenge to network inference. There are lots of false positives in the results of M-I and M-III. Many vegetation areas are predicted to be built-up. To our pleasure, the results of M-II are still robust.

After the above analysis, we found that it was difficult to predict images that are much different from the training samples. Many factors, including seasonal factors and human factors, can affect generalization performance. Due to the limited number of training samples and the limited learning ability of the deep learning network, certain features that contribute to generalization performance are difficult to extract. Therefore, it is necessary to provide some artificial features to the network, such as some Haralick features, proposed in this paper.

4.3 Quantitative Analysis

In the previous section, we qualitatively compared the generalization performance of the three methods. In this section, the relevant evaluation metrics from Fig. 8 are presented so that the generalization properties can be more fully understood.

The third image (2018/02/03) and the fifth image (2018/09/23), which is much different from the first image, were selected to make generalization comparisons. The evaluation metrics of each method for the two images are given in Tables 1 and 2, respectively. The evaluation metrics include precision, recall, IoU, mIoU, and accuracy of each class, which had already been proposed in Sect. 3.

The bold fonts in Tables 1 and 2 represent the highest evaluation index of the three methods. As you can see the metrics for M-I are all exceptionally poor. The precision, recall, and IoU are almost all zero. This suggests that M-I is extremely limited in its ability to generalize the water. It is difficult for deeplabv3+ itself to learn universal features from spectral information alone. As can be seen from the results of image 3, M-III does have some advantages in the extraction of built-up. The IoU of M-III in image 3 is 0.5197, which is 0.0106 higher than that of M-II. However, the performance of built-up extraction of M-III declined in image 5. The precision and IoU are both lower than those of M-II. Therefore, this indicates that M-II is more robust for built-up extraction. Surprisingly, M-II was consistently effective and stable in water extraction. All of the metrics of water extraction for M-II are significantly higher than for the other two methods. Hence, we can conclude that M-II is extremely effective in the generalization of water extraction. The last two rows in the tables show the overall classification performance of the three methods. Obviously, M-II maintained a significant performance advantage in the overall classification metrics. For example, the mIoU of M-II is nearly 20% points higher than that of M-I, and more than 10% points higher than that of M-III.

As we all know, the Receiver Operating Characteristic (ROC) curve is defined for binary class classification tasks and not for multi class classification tasks. In other words, there is no classical definition for precision and recall in multi class scenarios. As such, there is no standard method for drawing the ROC curve in the case of multi class problems. However, in order to show the performance of these three methods more visually, a new ROC curve drawing method is defined in this paper. First, the ROC curve for each class can be plotted separately. After that, we can average all the ROC curves (including background), and we can then obtain the final ROC curves. The final ROC curves of the three methods used here are presented in Fig. 9. The area under the curves (AUC) can be regarded as the metric of the classification.

Figure 9(a) presents the ROC curves for the three methods in image 1, which is the training dataset for the experiment. As can be seen from this figure, M-II is not as effective as M-I and M-III. The AUC of M-II is 3% lower than those of M-I and M-II. The result is reasonable, which has been discussed above. Nevertheless, the results for M-II are robust and excellent in respect of the next four images, which are shown using a green colored curve. From these ROC curves in Fig. 9, we can determine that the generalization performance of M-II is on the whole superior to those of M-I and M-III.

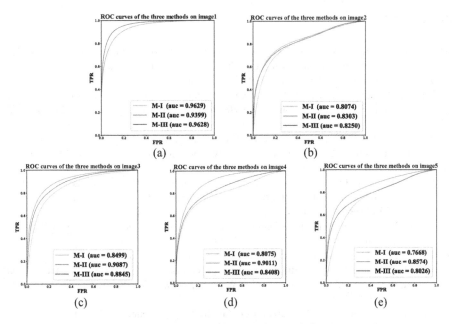

Fig. 9. The ROC curves for the three methods. (Color figure online)

5   Conclusions

In this paper, we studied the generalization of landcover classification. In order to expand the practicability of classification, three methods were proposed. Specifically, in addition to spectral features, three Haralick features were also selected.

The contrasting experiments show that the generalization performance is best when only using Haralick texture features, even if the method was not the most outstanding on the training imagery. This indicates that the features of artificial design have a significant effect on the classification and generalization of specific objects in remote sensing imagery. However, the method using both spectral features and Haralick features is not as good as the abovementioned method. The reason may be that there is a large amount of interference redundancy information in the spectrum that is not removed, which affects the generalization performance. It is worth mentioning that the basic direction for improving generalization of landcover classification has been found. The relevant results have been validated by experiments.

The work in this paper is just a preliminary exploration into this field, yet we look forward to further efforts in this direction. In the final analysis, it is still necessary to find a better fusion scheme to utilize the spectral and textural features effectively and complementarily, so that the generalization of classification can be further improved.

References

1. Sharma, A., Liu, X.-W., Yang, X.-J.: Land cover classification from multi-temporal, multi-spectral remotely sensed imagery using patch-based recurrent neural networks. Neural Netw. **105**, 346–355 (2018). https://doi.org/10.1016/j.neunet.2018.05.019

2. Tian, Y.-Q., Guo, P., Lyu, M.R.: Comparative studies on feature extraction methods for multispectral remote sensing image classification. In: Proceedings of IEEE International Conference on Systems, Man and Cybernetics, Hawaii, pp. 1275–1279 (2005)

3. Mahmoud, A., Elbialy, S., Pradhan, B., Buchroithner, M.: Field-based landcover classification using TerraSAR-X texture analysis. Adv. Space Res. **48**(5), 799–805 (2011). https://doi.org/10.1016/j.asr.2011.04.005

4. Shi, D., Yang, X.-J.: An assessment of algorithmic parameters affecting image classification accuracy by random forests. Photogram. Eng. Rem. Sens. **82**(6), 407–417 (2016). https://doi.org/10.14358/PERS.82.6.407

5. Yang, X.-J.: Parameterizing support vector machines for land cover classification. Photogram. Eng. Rem. Sens. **77**(1), 27–37 (2011)

6. Rakhlin, A., Davydow, A., Nikolenko, S.: Land cover classification from satellite imagery with U-Net and Lovász-Softmax loss. In: Proceedings of IEEE/CVF Conference on Computer Vision and Pattern Recognition Workshops (CVPRW), Salt Lake City, UT, USA, pp. 262–266 (2018)

7. Davydow, A., Nikolenko, S.: Land cover classification with superpixels and Jaccard index post-optimization. In: Proceedings of IEEE/CVF Conference on Computer Vision and Pattern Recognition Workshops (CVPRW), Salt Lake City, UT, USA, pp. 280–284 (2018)

8. Zhang, C., et al.: Joint deep learning for land cover and land use classification. Rem. Sens. Environ. **221**, 173–187 (2019). https://doi.org/10.1016/j.rse.2018.11.014

9. Kuo, T.-S., Tseng, K.-S., Yan, J., Liu, Y.-C., Wang, F.Y.-C.: Deep aggregation net for land cover classification. In: Proceedings of IEEE/CVF Conference on Computer Vision and Pattern Recognition Workshops (CVPRW), Salt Lake City, UT, USA, pp. 252–256 (2018). https://doi.org/10.1109/cvprw.2018.00046

10. Long, J., Shelhamer, E., Darrell, T.: Fully convolutional networks for semantic segmentation. In: Proceedings of the IEEE Conference on Computer Vision and Pattern Recognition Workshops (CVPRW), Boston MA, USA, pp. 3431–3440 (2015). https://doi.org/10.1109/tpami.2016.2572683

11. Badrinarayanan, V., Handa, A., Cipolla, R.: SegNet: a deep convolutional encoder-decoder architecture for robust semantic pixel-wise labelling. IEEE Trans. Pattern Anal. Mach. Intell. **39**(12), 2481–2495 (2017)

12. Ronneberger, O., Fischer, P., Brox, T.: U-Net: convolutional networks for biomedical image segmentation. In: Navab, N., Hornegger, J., Wells, William M., Frangi, Alejandro F. (eds.) MICCAI 2015. LNCS, vol. 9351, pp. 234–241. Springer, Cham (2015). https://doi.org/10.1007/978-3-319-24574-4_28

13. Zhang, Z., Liu, Q., Wang, Y.: Road extraction by deep residual U-Net. IEEE Geosci. Rem. Sens. Lett. **15**, 749–753 (2018). https://doi.org/10.1109/LGRS.2018.2802944

14. Chen, L.-C., Zhu, Y., Papandreou, G., Schroff, F., Hartwig, A.: Encoder-decoder with Atrous separable convolution for semantic image segmentation. In: Proceedings of the European Conference on Computer Vision (ECCV), Munich, Germany, pp. 801–818 (2018). https://doi.org/10.1007/978-3-030-01234-2_49

15. Haralick, R.M.: Statistical and structural approaches to texture. Proc. IEEE **67**(5), 786–804 (1979). https://doi.org/10.1109/PROC.1979.11328

16. Tong, X.-Y., et al.: Learning transferable deep models for land-use classification with high-resolution remote sensing images (2018). http://arxiv.org/abs/1807.05713

Determining Location and Detecting Changes Using a Single Training Video

Ryan Bluteau$^{(\boxtimes)}$ ⓘ, Boubakeur Boufama ⓘ, and Pejman Habashi ⓘ

School of Computer Science, University of Windsor, Windsor, ON N9B 3P4, Canada
{bluteaur,boufama,habashi}@uwindsor.ca
http://www.uwindsor.ca/science/computerscience/

Abstract. This paper proposes a new approach to find a robot's current location and to detect any changes in its path, using monocular vision. A recorded single obstacle-free training video is first obtained and saved. Then, a moving robot can use its camera to find its current location, within its path, by matching current frames with the ones from the training video. This frame-to-frame matching is performed using extracted feature points. Once a match is found, the corresponding frames are aligned (registered) using a homography that is calculated based the matched feature points. This allows to compensate for viewpoint changes between the observed and saved frames. Finally, we compare the regions of interest (ROIs) of the aligned frames, using their colour histograms. We carried out seventeen tests using this approach. The videos, for both training and testing, were recorded using off-the-shelf phone camera by walking down different paths. Four tests were performed in an outdoor environment, and 13 in an indoor environment. Our tests have shown excellent results, with an accuracy above 95% for most of them, for finding the robot's location and for detecting obstacles in the robot's path. Both training and testing videos used in our tests were realistic and very challenging, as they consisted of a mix of indoor and outdoor environments with cluttered backgrounds, repetitive floor textures and glare.

Keywords: Obstacle detection · Change detection · Background subtraction

1 Introduction

We propose a new change detection approach that uses a single training video, avoiding the lengthy training process in classical machine learning solutions. Change detection in computer vision relates to many fields, such as obstacle detection and background subtraction, with the main aim of detecting changes in a scene. This is especially important for autonomous vehicles or robots, surveillance systems, object tracking, etc. Often, approaches to vision-based techniques require quick computation while dealing with various areas of difficulty, such as glares and shadows, outdoor environments (like weather and dynamic lighting changes), camera quality and other issues.

© Springer Nature Switzerland AG 2020
C. Djeddi et al. (Eds.): MedPRAI 2019, CCIS 1144, pp. 65–78, 2020.
https://doi.org/10.1007/978-3-030-37548-5_6

The goal of obstacle detection is to detect obstructions in a path while being travelled. These obstructions can be things that generally stand out from the ground like walls, furniture, trees, vehicles, and people. Typical solutions usually create and maintain a model of the ground and are required to perform obstacle detection in real-time. The ground model is then used to classify obstacles which differ from the ground. Some difficulties in obstacle detection are changes in the floor patterns, dynamic colour changes, glares reflecting off shiny floors and even classifying obstacles with similar appearance to the ground model.

Background subtraction techniques aim at extracting the foreground from the background. This is done by creating a background model from a recorded scene with a stationary camera. Ideally, foreground extraction should be processed from the first few frames, but many methods require a large number of frames to first estimate the background. Once a model is created, theses techniques extract moving objects that are not part of the estimated background.

Our change detection approach utilizes concepts from both obstacle detection and background subtraction fields to detect new, unseen, obstacles, or any changes, along a path. For each potential robot's path, a single monocular video is obtained and is used as our training data. A training video is then represented by the extracted feature points of each of its frames. A dataset is constructed by combining all of these frames of feature points. During the testing stage, we first find the robot's current location by matching current frames to the dataset's frames. Then, the colour histograms of the ROIs of the corresponding frames are compared to determine possible changes in the path.

This paper is organized as follows. Section 2 describes the state-of-the-art in this area. The proposed new approach is presented in Sect. 3. Experiments and results are presented in Sect. 4. Finally, Sect. 5 concludes the paper.

2   Previous Works

2.1   Obstacle Detection

The method proposed in [21] uses a trapezoidal ROI placed at the bottom of the frame in the robot's direct path to model the hue and intensity (in the HSI colour space). They use a 5×5 gaussian filter to reduce the noise level of the image. They show a significant benefit of having a larger ROI due to the amount of ground modelled in the ROI, but also causes vulnerabilities from modelling potential obstacles in a larger area, if assumed to be obstacle-free. They classify each pixel as ground or obstacle in the entire frame if "the hue [or intensity] of the histogram bin value at the pixel's hue [or intensity] value is below the hue [or intensity] threshold" [21] (determined as 60 and 80 pixels, respectively). In order to use the ROI to model the ground, they must carefully maintain their assumptions of whether the ROI contains obstacles based on distance travelled (in relation to the ROI depth) and any turning motion. This leads them to implement a model which requires training by leading the robot through an obstacle-free path to create a history of histograms for future comparison. Raj et al. [10] use the bottom portion of the image to create a normalized histogram to classify obstacles. Both methods have three assumptions: (1) obstacles differ in appearance from the ground, (2) the ground is relatively flat, and (3) there are no overhanging obstacles. Michels et al. [17] vertically scan each frame using a small window to extract edge and corner features for detecting obstacles. The method requires training on numerous obstacles for estimating their distances through linear regression. Jia et al. [9] use two consecutive frames (TCF) and feature points to track movement. Heights and distances are estimated to classify whether or not feature points belong to obstacles. The method relies on the presence of accurate feature points on obstacles. Lee et al. [12] use edge detection to maintain a floor model and find obstacles. Then, they use an improved Inverse Perspective Mapping (IPM) for classification on a ROI, in the bottom third of the image. The authors in [14] use a combination of edge detection and obstacle boundaries found by sliding a window vertically on the image in the RGB and HSV spaces, with difficulty in complex floor patterns. The method proposed in [13] uses edge detection and an SVM classifier to detect (classify) vertical and horizontal lines to separate the wall and floor. The method has difficulties in complex floor patterns.

2.2 Background Subtraction

Mandellos et al. [15] use a ROI over a highway to detect moving traffic. The method requires hundreds of frames, depending on traffic, to create a model. In [3], authors proposed the ViBe method that determines foreground pixels based on the number of similar pixels. The method requires pixel history and randomly removes this history over time. In [11,16], authors implement the sigma-delta method which uses pixel history to calculate a median image. The foreground is then classified by comparing the motion likelihood (difference between median and current frames), to the temporal activity (variance) of each pixel.

St-Charles et al. [19] proposed the SubSENSE method that maintains and automatically updates parameters for the background model for minimal intervention, but requires a history of frames for the model. Babaee et al. [2] use SubSENSE (adaptable to any background subtraction technique) to first create a foreground mask. Then implemented an algorithm to keep a history of the background to refine the mask, from motion effects and bad camera quality, which is used to train a convolutional neural network (CNN).

Stauffer and Grimson [20] proposed the Gaussian mixture model (GMM) method, that uses k gaussian distributions for each pixel. It allows the modelling of several events over a pixel location using weights over time for maintenance, thus requiring many frames to generate accurate models. Zivkovic [22] improved the GMM method by using the standard deviation to better weigh distributions for an improved modelling over time. Chen et al. [6] perform image segmentation over a few frames and merge overlapping regions using histograms and a GMM to model each region. They use descriptors to classify pixels using Bhattacharyya distance. The method is shown to work using 60 frames of training.

The method in [5] produces a background image using 150 frames and a trained CNN on generated data to classify each pixel. The method requires training with labeled scenes. Cheng and Gong [7] use a generalization of 1-SVM to track neighbouring pixels requiring an online learning model. Bionco et al. [4] use genetic programming to combine outputs of several background subtraction methods using boolean logic. The method in [8] uses a weightless neural network (WNN) method CwisarDH which extends the WiSARD architecture [1] that requires a buffer history, but can be easily trained.

3 Methodology

Our proposed method consists of three main steps: (1) find a matching frame in the training set using feature points, (2) align (register) the frames using a homography transformation on the feature points, and (3) detect, within a ROI, any changes by comparing histograms.

These steps are summarized in Algorithm 1 and their details are provided in the following paragraphs. We also provide a flowchart of the overall approach in Fig. 1.

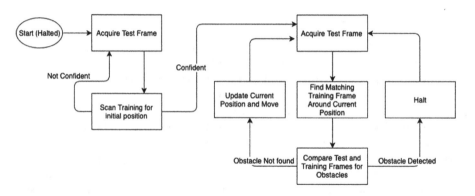

Fig. 1. Flow chart of our proposed method. The algorithm initially determines its whereabouts within the training video using some test frames. Once a position is determined, the algorithm enters a infinite loop and tests for obstacles while updating its position using the matched training frames. Note that frames used to determine the initial position can be used for obstacle detection as well, but are not needed.

3.1 Feature-Based Frame Matching

We first perform some preprocessing on the training data. We chose a frame size of 268×480 which is oriented vertically to allow more context for better feature points. Our feature points, ORB [18], are extracted from the entire training set labelled with their respective frame. The training set is a single video of the travelled paths (one video per path), where each frame is automatically ordered and labeled numerically.

Algorithm 1. Algorithm

1: **procedure** DETERMINELOCATION
2:      *loop*:
3:          $TestFrame1 \leftarrow TestSet$.getNextFrame()
4:          $TestFrame2 \leftarrow TestSet$.getNextFrame()
5:          [Note: Search entire training set, compare frames using feature points]
6:          $MatchingFrame1 \leftarrow TrainingSet$.findMatch($TestFrame1$)
7:          $MatchingFrame2 \leftarrow TrainingSet$.findMatch($TestFrame2$)
8:
9:          **if** distance($MatchingFrame1, MatchingFrame2$) < $Range$ **then**
10:             **return** $MatchingFrame2$.getPosition()
11:             **close**;
12:
13:         [Note: No valid match]
14:         $TestFrame1$.setDetection(true)
15:         $TestFrame2$.setDetection(true)
16:         **goto** *loop*.
17:
18:
19: **procedure** CHANGEDETECTION
20:     *loop*:
21:         $TestFrame \leftarrow TestSet$.getNextFrame()
22:         [Note: Search training in smaller range]
23:         $MatchingFrame \leftarrow TrainingSet$.findMatch($TestFrame$)
24:
25:         **if** $matchingFrame.empty()$ **then**
26:             $TestFrame$.setDetection(true)
27:             **goto** *loop*.
28:
29:         [Note: Register frames using their feature points]
30:         RegisterFrames($TestFrame, MachingFrame$)
31:         **if** AreaOfROI($TestFrame$) **is** too small **then**
32:             $TestFrame$.setDetection(true)
33:             **goto** *loop*.
34:
35:         [Note: Compare histograms of the ROI of each frame]
36:         $Result \leftarrow$ CompareROI($TestFrame, MachingFrame$)
37:         $TestFrame$.setDetection($Result$)
38:     **goto** *loop*.

A given test frame is processed in a similar manner as the training frames by resizing it and extracting its features. The test frame is then compared to a set of frames from the dataset, depending on a predefined range representing the frame context. We've determined a predefined range of roughly 1–2 s of video to be enough to account for pace changes between the training and the test videos. This range is centered around the currently determined position which allows for flexibility and avoids the assumption that all new test frames will be matched to succeeding training frames. We do not account for forks in the path since we assume the robot has a predefined path through the training video. However, we've tested scene recognition by combining all videos in our tests, see Fig. 2. Some videos contain very similar hallways on separate floors of the same building. We notice a drop in error near the match which represents roughly 350 frames from start to finish, hence the reason for considering a few seconds of video as the frame neighbourhood. We represent each frame by a positive number (an index) where the test frames are ordered by their sequence in the video feed and the training frames are placed in the order of their matching, to create a relationship from testing to training. In other words, we represent training frames as M_i and testing frames as F_i. We discuss how we define this relationship later in this section using a match score.

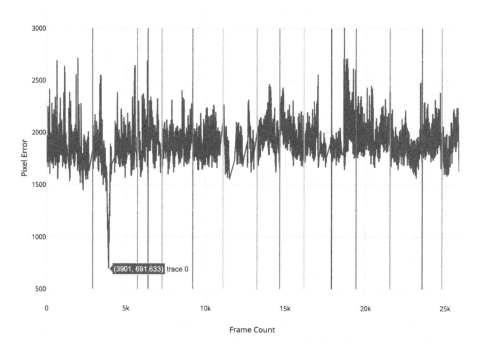

Fig. 2. We determine which scene (training video) a random test frame belongs. We graph the match score (otherwise known as the average pixel error or deviation of the match) on the Y-axis. The X-axis represents our labelled frames and is separated by scene using a vertical line (we combine all our training videos sequentially). The appropriate training frame and scene are matched with a significantly lower (better) match score. We have repeated this test with every other scene with similar results.

The initial matching is the most difficult step since we do not know where we are. Normally, all we need is to find a match of the first test frame in the training videos. To make this process more reliable, we actually consider the first few test frames F_1, F_2 .... In our experiments, two frames were enough to find a reliable match in a training video. Alternatively to scanning the training video, an initial match can be scanned using a grid search over the training video. First we use a matched score to define how well the current frame matches to a particular training frame. Using this score, we can select training frames with the best scores at a high level, then perform an in-depth search in these portions of the training video to find a more accurate position. The frame with the lowest match score is determined to be the best match. Once these two frames are matched, future frame matching will be much faster and easier, as it will be limited to a small frame range within our current position (frame context). For example, assuming F_2 was matched to M_{50}, the search range to match F_3 will be in the immediate neighbourhood of M_{50}, i.e., a few frames.

The comparison between two frames is obtained by the comparison of their feature points that we define as the match score. A simple brute force matching algorithm was used to match points between test and training frames. Alternatively, a flann based algorithm can be used with similar accuracy. Note that except for the matching of the first frame, subsequent frame matching only involves a few frames, making a brute-force technique appropriate and fast enough. We compute the pixel distance of each pair of matched feature point and remove pairs with distances larger than 40% of the length of the image diagonal. This is simply to remove large outliers for unnecessary error and can be adjusted based on the level of stability of the robot. From there we obtain the mean of each cluster of feature points (we consider the entire extraction of feature points of a given frame as a cluster of feature points). We align both cluster of feature points by their center using a simple translation. We create a covariance matrix H between the two clusters of points by using their matches (already calculated) and perform SVD on H. By removing the diagonal matrix produced in the decomposition, we can find the best rotation to register the two centered point clusters. The average distance between all the matched points is used as the match score to how well the two frames match. The lower this score, the better the match, and a perfect match at 0 (up to rotation and translation). Note that scale contributes to the final score, unlike rotation and translation. This allows us to differentiate nearby locations from farther locations using a sense of depth through scale while ignoring positional misalignments and shaky camera rotations.

3.2   Frame Registration

Once a test frame is matched to a training frame, we align (register) them via a homography-mapping. Using the best (or up to) 100 matched feature points, the homography is calculated using RANSAC algorithm for a robust estimation. This step technically only requires 4 matched points, though feature points are very inaccurate, hence the need for up to 100 and the use of RANSAC. Feature point algorithms can be adjusted to extract more feature points at the cost of either some inaccuracies or computation time. In our experiments, ORB provides the best compromise between speed and accuracy.

3.3   Histogram-Based Change Detection

Given a test frame that has been matched and registered to a training frame (as explained in the two previous paragraphs), we start the process of detecting changes using a ROI. Since the two frames are now aligned, their corresponding ROIs (see examples on Fig. 3, best seen in colour) should be covering roughly the same areas in both frames. The two histograms of the two ROIs are then built and compared.

Both frames are first blurred using a 9×9 Gaussian blur filter. This process slightly mixes the textures of the ground, hence reducing the variance of the colours. Then we convert the RGB values into the HSV colour space. We found that larger filters cause the variance to even out too much over the frame causing potential obstacles to blend in the frame and ultimately lost (in the context of variance). A reduction of the ROI in smaller blurred pieces allows for better use of localized variance without the fine details using a light filter.

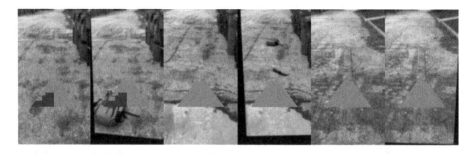

Fig. 3. Results of Test 14 showing detected changes in an outdoor environment. Detecting a backpack in the leftmost matching frames (best seen in colour).

Our ROI is a trapezoid placed in the center of the bottom half of the image. The registration of the frames allow the ROI to overlook the same portion of the scenes in both frames, which allows the ROI to be placed in the exact same pixel location of both frames. The size, shape, or placement of the ROI isn't particularly important since we simply want to cover enough space to find an obstacle that might collide with the robot. The size can be larger or smaller with no affect on the algorithm since the frames are registered, as long as the ROI remains within the direct path. However, if the size is too large, frame registration might shift the frame beyond the ROI's bounds and must be accounted for in calculations. To make the comparison of the corresponding ROIs robust, a ROI is split into a 9×4 grid of blocks. This way, we can also omit grid blocks that move beyond the frame's bounds for larger ROIs.

Change detection is found by comparing histograms of the corresponding grid blocks of the two frames. Histograms are compared using the variance of their difference, where each block consists of three normalized histograms, i.e., gray scale, Hue and Saturation histograms. The size of the histograms must be large enough to model some variance, but also have no limit to the size. A detection is determined if the sum of the variances of the three histograms for all the grid blocks is larger than a set threshold. The threshold can be easily determined through a few videos containing changes to simply adjust for background noise. To find the threshold, it can be increased until enough of the background is considered obstacle-free while still detecting the obstacle present. In particular, we have used the same threshold for all our tests of the same scene. In our experiments, we go beyond one system of grid blocks and utilize 3 differently-split systems. This increases the reliability of detection with a much higher accuracy and allows for larger grid blocks if needed. By shifting the split-point of the ROI, we can effectively obtain a different view of any possible detection. Each system will have all the pixels of each block labelled as obstacle or background. Finally, we combine all three ROI systems at a pixel level. If all three pixels (one from each system at the exact same position of the ROI) must be labelled obstacle to finally label the frame's pixel an obstacle.

4   Experimental Results

We implemented the proposed method in C++ with OpenCV, using built-in methods like ORB [18], BFMatcher, findHomography and SVD. The training and testing videos were recorded with a handheld phone camera, walking along a few paths to simulate a moving robot. The videos were recorded at 60FPS and we processed 4 frames for every second (we could have used more, but this was good enough for us). We extracted features in all frames of the training video (preprocessing) in advance using ORB. The neighbourhood search space for a matching frame in the training data was set to a range of 200 frames, centered around the previous match. The three detection parameters for each histogram and the final threshold were empirically estimated, but were unchanged for all tests in a given path.

We performed 17 tests on clips ranging from 10 to 50 s, walking down different paths. See Table 1 for results on each test. Under column Detections we provide the number of obstacles detected by the total number of obstacles. Accuracy is calculated as the percentage of frames classified properly (out of all total frames). The TP rate is the percentage of obstacle frames classified as obstacle. The TN rate is the percentage of obstacle-free frames classified as background. The obstacles that were tested are the followings: a grey and black backpack, water bottles (empty and full), Kleenex box, a looney, small white shiny case, a black umbrella, a black laptop case, a small orange bag, an orange ball and a light blue package. See Fig. 4 for examples of detections and miss-detections and see Fig. 5 for more detections.

4.1   Discussion and Comparison

Although our work closely relates to background subtraction and obstacle detection, neither of them can be easily compared to ours. Background subtraction

Table 1. Results of different tests run

ID	Context	Detections	Acc.	TP	TN
#1	Indoor-Train	3/3	0.9524	0.9167	0.9667
#2	Indoor-Test	3/3	0.8730	1.0000	0.8049
#3	Indoor-Train	3/4	0.9455	0.9545	0.9444
#4	Indoor-Test	5/6	0.9606	0.9375	0.9649
#5	Indoor-Test	3/3	0.9668	1.0000	0.9643
#6	Indoor-Test	3/3	0.9951	1.0000	0.9947
#7	Indoor-Train	7/7	0.9855	0.9355	1.0000
#8	Indoor-Test	7/7	0.9856	0.9583	0.9913
#9	Indoor-Test	1/1	0.9338	1.0000	0.9301
#10	Indoor-Train	3/4	0.9820	0.8571	1.0000
#11	Indoor-Test	4/4	0.7636	0.9375	0.7340
#12	Outdoor-Train	4/4	1.0000	1.0000	1.0000
#13	Outdoor-Test	3/3	0.9570	0.8333	0.9753
#14	Outdoor-Train	4/4	0.9759	1.0000	0.9728
#15	Outdoor-Test	4/4	0.9747	1.0000	0.9720
#16	Indoor-Train	3/3	1.0000	1.0000	1.0000
#17	Indoor-Test	3/3	0.9783	1.0000	0.9733

Fig. 4. Examples of detection. The first row is from Test 2, 9 and 17 from left to right. Detecting nothing, a backpack and a Kleenex box, respectively. The second row is from Test 11, 4 and 2 from left to right. Miss-detections due to glare, matching and homography alignment. (Best seen in colour).

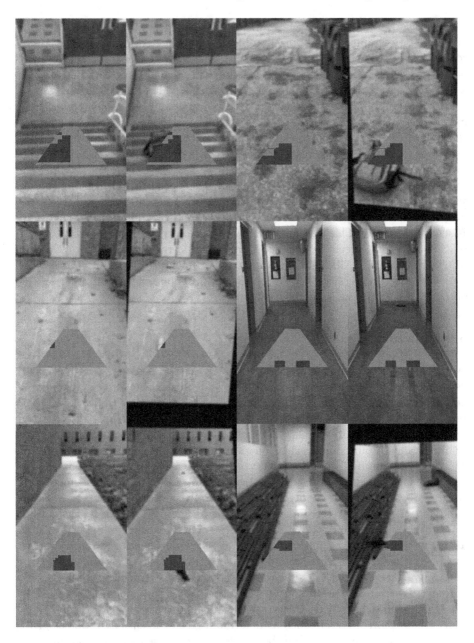

Fig. 5. Examples of detection. We detect a backpack in the first row, one or two water bottles in the second row, and an umbrella in the third row. (Best seen in colour).

approaches model the entire background before detecting any change. While we somehow model the background as well, our camera is constantly moving and we are dealing with hundreds of frames, representing whole paths. In particular, we cannot apply background subtraction methods to entire paths.

Obstacle detection approaches aim to differentiate the floor from all other objects. For example, authors in [9] applied obstacle detection for navigation in roads. They used KITTI dataset, CamVid Dataset and their own autonomous navigation vehicle. Unfortunately we cannot use these datasets, KITTI, CamVid and their own, as they do not include obstacle-free videos for our training.

In [12] they implement obstacle detection for small robots such as an automated home robot cleaner. They experimented using this robot and selected the following obstacles for testing as they mention in their paper: "a wire, a fan, a speaker with a thin plate at the bottom, a chair with U-shaped legs, a four-legged chair, a bed cover, a window sill, a unicolor transformer, a unicolor toolbox, and a garment." All their tests seem to be performed in the same indoor scene and a comparison is made with a conventional method. They tested 1079 images for a total precision, false positive rate, and recall of 81.4%, 5.9%, and 74.4%, respectively. This was shown as an improvement over the compared approach with a total precision, false positive rate, and recall of 57.4%, 14.2%, and 37.6%, respectively. Although the absence of obstacle-free training video makes the comparison impossible, our approach performs better when comparing the obtained results on the different data.

5   Conclusion

We proposed a method for detecting changes/obstacles along a robot's path, using monocular videos. The method has yielded excellent detection results at near real-time speed with a 2-frame per second processing time (detection stage). In addition to finding a robot's current position within the training set, the proposed method effectively detects changes and/or obstacles in a path. The use of histograms in our comparisons showed some difficulties with the presence of glare, but the method's performance was excellent in complex floor patterns as well as in outdoor environments. The main advantage of the proposed method is the use of a single training video. This is especially important when the creation of large datasets, required by machine learning techniques, is not an easy option.

Possible future work will be dedicated at demonstrating its applications to a moving robot along a path, while changes are detected at frame rate. We can further explore the histogram-based detection to better account for glares and dynamic colour changes. In order to adjust for these background changes, automated parameters updating will be explored through some limited use of machine learning techniques over the provided training video. Additional scenarios can be explored as well, such as determining the current environment given training videos of multiple scenes before determining the current location.

References

1. Aleksander, I., Thomas, W., Bowden, P.: Wisard.a radical step forward in image recognition. Sens. Rev. **4**, 120–124 (1984). https://doi.org/10.1108/eb007637
2. Babaee, M., Dinh, D.T., Rigoll, G.: A deep convolutional neural network for video sequence background subtraction. Pattern Recogn. **76**(C), 635–649 (2018). https://doi.org/10.1016/j.patcog.2017.09.040
3. Barnich, O., Droogenbroeck, M.: Vibe: a universal background subtraction algorithm for video sequences. IEEE Trans. Image Process. **20**, 1709–1724 (2011). https://doi.org/10.1109/TIP.2010.2101613
4. Bianco, S., Ciocca, G., Schettini, R.: How far can you get by combining change detection algorithms? CoRR abs/1505.02921 (2015). http://dblp.uni-trier.de/db/journals/corr/corr1505.html#BiancoCS15a
5. Braham, M., Droogenbroeck, M.V.: Deep background subtraction with scene-specific convolutional neural networks. In: 2016 International Conference on Systems, Signals and Image Processing (IWSSIP), pp. 1–4 (2016)
6. Chen, S., Zhang, J., Li, Y., Zhang, J.: A hierarchical model incorporating segmented regions and pixel descriptors for video background subtraction. IEEE Trans. Ind. Inf. **8**, 118–127 (2012). https://doi.org/10.1109/TII.2011.2173202
7. Cheng, L., Gong, M.: Realtime background subtraction from dynamic scenes, pp. 2066–2073 (2009). https://doi.org/10.1109/ICCV.2009.5459454
8. De Gregorio, M., Giordano, M.: Change detection with weightless neural networks, June 2014. https://doi.org/10.1109/CVPRW.2014.66
9. Jia, B., Liu, R., Zhu, M.: Real-time obstacle detection with motion features using monocular vision. Vis. Comput. **31**(3), 281–293 (2015). https://doi.org/10.1007/s00371-014-0918-5
10. Kompella, V., Bidargaddi, S.V., Kaipa, K., Ghose, D.: A tracked mobile robot with vision-based obstacle avoidance, pp. 12–13, January 2008
11. Lacassagne, L., Manzanera, A., Dupret, A.: Motion detection: fast and robust algorithms for embedded systems, pp. 3265–3268, December 2009. https://doi.org/10.1109/ICIP.2009.5413946
12. Lee, T., Yi, D.H., Dan Cho, D.I.: A monocular vision sensor-based obstacle detection algorithm for autonomous robots. Sensors **16**, 311 (2016). https://doi.org/10.3390/s16030311
13. Li, Y., Birchfield, S.T.: Image-based segmentation of indoor corridor floors for a mobile robot, pp. 837–843, November 2010. https://doi.org/10.1109/IROS.2010.5652818
14. Lorigo, L., Brooks, R., Grimsou, W.: Visually-guided obstacle avoidance in unstructured environments, vol. 1, pp. 373–379, October 1997. https://doi.org/10.1109/IROS.1997.649086
15. Mandellos, N.A., Keramitsoglou, I., Kiranoudis, C.T.: A background subtraction algorithm for detecting and tracking vehicles. Expert Syst. Appl. **38**(3), 1619–1631 (2011). https://doi.org/10.1016/j.eswa.2010.07.083
16. Manzanera, A., Richefeu, J.C.: A robust and computationally efficient motion detection algorithm based on sigma-delta background estimation, pp. 46–51, December 2004
17. Michels, J., Saxena, A., Ng, A.Y.: High speed obstacle avoidance using monocular vision and reinforcement learning. In: Proceedings of the 22nd International Conference on Machine Learning, ICML 2005, pp. 593–600. ACM, New York (2005). https://doi.org/10.1145/1102351.1102426

18. Rublee, E., Rabaud, V., Konolige, K., Bradski, G.: ORB: an efficient alternative to SIFT or SURF, pp. 2564–2571, November 2011. https://doi.org/10.1109/ICCV. 2011.6126544
19. St-Charles, P.L., Bilodeau, G.A., Bergevin, R.: Flexible background subtraction with self-balanced local sensitivity, June 2014. https://doi.org/10.1109/CVPRW. 2014.67
20. Stauffer, C., E. L. Grimson, W.: Adaptive background mixture models for real-time tracking. In: Proceedings of IEEE Conference on Computer Vision and Pattern Recognition, vol. 2, January 2007
21. Ulrich, I., Nourbakhsh, I.R.: Appearance-based obstacle detection with monocular color vision. In: Proceedings of the Seventeenth National Conference on Artificial Intelligence and Twelfth Conference on Innovative Applications of Artificial Intelligence, pp. 866–871. AAAI Press (2000). http://dl.acm.org/citation.cfm? id=647288.721755
22. Zivkovic, Z.: Improved adaptive Gaussian mixture model for background subtraction, vol. 2, pp. 28–31, September 2004. https://doi.org/10.1109/ICPR.2004. 1333992

Improving Deep Learning Parkinson's Disease Detection Through Data Augmentation Training

Catherine Taleb[1(✉)], Laurence Likforman-Sulem[2],
and Chafic Mokbel[1]

[1] University of Balamand, Balamand, El-Koura, Lebanon
catherine.taleb@std.balamand.edu.lb,
chafic.mokbel@balamand.edu.lb
[2] LTCI/Telecom Paris/Institut Polytechnique de Paris, Paris, France
likforman@telecom-paris.fr

Abstract. Deep learning has been successfully applied to different classification applications where large data are available. However, the lack of data makes it more difficult to predict Parkinson's disease (PD) with the deep models, which requires enough number of training data. Online handwriting dynamic signals can provide more detailed and complex information for PD detection task. In our previous work [1], two different deep models were studied for time series classification; the convolutional neural network (CNN) and the convolutional neural network- bidirectional long short term memory network (CNN-BLSTM). Different approaches were applied to encode pen-based signals into images for the CNN model while the raw time series are used directly with the CNN-BLSTM model. We have showed that both CNN model with spectrogram images as input and CNN-BLSTM model, improve the performance of time series classification applied for early PD stage detection. However, these approaches did not outperform classical support vector machine (SVM) classification applied on pre-engineered features. In this paper we investigate transfer learning and data augmentation approaches in order to train these models for PD detection on large-scale data. Various data augmentation methods for pen-based signals are proposed. Our experimental results show that the CNN-BLSTM model used with the combination of Jittering and Synthetic data augmentation methods provides promising results in the context of early PD detection, with accuracy reaching 97.62%. We have illustrated that deep architecture can surpass the models trained on pre-engineered features even though the available data is small.

Keywords: PDMultiMC dataset · Parkinson's disease (PD) · CNN · CNN-BLSTM · Handwriting · Data augmentation · Transfer learning

1 Introduction

Deep learning have shown excellent performance on classification problems where large datasets are available. However, it is challenging to apply deep learning to problems where only small datasets are available like medical data [4]. Training an

© Springer Nature Switzerland AG 2020
C. Djeddi et al. (Eds.): MedPRAI 2019, CCIS 1144, pp. 79–93, 2020.
https://doi.org/10.1007/978-3-030-37548-5_7

adequately sized neural network with a small dataset can cause the network to memorize all training examples, in turn leading to poor performance on a holdout dataset [5]. This phenomenon, also known as overfitting, can be solved using different techniques such as collecting more labeled data (which is in our case hard to obtain), using transfer learning method, or using data augmentation. Transfer learning is a machine learning technique where a model trained on one task (a source domain) is re-purposed on a second related task [14]. Data augmentation is the process of generating artificial data from the original ones. Such approaches have been applied in different domains including handwritten recognition of manuscripts [13]. In our case here, the key challenge is to maintain the correct label. It's important to find the proper data augmentation method that will preserve the correct label. In this paper, we are working with pen-based dynamic signals. However, unlike in image recognition problems, data augmentation techniques have not been completely investigated for the time series classification task [9]. In this paper, we propose transfer learning and data augmentation methods for time series to overcome the overfitting problem and to increase the recognition accuracy and robustness of Parkinson's disease (PD) detection system built in [1]. The paper is organized as follows. In the next section an overview of related work is provided. The datasets and the models used are presented in Sects. 3 and 4. Sections 5 and 6 explore the existing strategies to avoid overfitting and the possible combinations of the models respectively. Section 7 gives the experimental results. Finally the paper ends with conclusions and some perspectives.

2 Related Work

Some researchers have indicated that handwriting can be used to diagnose Parkinson's disease in the early stage, where the motor symptoms are not yet severe [16]. A SVM model trained on pre-engineering features was built in our previous work [2]. We found that handwriting can be a tool for PD diagnosis with 97% prediction accuracy when features related to the correlation between kinematic and pressure are used [2]. However, hand-crafted features model required expert knowledge of the field [15]; which motivated us to learn pen-based features by means of deep learning. In our previous work [1], an automatic classification algorithm for PD detection is developed based on online handwriting. We have proposed two deep learning models for end to-end time series classification: the CNN and the CNN-BLSTM. Three different frameworks were applied to encode time series into images for the CNN model: time series-based images proposed by Pereira et al. [3], Gramian angular field images, and spectrogram images. While the first two approaches normalize the time series into a fixed dimension image without extracting local information, the spectrogram images computes local short term information as existing in the non-stationary online handwriting signals before the application of normalization.

For the CNN-BLSTM model, the raw time series are directly used with no need to convert them into images. This approach has been experimented to validate the importance of considering the local information before integrating on the time scale [1].

We demonstrated the importance of both: a deep architecture based on the combination of 1D CNN and BLSTM recurrent layers, and a CNN model with spectrograms as input in PD detection achieving around 83.33% of classification accuracy considering the maximum voting combination approach described in [1]. In order to get the best time series features combination, a suboptimal incremental approach has been used. The feature providing the highest classification accuracy is first selected. Then, features are added incrementally by selecting, at every iteration, the one yielding the highest classification accuracy. The iterations stop when no more increase in performance is observed. Our results clearly show that when explicitly considering the local short term information on the time axis of the non-stationary online handwriting signals, the deep learning models provide better performance [1].

3 Dataset

To attain the target of detecting PD, we have collected a multimodal database called PDMultiMC that includes handwriting samples collected from 21 PD patients and 21 control subjects using Wacom intuos 5 tablet. The trace of the pen tip (x-y-z coordinate), the pressure of the pen tip on the surface, the angles of the pen relative to the tablet (altitude and azimuth), and timestamp were collected for each subject. The handwriting tasks recorded for each of the 21 controls and 21 PD patients in their "on-state" (i.e. taking their medication as regularly) were studied and analyzed. A complete task sheet is shown in Fig. 1. The template is divided into 7 tasks. They consist in drawing loops, triangular and rectangular waves, writing Monday, Tuesday, first and last name. The pen-based extracted signals are studied here instead of the drawings [1].

4 Model Architectures

We found in [1] that both the CNN model with the combination of spectrogram images referring to X, Y, Z, pressure, and altitude features as input and the CNN-BLSTM model with the combination of X, Y, Z, pressure, altitude and azimuth features time series, return the best PD detection accuracy. We applied in [1] the 3-folds cross validation (CV) with stratified sampling method in order to insure the same class distribution and number of samples in all the folds. The model architectures are represented in Figs. 2 and 3 respectively. The CNN model consists of 2 convolution layers and 2 pooling layers. Starting with a 64×64 pixel image with one channel (Grayscale), all the convolutional layers employ kernels of size 5×5 with stride of 1 pixel, and all the pooling layers are 2×2 max pooling. The convolutional layers convert the image to 64 feature maps of size 16×16. After using convolution layers to extract the spatial features of an image, we apply fully connected layers for the final classification [1].

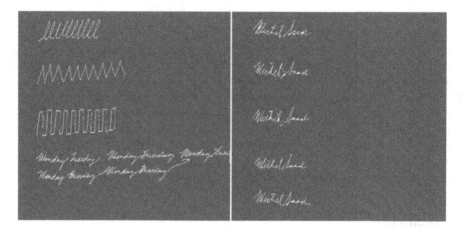

Fig. 1. Template used to assess the handwritten skills of a given individual. The template is divided into 7 tasks. They consist in drawing loops, triangular and rectangular waves, writing Monday, Tuesday, first and last name.

The CNN-BLSTM model involves using CNN layers for feature extraction on input data combined with BLSTMs to support sequence prediction. Instead of converting the time series into images, the entire raw time series are used here as input to the model. The convolutional layers are constructed using one-dimensional kernels that move through the sequence [1]. Based on these models and the best features combinations, two strategies will be applied to solve the overfitting problem due to the small dataset that we are working on.

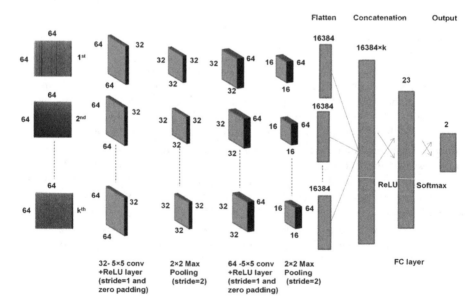

Fig. 2. Architecture of the k-input CNN model with Spectrogram images as input. The k inputs come from distinct features.

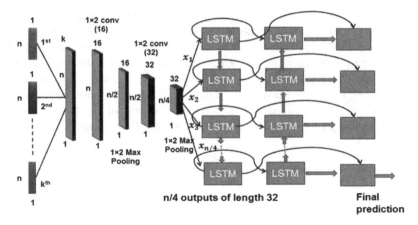

Fig. 3. The CNN-BLSTM model on multivariate time series. The output of the 1-d CNN is fed to a BLSTM as a sequence.

5   Strategies to Avoid Overfitting

In this paper the best deep learning model for time series classification found in our previous work [1] is selected with the best features combination (among features x, y, z, pressure, etc...). Based on this result, transfer learning and data augmentation approaches are applied to avoid the overfitting caused by the limited number of patient data in this study.

5.1   Transfer Learning Process

The first approach used to solve the overfitting problem is the transfer learning method. Some works have shown that transfer learning can be used efficiently with convolutional neural networks [6]. For this reason, in this work we apply transfer learning process on the CNN model represented in Fig. 2. By using pre-trained models which have been previously trained on large datasets, we can directly use the weights and architecture obtained and applies the learning on our problem statement [8]. Here we train the CNN model on a larger handwriting dataset, namely the PaHaw dataset that we can easily access [11]. Checking the PaHaW template in [11], we observe that PaHaW and PDMultiMC datasets are somehow similar: tasks in both sets contain loops. The differences between the 2 sets are that the Z coordinate feature is missing in PaHaW, and the number of tasks is 8 instead of 7. To match the two datasets we eliminate task 8 in PaHaW and the Z coordinate feature in PDMultiMC. The whole PaHaW dataset is used for pre- training in this work.

Different transfer learning strategies were studied and compared to validate the gains of transfer learning over training our CNN model from scratch. These strategies are summarized in Fig. 4. The first transfer learning strategy freezes all the PaHaW-trained model layers and a new softmax classifier is trained using the training images of PDMultiMC dataset since the softmax contains relatively few parameters, it can be trained from a relatively small number of examples [7]. The second strategy freezes only a part of the PaHaW-trained model. As we know, lower layers of the convolutional base refer to general features, while higher layers refer to specific features [8]. We studied 2 partial freeze strategies; where the first one freezes the whole convolutional base of the PaHaW-trained model and the part closer to the classifier is retrained using the training images of PDMultiMC dataset, and the second one freezes only the first layers of the convolutional base and retrains the rest of the model. Last, we consider full freezing of all layers of the PaHaW-trained CNN model.

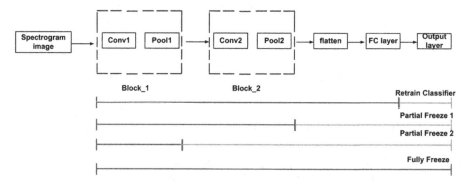

Fig. 4. Different transfer learning strategies are studied. Green indicates that blocks are retrained, and red indicates that blocks are frozen. (Color figure online)

5.2   Data Augmentation Applied to Time Series

Another way to prevent overfitting is to enlarge the training sets by generating synthetic (or artificial) examples. Time series that we are working with are collected from Wacom tablet's sensors. It's important to find the proper data augmentation method that will increase the recognition accuracy and robustness of the recognition system. There are two basic data augmentation approaches used in image processing: geometric transformation (shift, scale, rotation/reflection, Time-Wrapping, etc.) and noise addition [4]. Minor changes due to the geometric transformation or noise addition will not alter the data labels because they are likely to happen in real world observations (when pen sensors are not 100% precise) [4].

The Data Augmentation Techniques Used. Jittering, scaling, Time-Warping, and synthetic data generation techniques are used to generate new time series samples. Figure 5 presents the raw input time series and the augmented ones using jittering, scaling, time warping, and Synthetic data generation for a given subject and task (here it refers to task 1). These methods do not crop time series into shorter subsequences. This enables the network to learn discriminative properties from the whole time series in an end-to-end manner [9].

Jittering. It is considered as a way of simulating additive sensor noise. We focus on adding Gaussian noise to each feature time series of the original training data to obtain new training samples [10]. It can be considered as applying different noise to each sample of the time series. In order to ensure that the amplitude value of the sample will not be changed with the addition of noise, we generate the Gaussian noise with $\mu = 0$ [10]. In order to explore the effect of noise intensity (standard deviation (STD)) and the augmented multiple (m) on the work of time series data augmentation, different values of STD and m are studied. The amount of noise added is a hyper-parameter. Too little noise has no effect, whereas too much noise makes the mapping function too challenging to learn or may alter the labels because it introduces rapid fluctuations which look similar to tremor [4].

Scaling. Scaling changes the magnitude of the data in a window by multiplying by a random scalar [4]. It is considered as a way of simulating multiplicative sensor noise. We also focus on multiplying Gaussian noise (with a non-zero mean) to each feature time series of the original training data to obtain new training samples [4]. It can be considered as applying constant noise to the entire samples of a time series. Different values of m and STD are studied.

Time-Warping. Time-warping is a way to perturb the temporal location by smoothly distorting the time intervals between samples [4].

Generating Synthetic Data. To create the synthetic time series, some authors propose to average a set of time series and to use the averaged time series as a newly created example [9]. In this work, we are working with time series of variable lengths. First of all the training data will be separated into subsets of the same class label, then the size of each subset is calculated and the maximum is selected and defined by G [9]. The number of synthetic data per class Sl is equal to 2G-Hl; where Hl refers to the size of class l. The number of added synthetic data will rebalance classes in case they are imbalanced; which is not our case. The next step is to assign the weights for each subset separately based on the following steps: starting with a random initial time series chosen from the subset, it is assigned with a weight equal to 0.5 [9]. Then the 5 nearest neighbors using the Dynamic Time Warping (DTW) distance are searched. Randomly 2 out of these 5 neighbors are selected and assigned with a weight equal to 0.15 each [9]. Therefore, in order to have a normalized sum of weights, the rest of time series in the subset will share the rest of the weight 0.2. The new generated time series length is equal to the initial time series chosen.

6 Combination Approach

The experiments in this part are divided into two rounds: single assessment and combined assessment [3]. In the single assessment, we analyze each task separately, while in the combined assessment we combine the outputs of the 7 models in order to find the final label (also called overall performance) [1]. Each model corresponds to one task. Each model outputs two values corresponding to the probabilities that the input time series, associated to the given task, are performed by a parkinsonian or a control subject respectively.

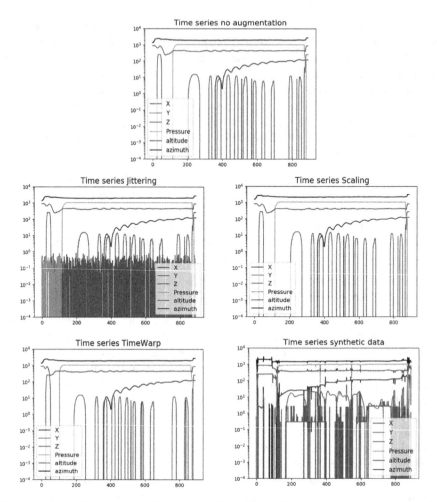

Fig. 5. Raw input time series and time series obtained by various data augmentation approaches such as: jittering, scaling, time-warping, and synthetic data generation.

For the transfer learning approach, maximum voting will be used to obtain the final label. However, in case of data augmentation approach, an MLP model that combines the probability vectors provided by the 7 models will be used instead of majority voting in order to acquire the final probability vector for classification decision. The MLP model is composed of an input layer of 14 nodes, a single hidden layer of 40 nodes with Rectified Linear Unit (ReLU) activation function, and 2 output nodes (corresponding to PD and control) with softmax activation function.

7 Experiments and Discussions

We will investigate transfer learning and data augmentation approaches based on the CNN and CNN-BLSTM models for time series classification in order to perform PD detection on large-scale data and to increase the recognition accuracy and robustness of recognition system. Different parameter values (STD and m) are applied and compared for data augmentation. For jittering a STD value sampled from a Gaussian distribution with 0.3 STD. This value was chosen not large neither small in order to not alter the labels [4]. For scaling, a random scalar is sampled from a Gaussian distribution with a mean of 1 and 0.1 STD. For Time-Warping, random sinusoidal curves are generated using arbitrary amplitude, frequency, and phase values [4]. We achieved the best accuracy when the training data is augmented to 2 times. The new times series are either used directly with the CNN-BLSTM model, or converted into spectrogram images with the CNN model as described in [1].

First, we compare the different transfer learning strategies described in Sect. 5 across the CNN model; where maximum voting is applied to merge the results provided by the 7 models (referring to the 7 tasks). The performance in Table 1 represents the average of 3 runs (3-folds CV). Comparing the transfer learning strategies, fully freezing performs worse than other strategies; where incremental performance may be observed when more convolutional layers are included in fine-tuning (partial freeze 1 and partial freeze 2). However, we expect that using PaHaW database to pre-train the CNN model will return a better performance than training from scratch. This can be due to the absence of Z coordinate feature in the PaHaW database, and it seems that this feature plays an important role in classification.

Table 1. Comparison of various transfer learning strategies across the CNN model; where maximum voting is used as combination approach.

Model	Data input	Transfer learning strategy	Best features combination	Overall Per. (%)
k-input CNN	Spectrogram images	From scratch (no transfer learning)	X+Y+Z+Pressure +Altitude	**Acc:83.33** Sens:85.71 Spec:80.95
k-input CNN	Spectrogram images	Retrain Classification layer	X+Y+Pressure+ Altitude	Acc:54.76 Sens:28.57 Spec:80.95
k-input CNN	Spectrogram images	Partial Freeze 1	X+Y+Pressure+ Altitude	Acc:66.67 Sens:66.67 Spec:66.67
k-input CNN	Spectrogram images	Partial Freeze 2	X+Y+Pressure+ Altitude	Acc:66.67 Sens:66.67 Spec:66.67
k-input CNN	Spectrogram images	Fully Freeze	X+Y+Pressure+ Altitude	Acc:45.24 Sens:71.43 Spec:19.05

Moving to data augmentation strategy, the main results of the proposed techniques are presented in Table 2. The CNN and the CNN-BLSTM models are used here, and a MultiLayer Perceptron (MLP) model is applied to combine the probability vectors provided by the 7 models (each one corresponding to one task), in order to provide the final classification decision. Scaling fails to improve the CNN-BLSTM performance because changing in the intensity of the signal may alter the labels [4]. On the other hand, jittering, Time-Warping, and creating synthetic time series by averaging a set of time series used with CNN-BLSTM model improve the accuracy of PD classification by 7.15% accuracy. Data augmentation improves the CNN-BLSTM performance and fails to improve the CNN performance because the CNN-BLSTM deals with time series directly without encoding them into spectrogram images (the case of CNN), which will benefits the most from the data augmentation techniques for time series.

Training and testing curves for CNN-BLSTM model with Jitter, Time-Warping, and averaging time series data augmentation techniques, and with MLP combination approach are depicted in Fig. 6. The accuracy plots show that data augmentation improves the accuracy of our deep learning model and helps in reducing overfitting. Task-wise system accuracies for the developed models in this study and the SVM model developed in our previous study [2] are represented in Table 3; where D1, D2, D3, and D4 models refer to SVM, CNN-BLSTM with Jittering augmentation, CNN-BLSTM with Time-Warping augmentation, and CNN-BLSTM with synthetic augmentation models *respectively*. It can be observed from Table 3 that "all tasks" reports highest accuracies across all the 4 models (D1, D2, D3, and D4). Additionally, we can observe that Task 2 (triangular wave) and Task 3 (rectangular wave) reports highest accuracies across all the 4 models. These two tasks are considered long and somehow complex. Copying these cursive tasks needs higher cognitive force and explains the effect of disease on handwriting [2]. The same conclusion is found in [1] and [2]. We also carry out experiments by combining the results obtained from the CNN-BLSTM model with different data augmentation methods (D2, D3, and D4 in Table 3) using a MLP model composed of an input layer of 4 nodes, a single hidden layer of 30 nodes with Rectified Linear Unit (ReLU) activation function, and 2 output nodes (corresponding to PD and control) with softmax activation function. The performance measures realized in these experiments are summarized in Table 4 where it can be seen that combining the results of various data augmentation methods show better performance than that a single data augmentation. The highest accuracy is 97.62% obtained when combining Jittering and Synthetic data augmentation methods. We can see that the existence of Time-Warping augmentation method in the combination fails to improve the performance. From a clinical point of view, inter-samples timing disturbances occurs due to the neuro-motor dysfunctions affecting wrist and finger movement of PD patients [11, 12]. As mentioned before, the temporal locations of the samples are changed by Time-Warping; which will look similar to inter-samples time disturbances. The best final model that detects PD with an accuracy of 97.62% is summarized in Fig. 7, where Jittering and Synthetic data augmentation techniques are applied separately on 'All-tasks" system. Two MLPs models (MLP1 and MLP2) are applied, where each one is used to combine the probability vectors (each of size 2) obtained by the 7 CNN-BLSTM models (with the best feature set (X, Y, Z, pressure, altitude, and azimuth) found in [1]) that are trained with distinct data augmentation approach. At a later stage, another MLP model (MLP3) is used to combine the probability vectors provided by each of MLP1 and MLP2 (each of size 2) in order to get the final prediction. This model was trained with Nvidia GTX 1080 GPU of 8 GB memory. The time required for the training process is around 1 day, where 203,636 parameters have been learned. A comparison of performance obtained in this study with other studies is presented in Table 5. In [2, 17, 18] the authors have applied SVM models that are trained on hand-crafted features for PD detection. Drotar et al. [17] found that a combination of kinematic, temporal, pressure, and intrinsic features return a classification accuracy of 89.09%, where Taleb et al. [2] report a higher accuracy of 96.87% when a set of features related to the correlation between kinematic and pressure are used. Mucha et al. [18] proposed another promising approach that returns an accuracy of 97.14% when a combination of kinematic and temporal features that are extracted for both "on-paper" and "in-air" is used. In addition, Pereira et al. [3] and Taleb et al. in this study proposed to use deep learning to learn features from online handwriting exams. In [3] Pereira has proposed to encode the handwriting signals into images and fed into a CNN model. This approach reaches an accuracy of 93.42%. Finally, in this work a CNN-BLSTM model with the combination of 2 different data augmentation techniques (Jittering and Synthetic data) returns an accuracy of 97.62%. Table 5 shows that our deep learning and SVM models report highest performance across all the mentioned works although results are not always measured on the same database. Future work will consist in testing our models on other PD databases (PahaW, HandPD) in order to confirm our conclusion.

Table 2. 3-folds CV performance measures obtained after applying data augmentation and MLP for classification decision.

Model	Data input	Augmentation technique	Best features combination	Overall Per. (%)
k-input CNN	Spectrogram images	Jitter	X+Y+Z+Pressure+ Altitude	Acc:83.33 Sens:85.71 Spec:80.95
k-input CNN-BLSTM	Raw Time series	Jitter	X+Y+Z+Pressure+ Altitude+Azimuth	**Acc:90.48** Sens:95.24 Spec:85.71
k-input CNN-BLSTM	Raw Time series	Scaling	X+Y+Z+Pressure+ Altitude+Azimuth	Acc:59.52 Sens:19.05 Spec:100
k-input CNN-BLSTM	Raw time series	Time-Warping	X+Y+Z+Pressure+ Altitude+Azimuth	**Acc:90.48** Sens:90.48 Spec:90.48
k-input CNN-BLSTM	Raw Time series	Synthetic data	X+Y+Z+Pressure+ Altitude+Azimuth	**Acc:90.48** Sens:85.71 Spec:95.24

Table 3. Task-wise system and all-tasks system accuracies (in %) for various models and training schemes. D1: SVM, D2: CNN-BLSTM/Jitter, D3: CNN-BLSTM/Time-Warping, D4: CNN-BLSTM/Synthetic data.

Task	D1	D2	D3	D4
Repetitive cursive letter 'l'	**87.5**	59.52	57.14	47.62
Triangular wave	**93.75**	80.95	83.33	78.57
Rectangular wave	**90.63**	71.43	69.05	76.19
Repetitive "Monday"	**87.5**	78.57	66.67	76.19
Repetitive "Tuesday"	**87.5**	57.14	47.62	59.52
Repetitive "Name"	**84.38**	57.14	42.86	50
Repetitive "Family Name"	**84.38**	69.05	71.43	64.29
All tasks (MLP combination)	**96.87**	**90.48**	**90.48**	**90.48**

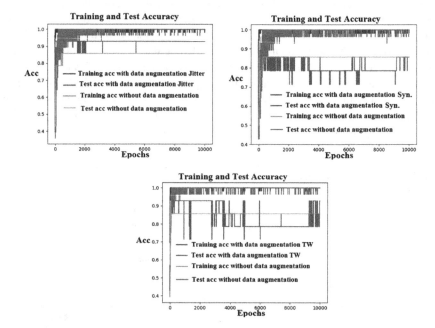

Fig. 6. Training and testing curves for CNN-BLSTM model with Jitter, Time-Warping, and averaging time series (or Synthetic) data augmentation techniques and MLP combination approach.

Table 4. "All tasks" system performance measures (in %) for different combinations of data augmentation techniques.

Metric	D2+D3	D2+D4	D3+D4	D2+D3+D4
Accuracy	92.86	**97.62**	92.86	92.86
Sensitivity	90.48	**95.24**	95.24	95.24
Specificity	95.24	**100**	90.48	90.48

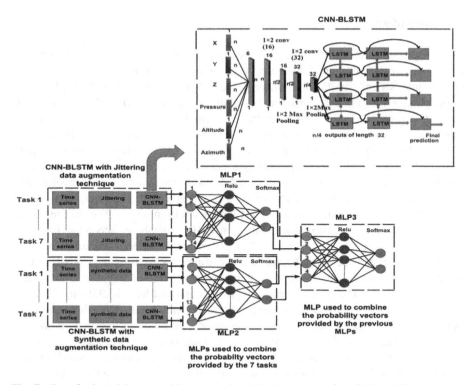

Fig. 7. Best final model that combines through MLPs the outputs of 14 CNN-BLSTM systems trained with augmented data.

Table 5. Comparison table between the developed method and the previous studies.

Ref.	Database	Model	Features	Perf. (%)
Drotar [17]	PaHaW	SVM	Kinematic, temporal, spatial, entropy, EMD, pressure (on-paper)	Acc:89.09
				Sens:N/A
				Spec:N/A
Taleb [2]	PDMultiMC	SVM	Kinematic, stroke, pressure, entropy, EMD (on-paper)	Acc:**96.87**
				Sens:93.75
				Spec:100
Mucha [18]	PaHaW	SVM	Kinematic, temporal (on-paper and in-air)	Acc: **97.14**
				Sens: 95.50
				Spec: 100
Pereira [3]	HandPD	CNN-ImageNet	CNN-based features (on-paper and in-air)	Acc:93.42
				Sens:97.84
				Spec:89.00
Proposed model	PDMultiMC	CNN-BLSTM	CNN-based features (on-paper and in-air)	Acc: **97.62**
				Sens: 95.24
				Spec: 100

8   Conclusion

In this paper, an automatic classification system for PD detection is developed based on online handwriting. In a previous work we proposed 2 based learning models for end to-end time series classification, namely the CNN and the CNN-BLSTM. Deep learning models require a large number of training samples to work well alike the SVM that is less sensitive to the number of training samples. This means that PD classification using deep learning is a challenging task due to the limited data availability. To cope with the limited data, two main classes of approaches were reported in this paper. Firstly, multiple transfer learning strategies across the CNN model for time series classification were investigated and compared. It was found that the more convolutional layers included in the fine-tuning, the better performance we get. However, there are no gains of transfer learning over training our CNN model from scratch. We believe this is due to the absence of Z coordinate feature in PaHaW database. Secondly, jittering, scaling, Time-Warping, and synthetic data generation techniques are used for data augmentation. The challenging PD task is successfully tackled using the CNN-BLSTM model described in Sect. 4 and the combination of jittering and synthetic data augmentation methods. The accuracy performance is improved from 83.33% to 97.62%.

It is important to summarize a number of observations and conclusions obtained from this study. First of all, the importance of Z coordinate feature in Parkinson's disease classification, and the effectiveness of data augmentation over transfer learning at reducing error and decreasing overfitting were shown. In addition, Time-Warping technique fails to improve the performance of PD classification due to the distortion of time intervals between samples that look similar to inter-samples time disturbances; which is one of the early marks of PD. Also, data augmentation methods applied for time series classification can increase deep learning model performance when time series are used directly with no need to convert them into images. Finally, it was illustrated that deep architecture with data augmentation can surpass the models trained on pre-engineered features even though the available data is small. We have proved in this study that data augmentation method can improve the performance of PD detection with deep learning models. As a future work, we will do experiments on SVM with the augmented data in order to examine if this method is also effective for other machine learning models and to approve the conclusion drawn in this paper.

Acknowledgments. This study has been approved by the institutional review board (IRB) of the University of Balamand and Saint George Hospital University Medical Center.

References

1. Taleb, C., Likforman, L., Khachab, M., Mokbel, C.: Visual representation of online handwriting time series for deep learning Parkinson's disease detection. In: 2019 3rd International Workshop on Arabic Script Analysis and Recognition (ASAR), Sydney, Australia (2019)
2. Taleb, C., Likforman, L., Khachab, M., Mokbel, C.: Feature selection for an improved Parkinson's disease identification based on handwriting. In: 2017 1st International Workshop on Arabic Script Analysis and Recognition (ASAR), Nancy, France (2017)

3. Pereira, et al.: Handwritten dynamics assessment through convolutional neural networks: an application to Parkinson's disease identification. Artif. Intell. Med. **87**, 67–77 (2018)
4. Um, T.T., et al.: Data augmentation of wearable sensor data for Parkinson's disease monitoring using convolutional neural networks. In: Proceedings of the 19th ACM International Conference on Multimodal Interaction - ICMI 2017 (2017)
5. Brownlee, J.: Train Neural Networks With Noise to Reduce Overfitting. Machine Learning Mastery (2019). https://machinelearningmastery.com/train-neural-networks-with-noise-to-reduce-overfitting/. Accessed 11 Sept 2019
6. Mormont, R., Geurts, P., Marée, R.: Comparison of deep transfer learning strategies for digital pathology. In: 2018 IEEE/CVF Conference on Computer Vision and Pattern Recognition (CVPR), Salt Lake City, UT, pp. 2262–2271 (2018)
7. Zeiler, D.M., Fergus, R.: Visualizing and Understanding Convolutional Networks, 28 November 2013. https://arxiv.org/abs/1311.2901
8. Marcelino, P.: Towards data science. Transfer learning from pre-trained models (2019). https://towardsdatascience.com/transfer-learning-from-pre-trained-models-f2393f124751. Accessed 11 Sept 2019
9. Fawaz, I.H., Forestier, G., Weber, J., Idoumghar, L., Muller, P.-A.: Data augmentation using synthetic data for time series classification with deep residual networks (2018). https://arxiv.org/abs/1808.02455
10. Wang, F., Zhong, S.-h., Peng, J., Jiang, J., Liu, Y.: Data augmentation for EEG-based emotion recognition with deep convolutional neural networks. In: Schoeffmann, K., et al. (eds.) MMM 2018. LNCS, vol. 10705, pp. 82–93. Springer, Cham (2018). https://doi.org/10.1007/978-3-319-73600-6_8
11. Drotar, et al.: Evaluation of handwriting kinematics and pressure for differential diagnosis of Parkinson's disease. Artif. Intell. Med. **67**, 39–46 (2016)
12. Gómez-Vilda, P., et al.: Parkinson disease detection from speech articulation neuromechanics. Front. Neuroinf. **11**, 56 (2017)
13. Chammas, E., Mokbel, C., Likforman-Sulem, L.: Handwriting recognition of historical documents with few labeled data. In: 13th IAPR International Workshop on Document Analysis Systems (DAS), pp. 43–48 (2018)
14. Sadouk, L.: CNN Approaches for Time Series Classification (2018). https://doi.org/10.5772/intechopen.81170
15. Gamboa, J.: Deep Learning for Time-Series Analysis (2017)
16. Spadoto, A.A., et al.: Improving Parkinson's disease identification through evolutionary-based feature selection. In: Annual International Conference of the IEEE, Engineering in Medicine and Biology Society, EMBC, pp. 7857–7860 (2011)
17. Drotar, P., et al.: Contribution of different handwriting modalities to differential diagnosis of Parkinson's disease. In: 2015 IEEE International Symposium on Medical Measurements and Applications (MeMeA), pp. 344–348 (2015)
18. Mucha, J., et al.: Identification and monitoring of Parkinson's disease dysgraphia based on fractional-order derivatives of online handwriting. In: 41st International Conference on Telecommunications and Signal Processing (TSP), Athens, Greece, pp. 1–4 (2018)

Human Action Recognition Using Stereo Trajectories

Pejman Habashi$^{(\boxtimes)}$, Boubakeur Boufama , and Imran Shafiq Ahmad

School of Computer Science, University of Windsor, Windsor, Canada
boufama@uwindsor.ca

Abstract. This paper proposes a new method that uses a pair of uncalibrated stereo videos, without the need for three-dimensional reconstruction, for human action recognition (HAR). Two stereo views of the same scene, obtained from two different cameras, are used to create a set of two-dimensional trajectories. Then, we calculate disparities between them and fuse them with the trajectories, to obtain our *disparity-augmented trajectories* that is used in our HAR method. The obtained results have shown on average a 2.40% improvement, when using disparity-augmented trajectories, compared to using the classical 2D trajectory information only. Furthermore, we have also tested our method on the challenging Hollywood 3D dataset and, we have obtained competitive results, at a faster speed than some state of the art methods.

Keywords: Human activity recognition · Disparity-augmented trajectory · Video content analysis

1 Introduction

Human activity recognition (HAR) referred to the process of automatically labelling the videos of human movements with the action names. Johansson et al. [1] attached markers to human joints before recording their movements in a video. Human subjects could easily say that the moving tags were attached to a human body, and they could name the type of activity that the actor was doing. This experiment proves that the task of HAR is rather trivial for humans, it does not provide any clues about whether the human brain uses 2D trajectories of markers or uses a 3D trajectory model, before the recognition process.

To solve the problem of human activity recognition, numerous approaches have been proposed. One approach is the use of sparse representation. In this method, each video is represented by a set of independent features. This method has gained a lot of popularity. However, most of the features proposed in the literature focused on low-level features [2–8], that are directly extracted from the pixel values. Some other works have used higher-level features, such as joint locations [9–12]. These methods assume that high-level features would yield better results.

© Springer Nature Switzerland AG 2020
C. Djeddi et al. (Eds.): MedPRAI 2019, CCIS 1144, pp. 94–105, 2020.
https://doi.org/10.1007/978-3-030-37548-5_8

In practice, extracting high-level features from cluttered scenes is not a trivial task. It sometimes requires the use of specialized equipment, like color markers on human joints [13], or special sensors, to create a depth map and to extract human skeleton from it [14,15].

On the other hand, it is easy to build a trajectory by tracking a set of interest points across video frames. In comparison to other sparse representation methods, trajectories are mid-level features and can produce competitive results. [16] proposed and compared different 2D trajectory-based HAR algorithms. In separate work, [17] proposed a better trajectory shape descriptor to be used for HAR.

In this paper, the disparity is used to boost the performance of trajectory-based HAR methods. Two slightly different views of the subject are required to create disparity maps. First, 2D trajectories are extracted from the left and right videos. Then, by matching these trajectories and mapping them to the rectified image planes, a disparity-augmented trajectory is created.

This paper demonstrates that adding the disparity information to the 2D trajectories, can be beneficial for human activity recognition. In particular, disparity-augmented trajectories have improved classification rates by 2.40% in our tests.

Both 2D and disparity-augmented trajectories are made of pixel locations across frames. To be used for classification, a descriptor, that can discriminate between different trajectories, should be defined based on the shape of trajectories. The descriptors used in this work were inspired by the ones used in [17].

To improve the performance of our proposed method, we have limited the processing to the regions of interest. The movements in the video used as a clue for finding regions of interest. In particular, the graph connected component analysis algorithm was used to select the active areas in frames.

The use of disparity augmented trajectories proposed in this paper, is not dependent on the HAR task, and it can be applied to other video categorization problems as well.

In summary, this paper proposes a new method to create disparity-augmented trajectories from stereo videos. The remainder of this paper is organized as follows. Section 2 reviews background works. Section 3 describes how the disparity information is added to the 2D trajectories. Section 4 has the details of the learning method used. Sections 5 and 6 present the experimental results and the conclusion, respectively.

2   Background Works

Wang et al. used trajectories in separate contributions [18,19]. In their works, a grid was used to dense sample video frames. Eigenvalues of the autocorrelation matrix was utilized to filter out the samples that were not easy to track. Dense optical flow field, proposed by Farnback [20], was applied to track these sample points in time. This flow was then employed to align the interest points neighborhoods before calculating the HOG and HOF features. They also proposed another trajectory shape descriptor, that did not outperform the other two.

Mademlis et al. [21] used disparity information to calculate HOG, HOF and MBH in different disparity zones before encoding them for activity recognition. Although their method improves the performance, but their use of disparity is limited to few disparity zones. Arguably the disparity can be used more efficiently for encoding task.

Hadfield et al. [22] used 3D Hollywood movies to create a challenging stereo dataset for human activity recognition. The authors estimated the calibration information using RANSAC method and repeating the process 100 times, before selecting the best estimation. Then, the extracted 3D information extracted was used to calculate 3.5D interest points. They have defined a 3D motion descriptors for each of these feature points and, they have normalized it to remove the effect of different camera rotations.

Matikainen et al. [23] used the technique of Kanade Lucas Tomasi (KLT) [24] to track a number of points and, created a trajectory for each of these points. Then, they used K-Means method to cluster the obtained trajectories in different clusters (words). They have also proposed to augment these trajectories by adding some affine transformation information, which represents the motion of various parts of the body. Finally, they have used a standard bag of words (BOW) method and SVM for clustering.

In another similar work, Messing et al. [25] used KLT to track keypoints of a video and created a generative model on the velocity history of these keypoints.

Sun et al. [26] proposed to track Scale Invariant Feature Transform (SIFT) points. They have used SIFT descriptors to match each keypoints across the frames. They have extracted features at different levels and used multichannel nonlinear SVM for human activity recognition.

Habashi et al. [16,17] demonstrated that good sparse trajectories could produce competitive results to low-level features, but with less computations. Besides, trajectories are a better choice for HAR as they encode the motion of a body, while low-level features usually encode the texture or movement within small neighborhoods in spatiotemporal space. This makes low-level features more dataset dependent.

3   Disparity-Augmented Trajectories

3.1   Preprocessing

To decrease the processing time, we have used a simple but effective method for detecting the regions of interest, here are the steps:

1. Estimate the background by a mixture of Gaussian
2. Subtract background from the current frame
3. Use morphological operations to highlight the moving parts of the video
4. Find the contours of motion
5. Finally, find rectangular regions of interest as follows:
   (a) Find a bounding box for each contour

(b) Create a graph, where each node is a bounding box and, connect two nodes if the corresponding boxes overlap or are close (closer than one eighth of the image height).

(c) Find the connected components of this graph by connected component labelling algorithm similar to [27]

(d) Combine the boxes of each connected components.

Trajectories are the trail of 2D or 3D spatial feature points in time. The disparity-augmented trajectories in this sense are similar to 3D trajectories except that they have the disparity in addition to 2D information. A trajectory T can be defined as an ordered list of locations, sampled over $l + 1$ time steps, with l being the trajectory length.

$$T = (p_0, p_1, p_2, ..., p_l), p_i \in \mathbb{R}^n, i = 0...l \tag{1}$$

To create a disparity-augmented trajectory, the corresponding 2D trajectories from two views of a scene are extracted and combined. Trajectories of each video are extracted as in [16] and, then disparity is added to our 2D trajectories allowing us to extend the method proposed in [17].

3.2 Finding Matching Trajectories

Each trajectory starting point, in the left and right videos, are encoded with a SIFT descriptor and the best match of this descriptor is found by using the method in [28]. Starting from the first frame of the video, for each descriptor in the left frame, its best match is found in the right frame. To make the matching robust, we repeat the process between the right to the left frames and, only keep the reciprocal matches.

3.3 Calculating Disparity-Augmented Trajectories

To ease the disparity calculation process, we have mapped the trajectories into the rectified image plane. Let us assume t_l and t_r represent the mapping of T_l and T_r (a pair of matched trajectories), and also each point on t_l and t_r represented by $q_i = (u_i, v_i)$ and $q_i' = (u_i', v_i')$ respectively. Then, the corresponding disparity augmented point (x_i, y_i, d_i) will be given by:

$$x_i = u_i \tag{2}$$
$$y_i = v_i \tag{3}$$
$$d_i = u_i - u_i' \tag{4}$$

The disparity augmented trajectories, then encoded by an extension of the methods proposed in [17].

4 Learning Phase

The trajectory shape representation method used, like other sparse representation methods, represents a video by a set of independent features. Formally, a video can be represented by a set of feature descriptors as:

$$S = \{D_k | D_k \in \mathbb{R}^N\} \tag{5}$$

where N is the dimension of the local descriptors.

Existing machine learning methods in general and SVM in particular, expect data as a vector of predetermined size. As a result, each set of these features should be represented by a vector. Different methods have been proposed in the literature. One of the conventional methods to convert sparse sets to a vector is based on the bag of words (BOW).

Another favorite technique, known as Fisher Vector Encoding (FVE), combines the generative and discriminative methods [29]. Unlike BOW that uses only the first order statistics, FVE uses first and second order statistics for encoding [19]. Instead of using K-Means for clustering, Expectation Maximization (EM) is used to cluster data into K Gaussian Mixtures. Then, the created Gaussian mixture model (GMM) is used to estimate the means, variances and prior probabilities of the mixtures.

5 Results and Discussion

This section first provides details on our experimental setup, then review the accuracy results we obtain and finally represents the time measurements.

5.1 Experimental Setup

Our tests were carried out on a Ubuntu machine, with eight 3.8 GHz cores and 8 Gb of RAM. The video processing part, including trajectory extraction, was implemented in C++, using OpenCV library. The trajectory aligning algorithm was implemented in Python.

After obtaining a set of trajectory descriptors for each video, and since [19] has shown the 'effectiveness' of *Fisher Vectors* over other methods, we have used *Fisher Vectors* to prepare data before passing it to a standard support vector machine (libSVM [30]).

Figure 1 has snapshots of the used dataset. The dataset has 27 different activity classes performed with different variations.

5.2 Disparity-Augmented Trajectories

Table 1 summarizes the obtained results for disparity-augmented trajectories. Each row represents a trajectory length. We have tested trajectory lengths that range between 9 and 23. As it can be seen, the added disparity information

Fig. 1. Sample images from our dataset (best seen in color) From top to butom left to right: standing up, hand shaking, walking toward camera, two-hand waving, high-five, shooting the ball, pulling heavy object and picking up something from floor, jumping over gap, exchanging object, sitting up and punching.

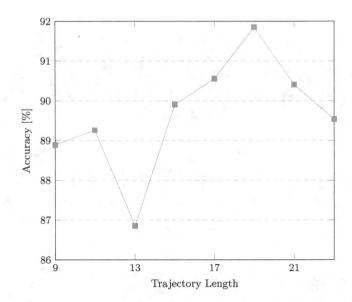

Fig. 2. Disparity-augmented trajectories accuracy. The effect of trajectory length on the accuracy

Table 1. Results of disparity-augmented trajectories for human activity recognition

Length	2D trajectory	DAT
9	85.30%	88.89%
11	85.30%	89.26%
13	87.95%	86.85%
15	87.07%	89.91%
17	89.09%	90.56%
19	**89.46%**	**91.85%**
21	87.38%	90.41%
23	86.48%	89.54%

increased the accuracy by 2.40% on average. The best obtained result (91.85%) was for trajectory length 19. Figure 2 represents the effect of trajectory length on the accuracy.

Figure 3 illustrates the confusion matrix of a sample run. Each row represents an actual class and each column represents a predicted class. The number of correct classifications is normalized between zero and one. It is also worth noting that the classes in our dataset are balanced, i.e., the number of samples for each activity classes is the same for all classes. The misclassified instances from the matrix give interesting information about the behavior of trajectories for HAR. For example, the most confused classes in this figure are "pointing" and "raise hand". The fact that for pointing to something, one should raise his/her hand shows that trajectories are capable of finding this similarity, but they are unable to distinguish between them in some cases. Another example is the classes "kicking a fixed object" and "kicking the ball". These classes have very similar motions and hence, they are expected to be confused by any motion-based HAR method.

From another viewpoint, it can be assumed that human activities have no precise definitions. In particular, many human activities do have some overlaps. For example, raising hand to point to something or waving. So, it is evident that there is a conceptual overlap over the definition of these classes and it is not easy to separate them conceptually.

5.3   Time Measurements

Our comparisons have shown that our disparity-augmented trajectory (DAT) method is faster than trajectory aligned methods (see Table 2). To test the time performance, five different random samples from the dataset were selected. Each reported time is the average of ten different runs. As it can be seen, the speed up gains vary between 1.5 to 4.5 times faster, depending on the selected activity samples. Overall, our proposed method is more than two times faster than the methods based on dense trajectories, as we are using sparse features.

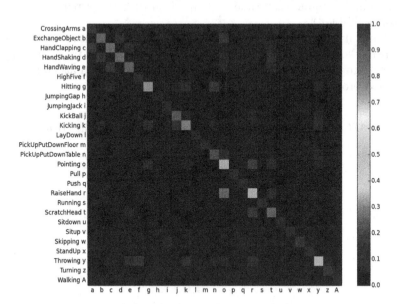

Fig. 3. The confusion matrix. Sample confusion matrix for 27 classes (indexed a to z and A). Each row represents the actual class, and each column is the predicted class.

Table 2. Time improvements obtained by using our method over trajectory aligned descriptors for different random samples, taken from our dataset.

Method	**DAT**	Trajectory aligned	Speed up
S1	19.67 s	46.89 s	238%
S2	32.13 s	51.95 s	161%
S3	7.33 s	33.68 s	459%
S4	42.70 s	66.17 s	155%
S5	13.09 s	41.31 s	311%
Sum	114.92 s	240.00 s	209%

5.4   Comparison

Table 3 shows the performance of our proposed method compared to the state of the art. The closest works to DAT are 2D dense trajectories [19]. We applied the algorithm proposed in [31] on sparse feature points and the result reported as sparse trajectories in Table 3. As it can be seen, our proposed method was able to outperform both dense and sparse trajectory methods, with a good margin. Moreover, the proposed method produced better result compared to HOG, and competitive results to HOF and MBH. It should be noted that HOG, HOF and MBH need more computation time in comparison with our disparity-augmented trajectories (Table 4).

We have also tested our method on Hollywood 3D dataset. As it can be seen, our method still yields superior results compared to the trajectory aligned descriptors proposed in [18] and reported in [22]. Our method also outperforms the method proposed by [22] in terms of accuracy.

Table 3. Comparison of our method against other state-of-the-art methods

	Method	Accuracy
Trajectory based	Sparse Trajectories	87.80%
	Dense Trajectory	88.74%
	DAT (Ours)	91.85%
Trajectory aligned	HOG	89.54%
	HOF	92.72%
	MBH	92.22%

Table 4. Comparisons of the obtained results on Hollywood 3D dataset. The first 5 rows are our DAT results with different trajectory lengths.

Length	Accuracy
7	21.50%
9	22.73%
11	**23.78%**
13	20.79%
15	19.80%
[18]	20.8%
[22]	21.8%

6 Conclusion

We have proposed a new method based on disparity-augmented trajectories for video content analysis where, we have fused the disparity information with motion-based features. Because disparities carry some kind of three-dimensional clues, our expectations for improvement in our HAR performance was confirmed. In particular, we have obtained better results on our HAR experiments, when compared to traditional trajectory-based methods, at a lower computational cost.

Furthermore, we have demonstrated that trajectories are useful for video content analysis in general, and for human activity recognition in particular. The added disparity information to trajectories has enhanced our overall results by 2.39%.

References

1. Johansson, G.: Visual perception of biological motion and a model for its analysis. Percept. Psychophysics **14**(2), 201–211 (1973)
2. Laptev, I., Lindeberg, T.: Interest point detection and scale selection in space-time. In: Griffin, L.D., Lillholm, M. (eds.) Scale-Space 2003. LNCS, vol. 2695, pp. 372–387. Springer, Heidelberg (2003). https://doi.org/10.1007/3-540-44935-3_26
3. Laptev, I.: On space-time interest points. Int. J. Comput. Vis. **64**(2–3), 107–123 (2005)
4. Dollár, P., Rabaud, V., Cottrell, G., Belongie, S.: Behavior recognition via sparse spatio-temporal features. In: 2005 2nd Joint IEEE International Workshop on Visual Surveillance and Performance Evaluation of Tracking and Surveillance, pp. 65–72. IEEE (2005)
5. Laptev, I., Marszalek, M., Schmid, C., Rozenfeld, B.: Learning realistic human actions from movies. In: 2008 IEEE Conference on Computer Vision and Pattern Recognition, CVPR 2008, pp. 1–8. IEEE (2008)
6. Bregonzio, M., Gong, S., Xiang, T.: Recognising action as clouds of space-time interest points. In: 2009 IEEE Conference on Computer Vision and Pattern Recognition, CVPR 2009, pp. 1948–1955. IEEE (2009)

7. Wang, H., Ullah, M.M., Klaser, A., Laptev, I., Schmid, C., et al.: Evaluation of local spatio-temporal features for action recognition. In: BMVC 2009-British Machine Vision Conference (2009)
8. Perš, J., Sulić, V., Kristan, M., Perše, M., Polanec, K., Kovačič, S.: Histograms of optical flow for efficient representation of body motion. Pattern Recogn. Lett. **31**(11), 1369–1376 (2010)
9. Li, L.-J., Su, H., Fei-Fei, L., Xing, E.P.: Object bank: a high-level image representation for scene classification & semantic feature sparsification. In: Advances in Neural Information Processing Systems, pp. 1378–1386 (2010)
10. Sadanand, S., Corso, J.J.: Action bank: a high-level representation of activity in video. In: 2012 IEEE Conference on Computer Vision and Pattern Recognition (CVPR), pp. 1234–1241. IEEE (2012)
11. Yao, A., Gall, J., Fanelli, G., Van Gool, L.J.: Does human action recognition benefit from pose estimation? In: BMVC, vol. 3, p. 6 (2011)
12. Jhuang, H., Gall, J., Zuffi, S., Schmid, C., Black, M.J.: Towards understanding action recognition. In: 2013 IEEE International Conference on Computer Vision (ICCV), pp. 3192–3199. IEEE (2013)
13. Ofli, F., Chaudhry, R., Kurillo, G., Vidal, R., Bajcsy, R.: Berkeley MHAD: a comprehensive multimodal human action database. In: 2013 IEEE Workshop on Applications of Computer Vision (WACV), pp. 53–60. IEEE (2013)
14. Shotton, J., et al.: Real-time human pose recognition in parts from single depth images. Commun. ACM **56**(1), 116–124 (2013)
15. Barnachon, M., Bouakaz, S., Boufama, B., Guillou, E.: Ongoing human action recognition with motion capture. Pattern Recogn. **47**(1), 238–247 (2014)
16. Boufama, B., Habashi, P., Ahmad, I.S.: Trajectory-based human activity recognition from videos. In: 2017 3rd International Conference on Advanced Technologies for Signal and Image Processing (ATSIP). IEEE (2017)
17. Habashi, P., Boufama, B., Ahmad, I.S.: A better trajectory shape descriptor for human activity recognition. In: Karray, F., Campilho, A., Cheriet, F. (eds.) ICIAR 2017. LNCS, vol. 10317, pp. 330–337. Springer, Cham (2017). https://doi.org/10.1007/978-3-319-59876-5_37
18. Wang, H., Kläser, A., Schmid, C., Liu, C.-L.: Dense trajectories and motion boundary descriptors for action recognition. Int. J. Comput. Vis. **103**(1), 60–79 (2013)
19. Wang, H., Schmid, C.: Action recognition with improved trajectories. In: 2013 IEEE International Conference on Computer Vision (ICCV), pp. 3551–3558. IEEE (2013)
20. Farnebäck, G.: Two-frame motion estimation based on polynomial expansion. In: Bigun, J., Gustavsson, T. (eds.) SCIA 2003. LNCS, vol. 2749, pp. 363–370. Springer, Heidelberg (2003). https://doi.org/10.1007/3-540-45103-X_50
21. Mademlis, I., Iosifidis, A., Tefas, A., Nikolaidis, N., Pitas, I.: Exploiting stereoscopic disparity for augmenting human activity recognition performance. Multimed. Tools Appl. **75**(19), 11641–11660 (2016)
22. Hadfield, S., Lebeda, K., Bowden, R.: Hollywood 3D: what are the best 3D features for action recognition? Int. J. Comput. Vis. **121**(1), 95–110 (2017)
23. Matikainen, P., Hebert, M., Sukthankar, R.: Trajectons: action recognition through the motion analysis of tracked features. In: 2009 IEEE 12th International Conference on Computer Vision Workshops (ICCV Workshops), pp. 514–521. IEEE (2009)
24. Lucas, B.D., Kanade, T., et al.: An iterative image registration technique with an application to stereo vision (1981)

25. Messing, R., Pal, C., Kautz, H.: Activity recognition using the velocity histories of tracked keypoints. In: 2009 IEEE 12th International Conference on Computer Vision, pp. 104–111. IEEE (2009)
26. Sun, J., Wu, X., Yan, S., Cheong, L.-F., Chua, T.-S., Li, J.: Hierarchical spatio-temporal context modeling for action recognition. In: 2009 IEEE Conference on Computer Vision and Pattern Recognition, CVPR 2009, pp. 2004–2011. IEEE (2009)
27. Vincent, L., Soille, P.: Watersheds in digital spaces: an efficient algorithm based on immersion simulations. IEEE Trans. Pattern Anal. Mach. Intell. **6**, 583–598 (1991)
28. Lowe, D.G.: Distinctive image features from scale-invariant keypoints. Int. J. Comput. Vis. **60**(2), 91–110 (2004)
29. Varol, G., Salah, A.A.: Efficient large-scale action recognition in videos using extreme learning machines. Expert Syst. Appl. **42**(21), 8274–8282 (2015)
30. Chang, C.-C., Lin, C.-J.: LIBSVM: a library for support vector machines. ACM Trans. Intell. Syst. Technol. **2**, 27:1–27:27 (2011). http://www.csie.ntu.edu.tw/~cjlin/libsvm
31. Wang, H., Klaser, A., Schmid, C., Liu, C.-L.: Action recognition by dense trajectories. In: 2011 IEEE Conference on Computer Vision and Pattern Recognition (CVPR), pp. 3169–3176. IEEE (2011)

Deep Convolutional Neural Network with 2D Spectral Energy Maps for Fault Diagnosis of Gearboxes Under Variable Speed

Md Junayed Hasan and Jongmyon Kim$^{(\boxtimes)}$

Department of Electrical and Computer Engineering, University of Ulsan,
Ulsan, South Korea
junhasan@gmail.com, jmkim07@ulsan.ac.kr

Abstract. For industrial safety, correct classification of gearbox fault conditions is necessary. One of the most crucial tasks in data-driven fault diagnosis is determining the best set of features by analyzing the statistical parameters of the signals. However, under variable speed conditions, these statistical parameters are incapable of uncovering the dynamic characteristics of different fault conditions of gearboxes. Later, several deep learning algorithms are used to improve the performance of the feature selection process, but domain knowledge expertise is still necessary. In this paper, a combination domain knowledge analysis and a deep neural network is proposed. By using the input acoustic emission (AE) signal, a two-dimensional spectrum energy map (2D AE-SEM) is created to form an identical fault pattern for various speed conditions of gearboxes. Then, a deep convolutional neural network (DCNN) is proposed to investigate the detailed structure of the 2D input for final fault classification. This 2D AE-SEM offers a graphical depiction of acoustic emission spectral characteristics. Our proposed system offers vigorous and dynamic classification performance through the proposed DCNN with a high diagnostic fault classification accuracy of 96.37% in all considered scenarios.

Keywords: Gearbox safety · Fault diagnosis · Convolutional neural network

1 Introduction

Gearbox fault diagnosis is a substantial issue regarding the safety and excellence of various apparatuses in many industries. Specifically, gearbox fault diagnosis is featured in many different mechanical schemes, including wind turbines, cars, gas turbines, and helicopters [1–3]. Because they function in tough atmospheres, gearboxes habitually encounter gear tooth pitting and root breaking issues [4]. Several of these disasters can cause severe damage to the completely automated motorized structure, resulting in large economic losses and even the loss of human life. An enhanced cost-effective fault identification approach for gearboxes under invariant speed conditions (revolutions per minutes (RMPs)) can ensure functioning dependability and lessen protection expenditures.

© Springer Nature Switzerland AG 2020
C. Djeddi et al. (Eds.): MedPRAI 2019, CCIS 1144, pp. 106–117, 2020.
https://doi.org/10.1007/978-3-030-37548-5_9

Data driven fault diagnosis is accomplished by accumulating data (i.e., vibration signals (VS) and acoustic emission signals (AE)), comprising an essential part of investigations structured over the previous decades [5–8]. Such research confirms that fault condition diagnosis can decrease preservation costs by improving the consistency of the machinery [6, 9, 10]. AE signals can secure fundamental information from low-energy signals [11–14]. This establishes AE signals as an effective method for data-driven fault diagnosis tactics over vibration analysis (VA). This analysis suggests an AE-based fault identification methodology for gearboxes. Several studies (i.e., short term fourier transform [15], wavelet analysis [16]) tried to prove the domain based solution for fault classification by analyzing the extracted features from signals, but due to the inappropriate time-window adjustment, and inability to capture the high frequency resolutions at high frequencies; the main purpose is not solved in a robust manner.

This work mainly addresses two limitations for gearbox fault diagnosis: a) the necessity of domain level expertise for designing the best feature set for different fault conditions from statistical parameters under variable speed conditions, and b) the necessity of a deep dynamic algorithm (DDA) to investigate automated feature extraction in a reliable way to ensure industrial safety. The main focus of the proposed approach is to create a bridge between these two limitations using a singular-as-a-whole standalone algorithm. The proposed two-dimensional acoustic emission spectral energy map (2D AE-SEM) analyzes the root mean square (RMS) frequency distribution of individual signals to create an identical fault pattern under variable speed conditions. The energy density of this pattern increases incrementally with speed [5]. To capture the core fault pattern of the striking energies of this 2D AE-SEM from different speeds, a five-layer deep convolutional neural network (DCNN) is proposed. To establish the robustness of the proposed approach, various state-of-the-art algorithms (multiclass support vector machine + neural network using the statistical parameters [17] and spectral average + k-nearest neighbor algorithm (KNN) [18]) are considered for final comparisons.

The major contributions of the 2D AE-SEM + DCNN proposed in this work can be summarized as follows.

(1) We present a unique 2D AE-SEM-based fault pattern visualization for various speeds for gearboxes to investigate the potential of AE signals.
(2) This 2D AE-SEM is used as an input to the proposed five-layer deep convolutional neural network (DCNN) for fault classification in a speed invariant way. The proposed DCNN analyzes the input image pattern to discover the true feature information for final fault classification. Under different RPMs, experiments were used to validate our method by comparing with several state-of-the-art algorithms. The main purpose of using DCNN is to automatically distinguish the patterns for classifying different cracks.

The remaining part of our paper is organized as follows. Section 2 defines the details of the proposed methodology, including the gearbox data acquisition testbed. Section 3 describes the experimental result analysis to establish the robustness and dynamic attitude of the proposed algorithm. Finally, conclusions are drawn in Sect. 4.

2 Methodology

The proposed method consists mainly of three major sections. Data collection from an experimental testbed, forming a 2D AE Spectral Energy Map (2D AE-SEM), and the Deep Convolutional Neural Network (DCNN). The raw AE signal is collected from the AE sensors of the bearing housing end from two channels. Then, the AE signal is used to form the 2D AE-SEM as an input for the DCNN. The whole process is illustrated in Fig. 1.

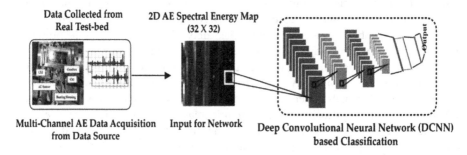

Fig. 1. The proposed 2D AE SEM + DCNN based gearbox health state classification approach.

2.1 Data Acquisition

In this experiment, we considered a simple gearbox with a gear ratio of 1.52:1. In the experimental testbed, two shafts are connected, specifically non-drive-end-shaft (NDS) and drive-end-shaft (DS). A three-phase induction motor is connected along with a displacement transducer at three different revolutions per minutes (RPM) (i.e., 300, 600, and 900 RPM) at the DS. The bearing house is attached to the motor shaft through the gearbox. At the NDS, a WSα AE [19] sensor is placed over the bearing house in the shaft [5, 20]. AE signals are collected though the AE sensor at a sampling rate of 100,000 Hz using a PCI-2 [21] system. The experimental testbed is illustrated in Fig. 2. The specification of the gears used in this data acquisition system is given in Table 1.

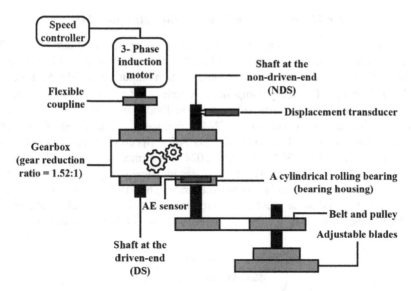

Fig. 2. Schematic of the experimental testbed for gearbox fault identification.

Table 1. Detailed gear specifications.

Gear Specification	Number of drive shaft teeth: 25
	Number of driven coaxial teeth: 38
	Tooth length: 9 mm

To create the different health conditions, an artificial defect is created on the shaft gear. The specifications of the faulty health conditions of the driven shaft gear are given in Table 2.

Table 2. Specifications of the defective coaxial driven shaft gear.

Health Condition	Picture	Defect Length (mm)
10% Crack (C10)		0.9
20% Crack (C20)		1.8
30% Crack (C30)		2.7

2.2   2D Acoustic Emission Spectral Energy Map (2D AE-SEM)

After collecting the raw AE signal, the unwanted noises are removed through a white-noise cancellation process. After that, the Fast Fourier transformation (FFT) is calculated to obtain the positive frequency response from the input signal. The AE spectrum has 50×10^4 positive frequency components, which is not a suitable input to DCNN. Therefore, the considered positive AE spectrum is divided into several frequency bins. From each bin, the root mean square (RMS) frequency is calculated. These RMS frequency values were used to create the 1D AE – Spectral Energy Map (1D AE-SEM). Finally, the 1D AE-SEM of length 1024 is reformed to create a 2D AE-SEM with a size of 32×32. This 2D AE-SEM creates identical patterns for different health conditions with regard to invariant speed scenarios. The 2D AE-SEM has reasonable dimensions to be used as an input to the proposed DCNN for final classification [5]. The total process of forming the 2D AE-SEM is given as a flowchart in Fig. 3.

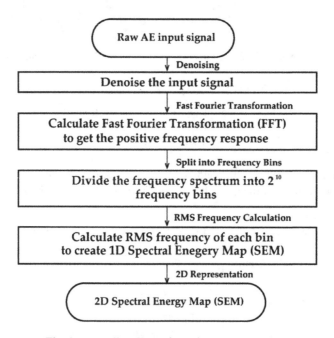

Fig. 3. Overall process of creating a 2D AE-SEM.

2.3   Deep Convolutional Neural Network (DCNN) for Fault Classification

A Deep Convolutional Neural Network (DCNN) is one of the most efficient supervised machine learning approaches [22]. In our work, since we are considering 2D AE-SEM, we used the DCNN to uncover the details of the 2D input. In DCNN, if the input data is $X = [x_1, x_2, \ldots \ldots x_m]$, then the total training sample size is m. Furthermore, the output vector is $Y = [y_1, y_2, \ldots \ldots y_m]$, which is supplementary to X. If P layers represent a

CNN, then each layer in the DCNN has F^p elements, which are utilized in convolution and max pooling [23]. The sigmoid activation function $\sigma(.)$ is considered.

The proposed DCNN architecture is illustrated in Fig. 4. The detailed specifications of the proposed DCNN are listed in Table 3.

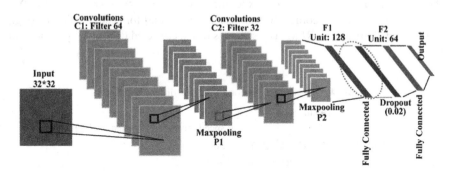

Fig. 4. The proposed structure of the DCNN.

Table 3. The dimensions of the Deep Convolutional Neural Network (DCNN)

Layers	Parameters	Observations	Height	Width	Depth	Trainable
Input		Preprocessed signals	32	32	3	
Conv1	Kernel	Filter	6	6		Yes
	Padding	Zero				
	Depth	Filter number			64	
MaxPool1	Kernel	Filter	3	3		No
	Padding	Zero				
Conv2	Kernel	Filter	3	3		Yes
	Padding	Zero				
	Depth	Filter number			32	
MaxPool2	Kernel	Filter	3	3		No
	Padding	Zero				
FC1	Nodes	Flatten as 1D	128			Yes
Dropout	Output		128			No
FC2	Nodes	Flatten as 1D	64			
Softmax	Nodes	Flatten into 1D	3			Classify

3   Result and Discussion

3.1   Dataset Description

For in-depth assessment of the proposed (2D AE-SEM + DCNN) fault classification approach, the following methods were used. The first method is the 2D AE-SEM-based invariant gearbox health state visualization. The second is DCNN-based RPM invariant performance analysis of health state classification and extensive comparisons with some state of art methods (i.e., multiclass support vector machine + neural network using the statistical parameters [17], spectral average + k-nearest neighbor algorithm (KNN) [18]). The standard AE dataset of gearbox crack faults from the experimental testbed is used throughout the whole experiment. We have used three different RPMs (300, 600, and 900) and recorded 100 signals of one second for each health type (e.g., C10, C20 and C30) at each RPM. The specifics of the collected dataset are presented in Table 4.

Table 4. Measured fault conditions for different datasets

	Health type	Shaft speed (rpm)	Sampling frequency (Hz)
Dataset 1	10% Crack (C10)	300	100,0000
	20% Crack (C20)	300	
	30% Crack (C30)	300	
Dataset 2	10% Crack (C10)	600	
	20% Crack (C20)	600	
	30% Crack (C30)	600	
Dataset 3	10% Crack (C10)	900	
	20% Crack (C20)	900	
	30% Crack (C30)	900	

3.2   Analysis of the 2D Acoustic Emission Spectral Energy Map

According to the previous discussion, the main reasons for constructing the 2D AE-SEM are (a) to create an invariant scenario for different RPMs under different health conditions, and (b) to deliver the benefits of 2D image structures to the DCNN with a minimum visibility of similar patterns.

Figure 5 exhibits the 2D AE-SEMs for different health conditions. For each RPM, the images of different health conditions show some identical information. From Fig. 5 (a), we can observe that for the C10 health condition, the striking energy of the RMS frequency in the 2D AE-SEM maintains some matching patterns. When the RPM increased, the energy striking density also increased. Thus, the amount of white strikes increases. From Fig. 5(b) and (c), we observe a similar situation for health states C20 and C30 respectively. Due to high RPM, the density of the striking energy increases. Thus, the similarity of these patterns has been carefully uncovered and handled through the proposed DCNN for the final classification analysis.

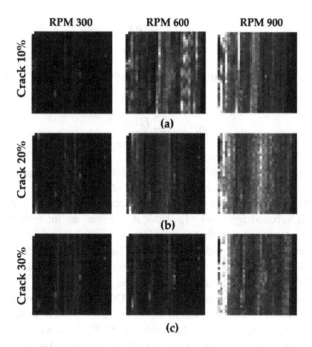

Fig. 5. From all the working conditions given in Table 4, the 2D AE-SEMs for different health conditions are displayed, i.e., (a) C10 (b) C20, and (c) C30 for different RPMs.

3.3   Diagnostic Performance of a Deep Convolutional Neural Network

To validate the proposed approach, we considered three different datasets (described in Table 4). These datasets contain different speeds with similar health conditions. The rpm invariance of this method is confirmed by examining three separate scenarios. In the first scenario, dataset 1 is used for training the DCNN, and datasets 2 and 3 are used for classification tests. In the second scenario, dataset 2 is used for training, and datasets 1 and 2 are used for testing. Similarly, in scenario 3, dataset 3 is used for training while the other two datasets are utilized for testing and classification. For evaluation of the analytical performance, we considered the F1 score as the basic classification performance matrix (F1), average classification accuracy (AC), and overall classification accuracy (OC) [5, 24]. The main reason for considering the F1 score for classification accuracy measurement is to balance between the Recall and Precision scores.

$$F1 = \frac{T_{positive}}{T_{positive} + \frac{F_{negetive} + F_{positive}}{2}} \times 100(\%) \tag{1}$$

Here, $T_{positive}$ is the number of correctly classified samples from a particular class and $F_{negative}$ is the number of incorrectly classified sample from a particular class. The final result is calculated as a percentage. After computing the final F1 score of a particular health condition, the average classification accuracy (AC) is measured following Eq. (2).

$$AC = \frac{\sum F1}{\sum T_{Classes}} \tag{2}$$

Finally, the overall classification accuracy, based on a particular scenario (OC), is obtained as Eq. (3).

$$OC = \frac{\sum TD_{AC}}{\sum T_{Scenario}} \tag{3}$$

Here, $\sum TD_{AC}$ defines the total of the CA test dataset, and $\sum T_{Scenario}$ describes the total number of test datasets existing in a discrete scenario.

Table 5 records the details of the analytical accomplishment of the proposed 2D AE-SEM + DCNN based approach. In Table 4, we see an interesting trend. From Figs. 5(a), (b), and (c), we see that the striking energy rises while RPM increases. Dataset 1 represents the lowest RPM here. Thus, from the 2D AE-SEM, we observe that rather than dataset 1, the patterns are more densely repeated in datasets 2 and 3. For scenario 1 in Table 5, when the DCNN is trained with dataset 1, the OC becomes 94.62%. When we move to scenario 2, where the DCNN is trained with dataset 2, the OC increases to 96.99%. Finally, when the network is trained with dataset 3, the performance increases to its optimal value, which is 97.5%. This means that while there is a repetitive pattern, the network learns details much better for classification. The average classification accuracy is 96.37% at the end.

Table 5. Analytical implementation of the proposed model for various scenarios

Scenario	Training dataset	Test dataset	F1 (%)			CA (%)	OC (%)
			C10	C20	C30		
1	Dataset 1	Dataset 2	95.22	94.39	94.41	94.67	94.62
		Dataset 3	94.93	94.17	94.59	94.56	
2	Dataset 2	Dataset 3	96.41	95.39	95.37	97.72	96.99
		Dataset 1	96.29	96.71	95.74	96.25	
3	Dataset 3	Dataset 1	97.83	98.2	97.49	97.84	97.5
		Dataset 2	97.72	97.32	96.43	97.16	
Average						**96.37**	

For this experiment, we used 500 epochs for training and testing. While training the network for each scenario, we considered 80% of the data for training and 20% for validation from the training dataset. For performance evaluation, 8–fold cross-validation is used. While training the network for each scenario, the loss function Adam performed better than the stochastic gradient decent (sgd). Figure 6 shows the loss curve performance analysis (sgd vs. Adam) for dataset 1 and dataset 2 while training the DCNN for scenario 1 and scenario 2, respectively.

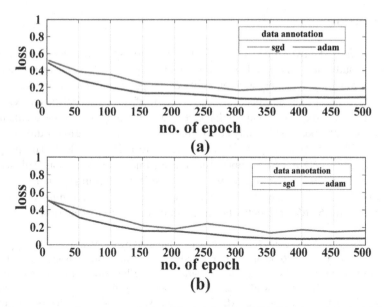

Fig. 6. Loss curve performance analysis while training the DCNN (sgd vs. Adam), (a) dataset 1 for scenario 1, and (b) dataset 2 for scenario 2.

3.4   Comparison Analysis

To demonstrate the robustness of the proposed approach, we made several comparisons with state-of-the-art approaches, i.e., the multiclass support vector machine + neural network using the statistical parameters [17] and the spectral average + k-nearest neighbor algorithm (KNN) [18]. The comparison of classification accuracy (F1 score (%) and the average classification accuracy (AC)) is described in Table 6. From Table 6, we see that our proposed approach outperformed these state of art approaches by at least 4.74% accuracy for each scenario. To ensure a fair comparison, similar settings for the training and testing data as given in Table 4 are used.

Table 6. Comparison analysis of different methods

Scenario	Method	F1 (%)			AC (%)	Improved (%)
		C10	C20	C30		
1	[17]	89.4	88.9	91.4	89.9	**4.74**
	[18]	48.52	47.22	47.9	47.88	**46.76**
	Proposed	95.08	94.28	94.5	94.64	–
2	[17]	89.91	87.2	88.6	88.57	**8.42**
	[18]	49.11	48.73	47.44	48.43	**48.56**
	Proposed	96.35	96.05	95.56	96.99	–
3	[17]	90.2	88.7	90.43	89.78	**7.72**
	[18]	48.37	47.39	48.27	48.01	**49.49**
	Proposed	97.78	97.76	96.96	97.5	–

4 Conclusion

This work proposed a two-dimensional acoustic emission spectral energy map (2D AE-SEM) with fault diagnosis based on a five-layer deep convolutional neural network (DCNN) for ensuring the safety and reliability of the gearbox, which is invariant to the shaft speed. In traditional approaches, consideration of the statistical parameters from signals and defect frequency analysis have several difficulties regarding premeditated differences in shaft speed. This study considered an invariant scenario for different fault conditions with respect to various RPMs by creating a 2D AE-SEM. The proposed DCNN utilized the 2D AE-SEM input structure for final fault condition analysis. The proposed method achieved an overall 96.37% classification accuracy. In addition, this work out-performed two state-of-the-art approaches with an overall improvement of at least 4.74%, and 46.76%, respectively, in the three considered scenarios.

Acknowledgements. This research was financially supported by the Ministry of Trade, Industry & Energy (MOTIE) of the Republic of Korea and Korea Institute for Advancement of Technology (KIAT) through the Encouragement Program for The Industries of Economic Cooperation Region (P0006123). This work was partly supported by the Korea Institute of Energy Technology Evaluation and Planning (KETEP) and the Ministry of Trade, Industry & Energy (MOTIE) of the Republic of Korea (No. 20172510102130)

References

1. Zhao, M., Kang, M., Tang, B., Pecht, M.: Deep residual networks with dynamically weighted wavelet coefficients for fault diagnosis of planetary gearboxes. IEEE Trans. Ind. Electron. **65**, 4290–4300 (2018)
2. Chen, X., Feng, Z.: Time-frequency demodulation analysis for gearbox fault diagnosis under nonstationary conditions. In: 2016 IEEE International Conference Prognostics and Health Management ICPHM 2016, pp. 1–6 (2016)
3. Du, Z., Chen, X., Zhang, H., Yan, R.: Sparse feature identification based on union of redundant dictionary for wind turbine gearbox fault diagnosis. IEEE Trans. Ind. Electron. **62**, 6594–6605 (2015)
4. Chaari, F., Fakhfakh, T., Haddar, M.: Dynamic analysis of a planetary gear failure caused by tooth pitting and cracking. J. Fail. Anal. Prev. **6**, 73–78 (2006)
5. Tra, V., Kim, J., Khan, S.A., Kim, J.-M.: bearing fault diagnosis under variable speed using convolutional neural networks and the stochastic diagonal Levenberg-Marquardt algorithm. Sensors **17**, 2834 (2017)
6. Sohaib, M., Kim, C.-H., Kim, J.-M.: A hybrid feature model and deep-learning-based bearing fault diagnosis. Sensors. **17**, 2876 (2017)
7. Zhao, S., Liang, L., Xu, G., Wang, J., Zhang, W.: Quantitative diagnosis of a spall-like fault of a rolling element bearing by empirical mode decomposition and the approximate entropy method. Mech. Syst. Signal Process. **40**, 154–177 (2013)
8. Yu, X., Ding, E., Chen, C., Liu, X., Li, L.: A novel characteristic frequency bands extraction method for automatic bearing fault diagnosis based on Hilbert Huang transform. Sens. (Switzerland). **15**, 27869–27893 (2015)
9. Yin, S., Ding, S.X., Zhou, D.: Diagnosis and prognosis for complicated industrial systems - Part I. IEEE Trans. Ind. Electron. **63**, 2501–2505 (2016)

10. Yin, S., Ding, S.X., Zhou, D.: Diagnosis and prognosis for complicated industrial systems - Part II. IEEE Trans. Ind. Electron. **63**, 3201–3204 (2016)
11. Eftekharnejad, B., Carrasco, M.R., Charnley, B., Mba, D.: The application of spectral kurtosis on acoustic emission and vibrations from a defective bearing. Mech. Syst. Signal Process. **25**, 266–284 (2011)
12. Widodo, A., et al.: Fault diagnosis of low speed bearing based on relevance vector machine and support vector machine. Expert Syst. Appl. **36**, 7252–7261 (2009)
13. Pandya, D.H., Upadhyay, S.H., Harsha, S.P.: Fault diagnosis of rolling element bearing with intrinsic mode function of acoustic emission data using APF-KNN. Expert Syst. Appl. **40**, 4137–4145 (2013)
14. Caesarendra, W., Kosasih, P.B., Tieu, A.K., Moodie, C.A.S., Choi, B.K.: Condition monitoring of naturally damaged slow speed slewing bearing based on ensemble empirical mode decomposition. J. Mech. Sci. Technol. **27**, 2253–2262 (2013)
15. Kim, B.S., Lee, S.H., Lee, M.G., Ni, J., Song, J.Y., Lee, C.W.: A comparative study on damage detection in speed-up and coast-down process of grinding spindle-typed rotor-bearing system. J. Mater. Process. Tech. **187–188**, 30–36 (2007)
16. Tahir, M.M., Khan, A.Q., Iqbal, N., Hussain, A., Badshah, S.: Enhancing fault classification accuracy of ball bearing using central tendency based time domain features. IEEE Access **5**, 72–83 (2017)
17. Jin, X., Zhao, M., Chow, T.W.S., Pecht, M.: Motor bearing fault diagnosis using trace ratio linear discriminant analysis. IEEE Trans. Ind. Electron. **61**, 2441–2451 (2014)
18. Del Campo, V., Ragni, D., Micallef, D., Diez, J., Simão Ferreira, C.J.: Vibration-based wind turbine planetary gearbox fault diagnosis using spectral averaging. Wind Energy **18**, 1875–1891 (2015)
19. Physicalacoustics – sensors. https://www.physicalacoustics.com/by-product/sensors/WDI-AST-100-900-kHz-Wideband-Differential-AE-Sensor
20. Islam, M.M.M., Myon, J.: Time–frequency envelope analysis-based sub-band selection and probabilistic support vector machines for multi-fault diagnosis of low-speed bearings. J. Ambient Intell. Humaniz. Comput. (2017). https://doi.org/10.1007/s12652-017-0585-2
21. Physicalacoustics - PCI 2. https://www.physicalacoustics.com/by-product/pci-2/
22. Malek, S., Melgani, F., Bazi, Y.: One-dimensional convolutional neural networks for spectroscopic signal regression. J. Chemom. **32**, 1–17 (2017)
23. Zhang, R., Tao, H., Wu, L., Guan, Y.: Transfer learning with neural networks for bearing fault diagnosis in changing working conditions. IEEE Access **5**, 14347–14357 (2017)
24. Hasan, M.J., Islam, M.M.M., Kim, J.M.: Acoustic spectral imaging and transfer learning for reliable bearing fault diagnosis under variable speed conditions. Meas. J. Int. Meas. Confed. **138**, 620–631 (2019)

Bayesian Convolutional Neural Network: Robustly Quantify Uncertainty for Misclassifications Detection

Cedrique Rovile Njieutcheu Tassi[✉]

Institute of Optical Sensor Systems, German Aerospace Center (DLR),
Rutherfordstraße 2, 12489 Berlin, Germany
Cedrique.NjieutcheuTassi@dlr.de

Abstract. For safety and mission critical systems relying on Convolutional Neural Networks (CNNs), it is crucial to avoid incorrect predictions that can cause accident or financial crisis. This can be achieved by quantifying and interpreting the predictive uncertainty. Current methods for uncertainty quantification rely on Bayesian CNNs that approximate Bayesian inference via dropout sampling. This paper investigates different dropout methods to robustly quantify the predictive uncertainty for misclassifications detection. Specifically, the following questions are addressed: In which layers should activations be sampled? Which dropout sampling mask should be used? What dropout probability should be used? How to choose the number of ensemble members? How to combine ensemble members? How to quantify the classification uncertainty? To answer these questions, experiments were conducted on three datasets using three different network architectures. Experimental results showed that the classification uncertainty is best captured by averaging the predictions of all stochastic CNNs sampled from the Bayesian CNN and by validating the predictions of the Bayesian CNN with three uncertainty measures, namely the predictive confidence, predictive entropy and standard deviation thresholds. The results showed further that the optimal dropout method specified through the sampling location, sampling mask, inference dropout probability, and number of stochastic forward passes depends on both the dataset and the designed network architecture. Notwithstanding this, I proposed to sample inputs to max pooling layers with a cascade of Multiplicative Gaussian Mask (MGM) followed by Multiplicative Bernoulli Spatial Mask (MBSM) to robustly quantify the classification uncertainty, while keeping the loss in performance low.

Keywords: Convolutional Neural Networks (CNNs) · Bayesian CNNs · Dropout sampling · Uncertainty quantification · Uncertainty quality

1 Introduction

Although CNNs have become the de-facto standard to solve challenging visual recognition and scientific data analysis problems, they can be uncertain in their predictions. It is however crucial for safety and mission critical systems relying on CNNs to avoid incorrect predictions that can cause accident, crash, financial crisis or false

© Springer Nature Switzerland AG 2020
C. Djeddi et al. (Eds.): MedPRAI 2019, CCIS 1144, pp. 118–132, 2020.
https://doi.org/10.1007/978-3-030-37548-5_10

diagnostics in medicine. In this context, methods to quantify uncertainty are required to enable those systems to trust or reject their predictions.

Current methods to estimate uncertainty rely on Bayesian CNNs that approximate the posterior via dropout sampling [1, 2]. Even if Bernoulli [3, 4] and Gaussian [5] sampling were investigated in [6] to approximate Bayesian inference, sampling from other dropout variants such as spatial dropout [7], max pooling dropout [8], or sampling with a cascade of Gaussian followed by Bernoulli mask has not yet been investigated in depth, especially in max and convolutional layers.

The aim of this paper is to robustly quantify the predictive uncertainty for false classifications detection. Since the uncertainty quality depends on the Bayesian inference approximate, the optimal dropout method is required to best fit the true unknown posterior. That is, the optimal inference dropout probability, sampling mask, sampling location, and number of stochastic forward passes should be found. The best measure for quantifying uncertainty and method for combining ensemble members should also be found.

The main contributions of this paper are summarized as follows: First, I evaluated the accuracies and uncertainty qualities of Bayesian CNNs with different dropout methods on three datasets using three different network architectures. Then, I proposed to approximate Bayesian inference by sampling inputs to max pooling layers with a cascade of MGM followed by MBSM. Lastly, I investigated how the uncertainty measures and methods for combining ensemble members help to detect misclassifications of in-distribution and out-of-distribution examples.

2   Related Works

2.1   Uncertainty Estimation

Lakshminarayanan et al. [9] proposed a deep ensemble of deterministic CNNs for uncertainty estimation. On the other hand, Gal and Ghahramani [1, 2] showed that dropout sampling can be interpreted as an approximate of Bayesian inference and can therefore be used to quantify uncertainty as applied in [10]. McClure and Kriegeskorte [6] sampled activations/weights with MGM to capture uncertainty. However, current studies applied sampling only in fully connected multi-layers. Since fully connected multi-layers are increasingly reduced to single-layers or completely removed in modern architectures [11], sampling in convolutional or pooling layers should be investigated for uncertainty estimation. Besides, the effect of dropout sampling with other dropout methods should be investigated.

2.2   Dropout Methods

To account for overfitting and increase the generalization ability of deep networks, the procedure of dropping activations was proposed in [3, 4]. Wang et al. [5] proposed to model activations as random Gaussian variables. Tompson et al. [7] proposed to drop feature maps instead of activations. Wu and Gu [8] studied the effect of dropout in max pooling layers. These dropout methods were empirically evaluated in this work to find the one that best approximates Bayesian inference.

3 Bayesian Convolutional Neural Network

Let the training data $\mathcal{D} = \left\{ x_i \in \mathbb{R}^{HxWxC}, \ y_i \in [0,1]^K \right\}_{i=1}^{N}$ be a realization of independently and identically distributed random variables where x_i denotes the ith input and y_i its corresponding one-hot encoded categorical probability. Here, HxWxC denotes the dimension of input images; K refers to the number of classes and N denotes the number of samples within the training data. A CNN maps the input x (i is omitted for clarity) to the output y using the set of weights W. The CNN can therefore be seen as a probabilistic model, where the output $p(y|x, W)$ is a categorical distribution. By placing a prior $p(W)$ over the weights, the CNN can be converted to a Bayesian CNN. Since Bayesian inference in Bayesian CNNs is computationally intractable due to the large number of neurons, dropout have been proposed in [1, 15] to approximate the posterior $p(W|\mathcal{D})$ over the weights. That is, $p(W|\mathcal{D})$ is gauged with a dropout distribution $q(W)$ realized by sampling weights with masks drawn from known distributions such as Bernoulli and/or Gaussian. Practically, sampling from $q(W)$ consists of performing T forward passes so as to estimate the likelihood of x with T stochastic CNNs, where each CNN with the set of weights $\widehat{W}_{t \in [1, T]} \sim q(W)$ maps x to $p(y|x, \widehat{W}_t)$. That is,

$$p(y|x, W) \approx \bar{p}(y|x, \mathcal{D}) \approx \frac{1}{T} \sum_{t=1}^{T} p(y|x, \widehat{W}_t) \tag{1}$$

However, weights sampling can be approximated with activations sampling. Given the matrix F that includes the activations of a feature map, F is sampled by performing element-wise multiplication $(\star)$ with the sampling matrix M. That is,

$$\widehat{F} \triangleq F \star M \ where \ M \triangleq \begin{bmatrix} \xi_{0,0} & \cdots & \xi_{0,j} \\ \vdots & \ddots & \vdots \\ \xi_{i,0} & \cdots & \xi_{i,j} \end{bmatrix} \tag{2}$$

The sampled feature map $\widehat{F}$ have the same dimension with F and M. The quality of $q(W)$ depends on the sampling location and sampling mask, the method for combining ensemble members, and the inference dropout probability. Hence, the following questions should be addressed.

3.1 Which Dropout Sampling Mask Performs Best?

To answer this question, the following dropout sampling masks were evaluated:

Multiplicative Bernoulli Mask (MBM). The elements of this mask are sampled from a Bernoulli distribution with probability p of dropping activations. That is,

$$\xi_{i,j} \sim Bernoulli(p) \tag{3}$$

This mask can reduce the number of active neurons within a feature map, but the magnitude of active neurons will remain unchanged. Hence, it can modify the spatial structure of feature representations, while keeping their contrast unchanged.

Multiplicative Bernoulli Spatial Mask (MBSM). The elements of this mask are equal to a random variable ξ sampled from a Bernoulli distribution with probability p of dropping all activations within the given feature map. That is,

$$\xi_{i,j} \triangleq \xi_{j,i} \triangleq \xi \sim Bernoulli(p) \tag{4}$$

This mask drops feature maps instead of single activations. Hence, it cannot modify the spatial structure or contrast of feature representations, but can discard some feature representations.

Multiplicative Gaussian Mask (MGM). The elements of this mask are drawn from a Gaussian distribution with a mean of 1 and variance of σ^2. That is,

$$\xi_{i,j} \sim \mathcal{N}\left(1, \sigma^2\right) \text{ where } \sigma^2 = p/(1-p) \tag{5}$$

This mask can modify the magnitude of active neurons, but the number of active neurons will remain unchanged. Therefore, it can modify the contrast of feature representations, while keeping their spatial structure unchanged.

Cascade of Gaussian and Bernoulli Masks. This mask is a cascade of the MGM followed by MBM and/or MBSM. It can increase/decrease the number of active neurons and strengthen/weaken the magnitude of active neurons. Hence, it can modify the spatial structure and/or contrast of feature representations.

3.2 Where Should Activations Be Sampled?

To address this question, the following procedures were evaluated:

Before Max Pooling Dropout. This dropout procedure refers to sampling applied to inputs to all max pooling layers.

After Max Pooling Dropout. This dropout procedure refers to sampling applied after max pooling, but before convolutional or fully-connected layers/blocks.

3.3 How to Effectively Combine Ensemble Members?

To address this question, the following methods were evaluated:

Average. This method averages the predictions of all stochastic CNNs to estimate the ensemble output as showed in Eq. (1).

Plurality Vote. Here, the stochastic CNNs first votes for one class label. Then, all CNNs that voted for the class label with highest frequency are selected.

Majority Vote. This filtering method is similar to plurality voting. However, more than half of the stochastic CNNs must have voted for the class label with highest frequency, otherwise the output will be an uncertain class.

Sanity Check. This method filters the stochastic CNNs by selecting only predictions with high confidence and low entropy.

4 Classification Uncertainty Quantification

The following uncertainty measures were evaluated:

4.1 Predictive Confidence

The confidence $\mathcal{C}(x)$ of $\bar{p}(y|x, \mathcal{D})$ is formulated in Eq. (6). If $\mathcal{C}(x)$ is above the confidence threshold $\mathcal{C}_T$, the predicted label $\mathcal{L}(x)$ is estimated as showed in Eq. (7), else x is classified as belonging to an uncertain class. That is, predictions with $\mathcal{C}(x) > \mathcal{C}_T$ are trusted, while those with $\mathcal{C}(x) \leq \mathcal{C}_T$ are rejected.

$$\mathcal{C}(x) \triangleq \max_{\bar{p}}(\bar{p}(y|x, \mathcal{D})) \tag{6}$$

$$\mathcal{L}(x) \triangleq \arg\max_{\bar{p}}(\bar{p}(y|x, \mathcal{D})) \tag{7}$$

4.2 Predictive Entropy

The predictive entropy $\mathbb{H}(\bar{p}(y|x, \mathcal{D}))$ is defined in Eq. (8). If $\mathbb{H}(\bar{p}(y|x, \mathcal{D}))$ is below the entropy threshold $\mathbb{H}_T$, the predicted label $\mathcal{L}(x)$ is estimated as showed in Eq. (7), else x is classified as belonging to an uncertain class. That is, predictions with $\mathbb{H}(\bar{p}(y|x, \mathcal{D})) < H_T$ are trusted, whereas those with $\mathbb{H}(\bar{p}(y|x, \mathcal{D})) \geq \mathbb{H}_T$ are rejected.

$$\mathbb{H}(\bar{p}(y|x, \mathcal{D})) \triangleq - \sum_{c=1}^{K} (\bar{p}(y = c|x, \mathcal{D}) \cdot log_2(\bar{p}(y = c|x, \mathcal{D}))) \tag{8}$$

4.3 Disagreement Between Ensemble Members

The disagreement between the stochastic CNNs is achieved after T forward passes by computing the standard deviation over the probabilities $p(y = c|x, \mathcal{D})$. That is,

$$\sigma(p(y = c|x, \mathcal{D})) \triangleq \sqrt{\sum_{t=1}^{T} \left(p\left(y = c|x, \widehat{W}_t\right) - \overline{p}(y = c|x, \mathcal{D})\right)^2} \qquad (9)$$

Knowing the disagreement between ensemble members, a Bayesian CNN can trust its prediction, if and only if, the standard deviation $\sigma(p(y = c|x, \mathcal{D}))$ of the predicted label c is below the user predefined standard deviation threshold σ_T.

5 Experimental Setup

5.1 Datasets

Experiments were conducted on three datasets described as follows:

The Modified National Institute of Standards and Technology (MNIST) data [12], which contains gray-scaled images of ten digits (from 0 to 9). It includes 60000 images for training and 10000 images for testing. The digits are centered inside the images of 28×28 pixels. The number of images per digit is not equal.

The Canadian Institute For Advanced Research (CIFAR10) dataset [13], which includes 10 categories of colored images of common objects (e.g.: airplane, animals, etc.). It includes 50000 images for training and 10000 images for testing. The objects appear in various poses and are not always centered inside the images of 32×32 pixels. The number of images per category is uniformly distributed.

The German Traffic Signs Recognition Benchmark (GTSRB) dataset [14], which contains 43 classes of colored images of German traffic signs. It includes 39,209 samples for training and 12,630 samples for testing. The traffic signs appear in different poses and are not always centered inside the images. The images have sizes varying from 15×15 to 222×192 pixels. The number of images per traffic sign is not uniformly distributed.

5.2 Convolutional Neural Networks

Experiments were conducted on three architectures, namely modified versions of the VGG [15] (referred to as M-VGGNet), of the Inception [16] (referred to as M-InceptionNet), and of the Residual [17] (referred to as M-ResNet) networks. The architectures of the M-VGGNet and M-InceptionNet are depicted in Figs. 1 and 2, respectively. Hereby, x, $C_M^{3\times3}$, MP and FC_K refer to the input; the convolutional layer with M convolutional kernels of size 3×3 pixels interleaved with Rectified Linear Units (RELUs); the max pooling layer with pooling regions of size 2×2 pixels; and the K fully-connected neurons with softmax activation functions; respectively. The convolutional layers have stride of 1 with same padding. The max pooling layers have stride of 2 with same padding. The symbols q and h refer to the number of times the blocks are consecutively repeated. The M-ResNet is similar to the M-InceptionNet, but the channels concatenation operation ($\otimes$) is replaced with the elementwise additive operation. Thus, the feature maps of M-InceptionNets have more channels than those of M-ResNets. Table 1 reports the configurations of the CNNs for the three datasets.

Table 1. Configurations of the CNNs evaluated on MNIST, CIFAR10 and GTSRB datasets

	q [blocks]	h [blocks]	M [kernels]	K [classes]	x [pixels]
MNIST	3	1	48	10	28×28
CIFAR10	3	2	72	10	$32 \times 32 \times 3$
GTSRB	3	3	88	43	64×64

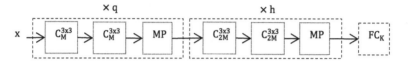

Fig. 1. The architecture of the Modified VGG Network (M-VGGNet)

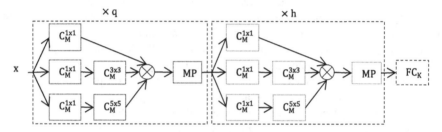

Fig. 2. The architecture of the Modified Inception Network (M-InceptionNet)

5.3 Training Methodology

The experiments were executed with the tensorflow framework. The CNNs were trained using the categorical cross-entropy and stochastic gradient descent with momentum of 0.9, learning rate of 0.02, L2 weight decay of 0.0005, and batch size of 128. The CNNs were trained with a dropout probability of 0.1 for 50 epochs using cascades of MGM followed by MBSM followed by MBM placed at inputs to max pooling layers. Then, they were retrained with a probability of 0.3 for 50 epochs. These CNNs were then used to run all experiments applying dropout before max pooling layers. They were then retrained with a probability of 0.3 for 10 epochs, but by placing the cascade masks after max pooling layers. The new CNNs were then used to run all experiments applying dropout after max pooling layers. All images were normalized by dividing their pixels values by 255. Images of the GTSRB were converted to grayscale and resized to 64×64.

5.4 Classification Uncertainty Measures

The architectures of the Bayesian CNNs were modified by placing validators after the fully connected layers. The validators operate on outputs of softmax layers and compute the predictive confidence, the predictive entropy, and/or the standard deviation.

They validate the predictions of Bayesian CNNs using the confidence, entropy and/or standard deviation thresholds. The thresholds introduce a trade-off between the detection of misclassifications and rejection of true predictions. To compromise between detection and rejection, the confidence, entropy and standard deviation thresholds were experimentally set to 0.7, 2 and 0.2, respectively.

5.5 Classification Uncertainty Quality Assessment

The uncertainty quality was assessed by evaluating the ability of the uncertainty measures to detect/reject misclassifications. The uncertainty measures are used by built-in validators (binary classifiers) to trust (true) or reject (false) the predictions of Bayesian CNNs. The False Positive Rate (FPR) and F-measure used to evaluate the validators are formulated in Eqs. (10) and (11), respectively.

$$FPR \triangleq \frac{FP}{FP + TN} \tag{10}$$

$$F\text{-}measure \triangleq 2 \cdot \frac{Precision \cdot Recall}{Precision + Recall} \tag{11}$$

$$Precision \triangleq \frac{TP}{TP + FP} \tag{12}$$

$$Recall \triangleq \frac{TP}{TP + FN} \tag{13}$$

The True Positive (TP) is the number of inputs correctly classified by the Bayesian CNN and trusted by the validator. The True Negative (TN) is the number of inputs misclassified by the Bayesian CNN, but rejected by the validator. The False Negative (FN) is the number of inputs correctly classified by the Bayesian CNN, but rejected by the validator. The False Positive (FP) is the number of inputs misclassified by the Bayesian CNN and trusted by the validator.

6   Experimental Results

The experiments aimed not to compare the three architectures or achieve state-of-the-art results on the three datasets, but to find the dropout method, combination method, and uncertainty measure that best captures the classification uncertainty, while avoiding extreme performance degradation.

6.1   Comparison of Dropout Methods

The Effect of Dropout Methods on Accuracies of Bayesian CNNs. Table 2 shows that inference approximations via dropout methods (except dropout applied before max pooling layers of M-VGGNets) decreased the accuracies of Bayesian CNNs evaluated on CIFAR10 and GTSRB test data. Conversely, inference approximations via dropout methods (except dropout applied after max pooling layers of M-VGGNets and M-InceptionNets) increased the accuracies of Bayesian CNNs evaluated on the MNIST test data. Hence, the optimal dropout method for inference approximation depends on the data. Still, the exceptions indicate that it depends also on the network architecture.

Table 2. The mean and standard deviation of accuracies [%] of Bayesian CNNs were reported as function of dropout methods. The columns' headers include the sampling locations, while the rows' headers include the sampling masks. The experiments were conducted on the MNIST, CIFAR10 and GTSRB test data using three architectures. The number of stochastic forward passes T was set to 20 and the inference dropout probability p to 0.1. Each experiment was repeated 5 times. The predictions of all stochastic CNNs sampled from Bayesian CNNs were averaged without filtering. The accuracies of the deterministic CNNs were also reported and used as baseline for comparison.

	M-VGGNet		M-InceptionNet		M-ResNet	
	After max pooling dropout	Before max pooling dropout	After max pooling dropout	Before max pooling dropout	After max pooling dropout	Before max pooling dropout
MNIST dataset						
Deterministic CNNs	**99.35**	**99.27**	**99.28**	**98.36**	**97.10**	**98.73**
MBM	99.35 ± 0.01	**99.30 ± 0.02**	99.28 ± 0.02	**99.10 ± 0.01**	97.37 ± 0.03	98.83 ± 0.01
MBSM	99.35 ± 0.01	99.29 ± 0.02	99.28 ± 0.02	98.33 ± 0.03	97.36 ± 0.04	98.78 ± 0.02
MGM	99.35 ± 0.01	**99.35 ± 0.01**	99.27 ± 0.02	**99.14 ± 0.01**	97.34 ± 0.02	98.88 ± 0.01
MGM ⋆ MBM	99.35 ± 0.01	**99.37 ± 0.04**	**99.29 ± 0.01**	**99.26 ± 0.02**	97.59 ± 0.05	**98.99 ± 0.02**
MGM ⋆ MBSM	99.34 ± 0.02	**99.36 ± 0.01**	99.29 ± 0.02	**99.12 ± 0.02**	97.55 ± 0.04	98.96 ± 0.03
MGM ⋆ MBSM ⋆ MBM	**99.36 ± 0.02**	**99.39 ± 0.04**	99.29 ± 0.03	**99.24 ± 0.02**	**97.73 ± 0.03**	**99.04 ± 0.03**
CIFAR10 dataset						
Deterministic CNNs	**85.92**	**83.86**	**86.07**	**82.43**	**81.01**	**82.55**
MBM	85.67 ± 0.16	83.49 ± 0.07	85.17 ± 0.08	81.79 ± 0.08	78.56 ± 0.14	81.39 ± 0.06
MBSM	85.67 ± 0.07	**84.08 ± 0.05**	85.39 ± 0.15	82.26 ± 0.08	79.76 ± 0.19	81.32 ± 0.10
MGM	85.60 ± 0.09	83.47 ± 0.09	85.04 ± 0.10	80.51 ± 0.12	78.01 ± 0.08	78.14 ± 0.09
MGM ⋆ MBM	85.35 ± 0.11	82.21 ± 0.10	83.23 ± 0.06	77.67 ± 0.15	73.04 ± 0.12	72.65 ± 0.23
MGM ⋆ MBSM	85.21 ± 0.25	83.35 ± 0.07	83.76 ± 0.19	79.69 ± 0.16	74.69 ± 0.09	74.41 ± 0.23
MGM ⋆ MBSM ⋆ MBM	84.58 ± 0.11	81.87 ± 0.09	81.31 ± 0.10	76.3 ± 0.18	67.99 ± 0.09	67.21 ± 0.17
GTSRB dataset						
Deterministic CNNs	**97.93**	**97.36**	**97.43**	**97.45**	**97.89**	**97.83**
MBM	97.09 ± 0.05	**97.98 ± 0.02**	95.96 ± 0.04	97.41 ± 0.06	97.49 ± 0.06	97.78 ± 0.02
MBSM	97.84 ± 0.03	**97.97 ± 0.01**	97.05 ± 0.03	97.36 ± 0.02	97.56 ± 0.06	97.82 ± 0.04
MGM	97.11 ± 0.03	**98.16 ± 0.04**	96.01 ± 0.02	96.94 ± 0.04	97.53 ± 0.09	97.69 ± 0.05
MGM ⋆ MBM	95.63 ± 0.08	**98.41 ± 0.01**	92.60 ± 0.06	96.59 ± 0.08	96.30 ± 0.03	97.52 ± 0.05
MGM ⋆ MBSM	96.75 ± 0.06	**98.17 ± 0.02**	94.77 ± 0.10	96.50 ± 0.10	96.32 ± 0.07	97.06 ± 0.05
MGM ⋆ MBSM ⋆ MBM	94.87 ± 0.06	**98.39 ± 0.03**	89.98 ± 0.12	96.07 ± 0.06	93.39 ± 0.15	96.58 ± 0.09

The Effect of Dropout Methods on Misclassifications Detection. Table 3 shows that Bayesian CNNs (except the M-VGGNet with MBSM) evaluated on the CIFAR10 and GTSRB test data better detected misclassifications by performing sampling after max pooling layers. In contrast, Bayesian CNNs (except the M-ResNet) evaluated on the MNIST test data better detected misclassifications by performing sampling before max pooling layers. Table 3 shows further that cascade masks often better captured uncertainty than single masks. However, even if the MGM ⋆ MBSM ⋆ MBM better captured uncertainty than other cascade masks, it drastically decreased the F-measure and therefore highlighted a danger associated with dropout methods. Notwithstanding this, the dropout method that sampled inputs to max pooling layers with MGM $\star$ MBSM was selected for further investigation so as to compromise between uncertainty quality and F-measure.

Table 3. The mean and standard deviation of false positive rates [%] and F-measures [%] (reported in brackets) of built-in validators were reported as function of dropout methods. The columns' headers include the sampling locations, while the rows' headers include the sampling masks. The experiments were conducted on the MNIST, CIFAR10 and GTSRB test data using three architectures. The number of stochastic forward passes T was set to 20 and the inference dropout probability p to 0.1. Each experiment was repeated 5 times. The predictions of all stochastic CNNs sampled from Bayesian CNNs were averaged without filtering. The built-in validators concurrently used the confidence, entropy and standard deviation thresholds for uncertainty quantification.

	M-VGGNet		M-InceptionNet		M-ResNet	
	After max pooling dropout	Before max pooling dropout	After max pooling dropout	Before max pooling dropout	After max pooling dropout	Before max pooling dropout
MNIST dataset						
MBM	59.46 ± 2.87 (99.58 ± 0.01)	23.58 ± 0.91 (99.19 ± 0.00)	52.44 ± 3.29 (99.51 ± 0.02)	18.14 ± 0.94 (98.63 ± 0.02)	46.77 ± 0.83 (98.32 ± 0.02)	42.95 ± 0.50 (99.07 ± 0.02)
MBSM	56.40 ± 2.89 (99.55 ± 0.01)	18.76 ± 2.16 (97.99 ± 0.02)	48.68 ± 3.24 (99.48 ± 0.01)	14.86 ± 1.67 (96.21 ± 0.04)	41.80 ± 1.88 (98.20 ± 0.05)	34.82 ± 1.41 (98.70 ± 0.01)
MGM	59.08 ± 2.81 (99.59 ± 0.01)	24.15 ± 0.83 (99.23 ± 0.02)	51.57 ± 4.24 (99.50 ± 0.03)	20.38 ± 0.54 (98.79 ± 0.01)	44.48 ± 0.97 (98.37 ± 0.02)	40.83 ± 0.35 (99.10 ± 0.02)
MGM $\star$ MBM	48.96 ± 3.53 (99.53 ± 0.02)	33.33 ± 2.10 (99.42 ± 0.02)	44.83 ± 2.18 (99.43 ± 0.04)	28.47 ± 1.86 (99.26 ± 0.03)	37.03 ± 1.90 (98.09 ± 0.09)	40.61 ± 2.54 (99.18 ± 0.03)
MGM $\star$ MBSM	44.20 ± 2.62 (99.49 ± 0.02)	22.10 ± 1.80 (99.13 ± 0.01)	44.12 ± 2.09 (99.39 ± 0.02)	17.14 ± 1.25 (98.58 ± 0.03)	31.17 ± 2.13 (97.94 ± 0.05)	32.92 ± 1.75 (98.82 ± 0.04)
MGM $\star$ MBSM $\star$ MBM	33.85 ± 2.86 (99.41 ± 0.02)	25.94 ± 2.49 (99.35 ± 0.02)	36.28 ± 1.16 (99.24 ± 0.02)	24.41 ± 1.44 (99.08 ± 0.03)	23.88 ± 1.16 (97.58 ± 0.07)	29.08 ± 4.56 (98.78 ± 0.07)
CIFAR10 dataset						
MBM	20.52 ± 0.36 (86.57 ± 0.09)	38.52 ± 0.38 (90.13 ± 0.13)	16.57 ± 0.35 (84.82 ± 0.11)	39.99 ± 0.19 (89.32 ± 0.08)	8.46 ± 0.38 (71.33 ± 0.15)	30.76 ± 0.50 (87.20 ± 0.05)
MBSM	9.87 ± 0.47 (78.50 ± 0.06)	10.17 ± 0.45 (78.82 ± 0.18)	8.78 ± 0.25 (78.93 ± 0.15)	12.79 ± 0.23 (78.98 ± 0.14)	2.68 ± 0.25 (57.35 ± 0.25)	3.31 ± 0.15 (59.80 ± 0.29)
MGM	20.00 ± 0.20 (86.58 ± 0.10)	27.68 ± 0.39 (87.88 ± 0.07)	14.72 ± 0.48 (83.81 ± 0.15)	29.37 ± 0.25 (85.81 ± 0.06)	6.44 ± 0.27 (67.98 ± 0.14)	13.12 ± 0.56 (76.26 ± 0.12)
MGM $\star$ MBM	7.74 ± 0.36 (76.46 ± 0.20)	18.17 ± 0.63 (84.16 ± 0.20)	4.02 ± 0.18 (68.52 ± 0.21)	22.74 ± 0.55 (81.01 ± 0.24)	0.90 ± 0.13 (36.65 ± 0.55)	8.24 ± 0.63 (65.43 ± 0.56)
MGM $\star$ MBSM	4.15 ± 0.16 (67.07 ± 0.12)	5.21 ± 0.39 (69.96 ± 0.16)	2.12 ± 0.37 (61.59 ± 0.22)	6.48 ± 0.47 (68.18 ± 0.34)	0.22 ± 0.05 (24.38 ± 0.45)	0.74 ± 0.13 (32.66 ± 0.36)
MGM $\star$ MBSM $\star$ MBM	1.75 ± 0.27 (52.07 ± 0.39)	3.42 ± 0.20 (64.22 ± 0.25)	0.62 ± 0.10 (41.27 ± 0.28)	4.57 ± 0.10 (96.88 ± 0.08)	0.01 ± 0.01 (5.45 ± 0.29)	0.38 ± 0.07 (22.56 ± 0.20)
GTSRB dataset						
MBM	6.59 ± 0.57 (96.25 ± 0.08)	7.12 ± 0.18 (96.65 ± 0.02)	3.93 ± 0.69 (84.96 ± 0.07)	23.88 ± 0.86 (96.94 ± 0.08)	0.82 ± 0.33 (86.12 ± 0.18)	19.66 ± 1.40 (97.81 ± 0.03)
MBSM	16.04 ± 0.40 (98.04 ± 0.02)	7.28 ± 0.23 (96.62 ± 0.02)	5.89 ± 0.69 (88.30 ± 0.16)	23.56 ± 1.25 (97.01 ± 0.04)	0.45 ± 0.16 (79.50 ± 0.26)	19.64 ± 1.59 (97.78 ± 0.09)
MGM	8.17 ± 1.13 (8.17 ± 1.13)	8.94 ± 0.69 (97.11 ± 0.04)	4.01 ± 0.75 (86.13 ± 0.07)	6.69 ± 1.25 (93.20 ± 0.06)	0.70 ± 0.24 (87.26 ± 0.16)	6.12 ± 0.85 (94.32 ± 0.11)
MGM $\star$ MBM	0.91 ± 0.17 (91.08 ± 0.06)	20.22 ± 0.90 (20.22 ± 0.90)	0.04 ± 0.05 (50.87 ± 0.17)	2.50 ± 0.39 (86.41 ± 0.14)	0.04 ± 0.09 (50.91 ± 0.34)	1.47 ± 0.44 (86.14 ± 0.08)
MGM $\star$ MBSM	1.41 ± 0.36 (93.03 ± 0.04)	5.37 ± 0.66 (96.38 ± 0.02)	0.06 ± 0.07 (54.22 ± 0.31)	0.46 ± 0.30 (73.60 ± 0.12)	0.0 ± 0.0 (41.89 ± 0.23)	0.27 ± 0.17 (57.07 ± 0.36)
MGM $\star$ MBSM $\star$ MBM	0.25 ± 0.07 (84.85 ± 0.06)	9.18 ± 0.41 (97.65 ± 0.03)	0.00 ± 0.00 (13.90 ± 0.22)	0.16 ± 0.15 (59.17 ± 0.28)	0.00 ± 0.00 (9.48 ± 0.18)	0.09 ± 0.11 (38.80 ± 0.23)

6.2   The Effect of the Number of Ensemble Members

Table 4 shows that the increase of the number of stochastic CNNs increases the accuracies of the Bayesian CNNs evaluated on the CIFAR10 test data and helps to better detect misclassifications. On the other hand, for Bayesian CNNs evaluated on the MNIST and GTSRB test data, the increase of the number of ensemble members does not necessarily increase the accuracies of the Bayesian CNNs and does not necessarily help to better detect misclassifications.

Table 4. The mean and standard deviation of the accuracies [%] of Bayesian CNNs, as well as, the false positive rates [%] and F-measures [%] (reported in brackets) of built-in validators were reported as function of different number of stochastic forward passes T. The inference dropout probabilities were set to 0.1. The validators concurrently used the confidence, entropy and standard deviation thresholds for uncertainty quantification. The experiments were conducted on the MNIST, CIFAR10 and GTSRB test data using three different architectures. Each experiment was repeated 5 times. The predictions of all stochastic CNNs sampled from Bayesian CNNs were averaged without filtering.

	M-VGGNet		M-InceptionNet		M-ResNet	
	Bayesian CNNs	Validators	Bayesian CNNs	Validators	Bayesian CNNs	Validators
MNIST dataset						
T = 20	99.35 ± 0.03	22.86 ± 0.99 (99.10 ± 0.00)	99.11 ± 0.02	17.27 ± 0.53 (98.58 ± 0.02)	98.96 ± 0.05	31.65 ± 2.48 (98.80 ± 0.03)
T = 40	99.35 ± 0.02	22.54 ± 0.76 (99.11 ± 0.01)	99.13 ± 0.02	17.44 ± 1.49 (98.59 ± 0.01)	**98.98 ± 0.01**	32.82 ± 1.08 (98.82 ± 0.02)
T = 60	99.35 ± 0.01	23.15 ± 0.95 (99.11 ± 0.01)	**99.13 ± 0.01**	16.29 ± 0.93 (98.58 ± 0.01)	98.97 ± 0.03	**31.54 ± 1.59** **(98.86 ± 0.01)**
T = 80	99.36 ± 0.02	23.66 ± 0.65 (99.10 ± 0.01)	99.12 ± 0.01	16.18 ± 0.58 (98.60 ± 0.01)	98.98 ± 0.02	32.53 ± 1.67 (98.85 ± 0.02)
T = 100	**99.36 ± 0.01**	22.75 ± 0.89 **(99.12 ± 0.02)**	99.11 ± 0.01	**15.77 ± 1.09** **(98.59 ± 0.02)**	98.98 ± 0.02	31.65 ± 0.64 (98.87 ± 0.03)
CIFAR10 dataset						
T = 20	83.32 ± 0.12	5.30 ± 0.42 (69.92 ± 0.28)	79.72 ± 0.11	6.77 ± 0.50 (68.03 ± 0.08)	74.42 ± 0.12	0.67 ± 0.16 (32.96 ± 0.46)
T = 40	83.54 ± 0.08	4.50 ± 0.33 (69.64 ± 0.20)	80.01 ± 0.14	5.40 ± 0.23 (67.47 ± 0.11)	75.18 ± 0.15	0.59 ± 0.07 (30.30 ± 0.29)
T = 60	83.59 ± 0.07	4.06 ± 0.20 (69.48 ± 0.24)	80.08 ± 0.09	4.94 ± 0.22 (67.35 ± 0.14)	75.22 ± 0.25	0.41 ± 0.10 (29.48 ± 0.34)
T = 80	83.63 ± 0.07	4.05 ± 0.22 (69.27 ± 0.08)	80.07 ± 0.11	4.79 ± 0.24 (67.28 ± 0.10)	75.52 ± 0.15	0.40 ± 0.07 (28.68 ± 0.16)
T = 100	**83.73 ± 0.06**	**3.81 ± 0.11** **(69.15 ± 0.20)**	**80.10 ± 0.05**	**4.57 ± 0.23** **(67.18 ± 0.18)**	**75.64 ± 0.17**	**0.34 ± 0.06** **(28.57 ± 0.21)**
GTSRB dataset						
T = 20	98.15 ± 0.03	6.17 ± 0.19 (96.37 ± 0.03)	96.51 ± 0.04	0.54 ± 0.27 (73.70 ± 0.11)	97.05 ± 0.04	0.16 ± 0.13 (56.96 ± 0.28)
T = 40	98.22 ± 0.03	5.52 ± 0.67 (96.38 ± 0.03)	96.66 ± 0.06	0.28 ± 0.18 75.52 ± 0.22	97.21 ± 0.07	0.23 ± 0.11 (57.53 ± 0.11)
T = 60	98.22 ± 0.02	6.06 ± 0.33 (96.37 ± 0.03)	96.73 ± 0.03	0.19 ± 0.18 (76.04 ± 0.16)	97.31 ± 0.03	0.18 ± 0.14 (57.61 ± 0.36)
T = 80	98.22 ± 0.04	5.78 ± 0.35 (96.38 ± 0.05)	**96.78 ± 0.01**	**0.10 ± 0.12** **(76.13 ± 0.13)**	**97.31 ± 0.03**	**0.12 ± 0.14** **(56.88 ± 0.29)**
T = 100	**98.23 ± 0.01**	**5.38 ± 0.45** **(96.38 ± 0.02)**	96.77 ± 0.03	0.25 ± 0.16 (76.19 ± 0.07)	97.28 ± 0.06	0.17 ± 0.14 (57.07 ± 0.17)

6.3   The Effect of the Inference Dropout Probability

Table 5 shows that the increase of the inference dropout probabilities increases the accuracies of Bayesian CNNs evaluated on the MNIST test data and helps to better detect misclassifications at the cost of sacrificing the F-measures. In contrast, for Bayesian CNNs evaluated on the CIFAR10 and GTSRB (except for the M-VGGNet) test data, the increase of the probabilities decreases both the accuracies of the Bayesian CNNs and the F-measures of the validators.

Table 5. The mean and standard deviation of accuracies [%] of Bayesian CNNs, as well as, false positive rates [%] and F-measures (%) (reported in brackets) of built-in validators were reported as function of different inference dropout probabilities p. The numbers of stochastic forward passes T were set to 60. The built-in validators concurrently used the confidence, entropy and standard deviation thresholds for uncertainty quantification. The experiments were conducted on the MNIST, CIFAR10 and GTSRB test datasets using three different architectures. Each experiment was repeated 5 times. The predictions of the stochastic CNNs sampled from Bayesian CNNs were averaged without filtering.

	M-VGGNet		M-InceptionNet		M-ResNet	
	Bayesian CNNs	Validators	Bayesian CNNs	Validators	Bayesian CNNs	Validators
MNIST dataset						
p = 0.1	99.35 ± 0.01	23.15 ± 0.95 (99.11 ± 0.01)	99.12 ± 0.01	16.29 ± 0.93 (98.58 ± 0.01)	98.97 ± 0.08	31.54 ± 1.59 (98.86 ± 0.01)
p = 0.2	99.40 ± 0.02	17.13 ± 1.36 (99.23 ± 0.02)	99.24 ± 0.02	19.72 ± 1.16 (98.84 ± 0.03)	99.07 ± 0.02	12.46 ± 1.24 (98.06 ± 0.05)
p = 0.3	**99.41 ± 0.02**	**11.83 ± 1.40** **(98.77 ± 0.05)**	**99.30 ± 0.03**	**12.14 ± 2.31** **(98.19 ± 0.03)**	99.09 ± 0.02	**5.29 ± 1.31** **(95.92 ± 0.04)**
CIFAR10 dataset						
p = 0.1	**83.59 ± 0.08**	**4.06 ± 0.20** **(69.48 ± 0.24)**	**80.08 ± 0.09**	**4.94 ± 0.22** **(67.35 ± 0.14)**	**75.22 ± 0.25**	**0.41 ± 0.10** **(29.48 ± 0.34)**
p = 0.2	81.59 ± 0.07	0.29 ± 0.10 (31.12 ± 0.16)	73.48 ± 0.09	0.35 ± 0.05 (25.79 ± 0.15)	57.62 ± 0.07	0.00 ± 0.00 (0.39 ± 0.07)
p = 0.3	76.68 ± 0.16	0.00 ± 0.00 (5.58 ± 0.36)	61.87 ± 0.21	0.01 ± 0.01 (3.37 ± 0.37)	38.45 ± 0.29	0.00 ± 0.00 (00.00 ± 0.00)
GTSRB dataset						
p = 0.1	98.22 ± 0.02	6.06 ± 0.33 (96.37 ± 0.03)	**96.73 ± 0.03**	**0.19 ± 0.18** **(76.04 ± 0.16)**	**97.31 ± 0.03**	**0.18 ± 0.14** **(57.61 ± 0.36)**
p = 0.2	98.42 ± 0.05	3.20 ± 0.20 (96.53 ± 0.04)	95.32 ± 0.07	0.00 ± 0.00 (10.02 ± 0.16)	91.53 ± 0.09	0.00 ± 0.00 (0.02 ± 0.02)
p = 0.3	**98.52 ± 0.03**	**0.85 ± 0.26** **(94.26 ± 0.03)**	91.53 ± 0.09	0.00 ± 0.00 (0.02 ± 0.02)	81.80 ± 0.31	0.00 ± 0.00 (0.00 ± 0.00)

6.4   Comparison of Methods for Combining Ensemble Members

Table 6 shows that the averaging of all stochastic CNNs sampled from the Bayesian CNNs better detect misclassifications than other combination methods described in Sect. 3.3.

Table 6. The mean and standard deviation of false positive rates [%] and F-measures (%) (reported in brackets) of validators were reported as function of the combination methods. The validators concurrently used the confidence, entropy and standard deviation thresholds for uncertainty quantification. The experiments were conducted on the MNIST, CIFAR10 and GTSRB test data using three architectures. The dropout probabilities p were set to 0.1 and the numbers of forward passes were set to 60. Each experiment was repeated 5 times.

	M-VGGNet		M-InceptionNet		M-ResNet	
	Bayesian CNNs	Validators	Bayesian CNNs	Validators	Bayesian CNNs	Validators
MNIST dataset						
Average	**99.35 ± 0.01**	**23.15 ± 0.95** (**99.11 ± 0.01**)	**99.13 ± 0.01**	**16.29 ± 0.93** (**98.58 ± 0.01**)	**98.97 ± 0.03**	**31.54 ± 1.59** (**98.85 ± 0.01**)
Plurality vote	99.36 ± 0.01	26.10 ± 1.24 (99.16 ± 0.01)	99.12 ± 0.01	18.75 ± 1.89 (98.66 ± 0.02)	98.96 ± 0.02	53.76 ± 1.23 (99.19 ± 0.03)
Majority vote	99.33 ± 0.01	25.15 ± 1.06 (99.18 ± 0.01)	99.10 ± 0.02	18.27 ± 1.61 (98.67 ± 0.02)	98.89 ± 0.03	49.56 ± 0.58 (99.23 ± 0.02)
Sanity check	99.15 ± 0.04	51.29 ± 3.18 (99.73 ± 0.02)	98.92 ± 0.02	63.07 ± 3.48 (99.52 ± 0.02)	98.98 ± 0.03	57.91 ± 2.63 (99.38 ± 0.03)
CIFAR10 dataset						
Average	**83.59 ± 0.08**	**4.06 ± 0.20** (**69.48 ± 0.24**)	**80.08 ± 0.09**	**4.94 ± 0.22** (**67.34 ± 0.14**)	**75.22 ± 0.25**	**0.41 ± 0.10** (**29.48 ± 0.34**)
Plurality vote	83.58 ± 0.10	56.41 ± 1.04 (90.18 ± 0.09)	80.07 ± 0.07	63.68 ± 0.69 (88.62 ± 0.16)	74.98 ± 0.23	58.89 ± 1.07 (84.35 ± 0.07)
Majority vote	79.61 ± 0.10	39.23 ± 0.81 (92.34 ± 0.08)	75.54 ± 0.12	44.20 ± 0.38 (91.04 ± 0.09)	62.23 ± 0.20	20.75 ± 0.52 (91.24 ± 0.12)
Sanity check	83.26 ± 0.12	11.77 ± 0.24 (79.31 ± 0.14)	79.87 ± 0.10	13.45 ± 0.08 (76.16 ± 0.14)	74.98 ± 0.23	1.54 ± 0.06 (43.12 ± 0.31)
GTSRB dataset						
Average	**98.22 ± 0.02**	**6.06 ± 0.33** (**96.37 ± 0.03**)	**96.73 ± 0.03**	**0.19 ± 0.18** (**76.04 ± 0.16**)	**97.31 ± 0.03**	**0.18 ± 0.14** (**57.61 ± 0.36**)
Plurality vote	98.18 ± 0.03	8.19 ± 0.17 (96.54 ± 0.03)	96.70 ± 0.06	88.77 ± 0.86 (98.33 ± 0.04)	97.27 ± 0.04	76.84 ± 1.68 (98.31 ± 0.05)
Majority vote	97.91 ± 0.02	7.05 ± 0.22 (96.68 ± 0.02)	94.65 ± 0.05	23.27 ± 0.67 (99.31 ± 0.03)	94.04 ± 0.02	10.63 ± 0.71 (99.39 ± 0.04)
Sanity check	96.66 ± 0.03	19.84 ± 0.85 (99.52 ± 0.02)	96.74 ± 0.03	0.43 ± 0.32 (78.71 ± 0.12)	97.30 ± 0.04	0.23 ± 0.11 (64.77 ± 0.23)

7 Comparison of Uncertainty Measures

Figure 3 shows that the curves of the false positive rates of built-in validators concurrently using the three uncertainty measures, namely the confidence, entropy and standard deviation thresholds, are always below that of other validators using single uncertainty measure. As a result, robustness to test data corrupted with additive Gaussian noises (AGNs) is best guaranteed by concurrently using the three uncertainty measures at the cost of sacrificing the F-measure of the validator.

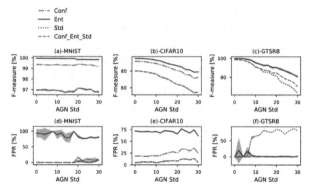

Fig. 3. The mean and standard deviation of false positive rates (FPRs) and F-measures of built-in validators were plotted as function of test data corrupted with additive Gaussian noises (AGNs). The validators used the confidence (Conf), entropy (Ent) and/or standard deviation (Std) thresholds for uncertainty quantification. The experiments were conducted on MNIST using M-ResNet with 9698 test images, on CIFAR10 using M-InceptionNet with 2580 test images and on GTSRB using M-VGGNet with 10781 test images. The dropout probabilities p were set to 0.3, 0.1, 0.1 for MNIST, CIFAR10, and GTSRB, respectively. The numbers of forward passes were set to 60. The selected test data were correctly classified by deterministic CNNs with low entropy and high confidence. The standard deviation of the AGN was iterated from 0 to 30 with a step of 2. The selected test images were perturbed with AGNs sampled at the iterations. Each experiment was repeated 5 times.

8   Discussion

Empirical results showed that different dropout methods resulted to different approximates and therefore to different uncertainty estimates, trading-off uncertainty quality and performance (classification accuracy and/or F-measure). However, the optimal dropout method specified through the sampling location, the sampling mask, the inference dropout probability, and the number of stochastic forward passes depends on the problem at hand (dataset) and the designed network architecture. Nothstanding this, I proposed to approximate inference by randomly sampling feature representations and strengthening/weakening activations to max pooling layers using the cascade of MGM followed by MBSM. I claimed that this sampling method emulated random max pooling layers, which at training forced independence between feature representations and therefore increased the inherent plasticity of the Bayesian CNNs thanks to the MBSM. Besides, it forced the Bayesian CNNs to learn noisy versions of extracted features thanks to the MGM. Hence, it give a good fit to the true unknown posterior, since the stochastic CNNs sampled at inference are often accurate. It avoids therefore extreme performance degradation, while robustly capturing the classification uncertainty. The empirical results showed further that the classification uncertainty is best captured by averaging the predictions of all stochastic CNNs and by concurrently using three uncertainty measures, namely the confidence, entropy and standard deviation thresholds. Besides, the results showed that 60 stochastic forward passes are enough to better capture uncertainty. Moreover, the increase of the inference dropout probability increases the uncertainty quality at the cost of sacrificing the performance.

The proposed sampling method for uncertainty quantification will be used in near future to reinforce learning of training data correctly classified by the Bayesian CNNs, but rejected by the validators due to violation of defined constraints. Doing so, the loss in performance will surely be recovered, while keeping/increasing the uncertainty quality. Ensembles of Bayesian CNNs will also be investigated in near future to reduce the loss in performance, while improving the uncertainty quality.

References

1. Gal, Y., Ghahramani, Z.: Dropout as a bayesian approximation: representing model uncertainty in deep learning. In: Proceedings of the 33rd International Conference on Machine Learning, vol. 48, pp. 1050–1059 (2016)
2. Gal, Y., Ghahramani, Z.: Bayesian convolutional neural networks with Bernoulli approximate variational inference (2016). http://arxiv.org/pdf/1506.02158v6
3. Hinton, G.E., Srivastava, N., Krizhevsky, A., Sutskever, I., Salakhutdinov, R.R.: Improving neural networks by preventing co-adaptation of feature detectors (2012). http://arxiv.org/pdf/1207.0580v1
4. Srivastava, N., Hinton, G., Krizhevsky, A., Sutskever, I., Salakhutdinov, R.: Dropout: a simple way to prevent neural networks from overfitting. J. Mach. Learn. Res. **15**, 1929–1958 (2014)
5. Wang, S.I., Manning, C.D.: Fast dropout training (2013). http://proceedings.mlr.press/v28/wang13a.html
6. McClure, P., Kriegeskorte, N.: Robustly representing uncertainty in deep neural networks through sampling (2018). http://arxiv.org/pdf/1611.01639v7
7. Tompson, J., Goroshin, R., Jain, A., LeCun, Y., Bregler, C.: Efficient object localization using convolutional networks (2015). http://arxiv.org/pdf/1411.4280v3
8. Wu, H., Gu, X.: Max-pooling dropout for regularization of convolutional neural networks (2015). https://arxiv.org/abs/1512.01400v1
9. Lakshminarayanan, B., Pritzel, A., Blundell, C.: Simple and scalable predictive uncertainty estimation using deep ensembles (2017). http://arxiv.org/pdf/1612.01474v3
10. Oliveira, R., Tabacof, P., Valle, E.: Known unknowns: uncertainty quality in Bayesian neural networks (2016). http://arxiv.org/pdf/1612.01251v2
11. Lin, M., Chen, Q., Yan, S.: Network in network (2014). http://arxiv.org/pdf/1312.4400v3
12. LeCun, Y., Bottou, L., Bengio, Y., Haffner, P.: Gradient based learning applied to document recognition. In: Proceedings of the IEEE (1998). https://doi.org/10.1109/5.726791
13. Krizhevsky, A.: Learning multiple layers of features from tiny images. Master's thesis, University of Toronto (2009)
14. Stallkamp, J., Schlipsing, M., Salmen, J., Igel, C. (eds.): The German traffic sign recognition benchmark: a multi-class classification competition. In: The 2011 International Joint Conference on Neural Networks, San Jose, CA, USA. IEEE (2011)
15. Simonyan, K., Zisserman, A.: Very deep convolutional networks for large-scale image recognition (2015). http://arxiv.org/pdf/1409.1556v6
16. Szegedy, C., et al.: Going deeper with convolutions (2014). http://arxiv.org/pdf/1409.4842v1
17. He, K., Zhang, X., Ren, S., Sun, J.: Deep residual learning for image recognition (2015). http://arxiv.org/pdf/1512.03385v1

Particle Filter for Trajectories of Movers from Laser Scanned Dataset

Md. Haidar Sharif[(⊠)]

University of Hail, Hail, Kingdom of Saudi Arabia
md.sharif@uoh.edu.sa

Abstract. Laser scanner takes away the problem of private life conservation as it does not record real world videos except scanned data points. So it shows many benefits over the use of video camera. This paper portrays an approach to detect and track movers from laser scanned datasets. Laser scanned data points from each scan are deemed as a video frame. Blobs are extracted from each frame. Support vector machine (SVM) and Hungarian method along with particle filter are used to get trajectories of movers. Experimental results on the identical laser scanned dataset demonstrate that the approach of SVM with Hungarian method using particle filter outperforms both the threshold based approach with Hungarian method using Kalman filter and the approach of SVM with Hungarian method using Kalman filter.

Keywords: Kalman filter · Particle filter · Laser scanner · SVM · Tracking

1 Introduction

Trajectories of movers (e.g., pedestrians and vehicles) are one of the key issues for surveillance and traffic systems analysis. For example, a surveillance system on the highways would expect to detect and track unusual activities to ensure high degree of public security and safety. A nonautomated and human functioned surveillance system is very expensive and erroneous. Those problems can be reduced by an automated surveillance system. In the urban life, sidewalk occupancy is a serious problem (e.g., see Fig. 1). Sidewalk occupancy leads to the passersby walk on the street which would cause many potential unpleasant traffic events. An automatic traffic-video analysis system expects good trajectories of movers. Trajectory analysis can provide the knowledge of potential risk for the movers on the roads and highways. Civil engineers may get knowledge of how the sidewalk can be constructed to provide an extreme comfort to the passersby. The detection of usual (e.g., [1,2]) and unusual (e.g., [3-9]) video events is a cardinal chore of a surveillance camera system. An automated camera system can provide good trajectories of movers. But camera systems include several detriments when compared with the laser scanner systems. Many laser scanners can be applied conjointly to widen the scanned area. Laser scanners can readily keep

C. Djeddi et al. (Eds.): MedPRAI 2019, CCIS 1144, pp. 133–148, 2020.
https://doi.org/10.1007/978-3-030-37548-5_11

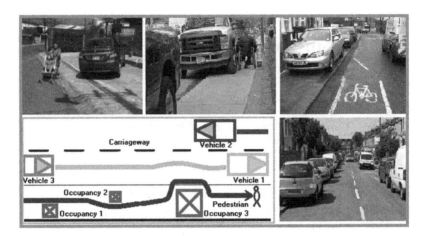

Fig. 1. Scenarios of sidewalk occupancy and rick of potential accident. Pedestrians change their designed walk ways due to sidewalk occupancy. Thus their trajectories reflect the reality. How to get automatically a high quality of trajectories of the movers from laser scanned data points of movers for traffic analysis?

watch over huge crowd via high-speed processor with low-cost data processing. Inconstant light illumination has no effect on them. Transfer of moving objects into real coordinate systems is very easy and fast with them. Thus their system is very convenient and efficient. In spite of that, from laser scanned data points the recognition and tracking of movers be a challenging task. In the literature, many algorithms have been proposed to recognize and/or track of movers from laser scanned data points. Table 1 depicts a brief overview of state-of-the-art methods. A common characteristic of those algorithms is that they are mainly based on clustering the laser scanned data points, without directly plotting the data points onto the image video frame. Because of algorithmic assumptions and large amount of data processing, the existing algorithms did not attend to their desire level of applicability. Henceforth, the consequence of developing efficient new algorithms to handle high quality of trajectories for movers is still very high.

It is a general task to get trajectories of movers from the laser scanned data points of objects. For instances, both Galip et al. [50] and Sharif et al. [65] presented an image processing based approach to get trajectories of movers from laser scanned data points. Laser scanned data points from each scan were deemed as a video frame. Blobs were extracted and then Hungarian method with Kalman filter was applied to get trajectories of movers from laser scanned datasets. But recognition of movers was performed based on various thresholds. Instead of using multiple thresholds, it would be nice to focus on supervised learning based methods to recognize movers from the laser scanned data points. Galip et al. [52] modeled the laser scanned data points of objects for support vector machine (SVM). Explicitly, SVM was used to recognize each mover as either a pedestrian or a vehicle. But the tracking was not performed. Sharif et al. [65] used SVM

Table 1. State-of-the-art methods for detecting and tracking of movers from miscellaneous laser scanned datasets. The signs ✓ and × point to corresponding intents included and excluded, respectively.

Years	Miscellaneous methods	Which mover was tracked from datasets?			Kalman Filter used?	Particle Filter used?
		Pedestrian	Vehicle	Pedestrian & Vehicle		
2003	Surmann et al. [10]	×	✓	×	×	×
	Wang et al. [11]	×	×	✓	×	×
2004	Mendes et al. [12]	×	×	✓	✓	×
	Vosselman et al. [13]	×	×	×	×	×
	Nakamura et al. [14]	✓	×	×	✓	×
2005	Topp et al. [15]	✓	×	×	×	×
	Xavier et al. [16]	×	×	×	×	×
	Zhao et al. [17]	✓	×	×	✓	×
2006	Cui et al. [18]	✓	×	×	✓	×
	Zhao et al. [19]	×	×	✓	×	×
	Serment et al. [20]	×	×	✓	✓	×
2007	Arras et al. [21]	✓	×	×	×	×
	Shao et al. [22]	✓	×	×	×	✓
	Cui et al. [23]	✓	×	×	✓	×
2008	Zhao et al. [24]	×	×	✓	×	×
	Arras et al. [25]	×	×	✓	✓	×
	Song et al. [26]	✓	×	×	×	✓
2009	Vu et al. [27]	×	×	✓	✓	✓
	Gate et al. [28]	×	×	✓	✓	×
	Gidel et al. [29]	✓	×	×	×	✓
2010	Mozos et al. [30]	✓	×	×	×	×
	Musleh et al. [31]	✓	×	×	×	×
	Gidel et al. [32]	✓	×	×	×	✓
2011	Shao et al. [33]	✓	×	×	×	×
	Fu et al. [34]	×	×	×	×	×
	Song et al. [35]	✓	×	×	×	✓
2012	Zhao et al. [36]	×	✓	×	×	×
	Garcia et al. [37]	×	✓	×	✓	×
	Song et al. [38]	✓	×	×	×	✓
2013	Fotiadis et al. [39]	✓	×	×	✓	✓
	Song et al. [40]	✓	×	×	×	✓
	Wada et al. [41]	✓	×	×	×	×
2014	Akamatsu et al. [42]	✓	×	×	✓	×
	Adiaviakoye et al. [43]	✓	×	×	×	✓
	Kim et al. [44]	×	✓	×	×	×
	Kaneko et al. [45]	✓	×	×	×	×
2015	Leigh et al. [46]	✓	×	×	✓	×
	Kim et al. [47]	×	✓	×	×	×
	Shalal et al. [48]	×	✓	×	×	×
	Hashimoto et al. [49]	✓	×	×	×	×
	Galip et al. [50]	×	×	✓	✓	×

(contniued)

Table 1. *(continued)*

Years	Miscellaneous methods	Which mover was tracked from datasets?			Kalman	Particle
		Pedestrian	Vehicle	Pedestrian & Vehicle	Filter used?	Filter used?
2016	Weinrich et al. [51]	✓	×	×	×	×
	Feyza et al. [52]	×	×	✓	×	×
	Kim et al. [53]	×	✓	×	×	×
	Tsugita et al. [54]	✓	×	×	✓	×
2017	Zou et al. [55]	×	×	✓	×	×
	Liu et al. [56]	✓	×	×	×	×
	Zhang et al. [57]	×	✓	×	×	×
	Ishi et al. [58]	×	×	✓	×	×
2018	Zou et al. [59]	×	×	✓	×	×
	Kim et al. [60]	×	✓	×	✓	×
	Gizlenmistir [61]	×	✓	×	×	×
	Liu et al. [62]	×	×	✓	✓	×
	Halmheu et al. [63]	×	✓	×	×	×
2019	Urano et al. [64]	×	✓	×	×	×
	Sharif et al. [65]	×	×	✓	✓	×
Proposed method		×	×	✓	×	✓

to solve the existing threshold estimation difficulty of Galip et al. [50]. However, both Galip et al. [50] and Sharif et al. [65] used Kalman filter, which is a linear quadratic estimator. Kalman filter would be the best to estimate linear system having Gaussian noise. It has low computational requirements. But if the system does not suit nicely into a linear model or if the sensor uncertainty does not fit with Gaussian model, then its performance decreases drastically. If the linearity or Gaussian conditions do not exist, its variants (e.g., Extended Kalman filter, Unscented Kalman filter) can be used. But those variants cannot give a reasonable estimate for highly nonlinear and non-Gaussian problems. Besides, movers' data points of laser scanners behave very differently in some regions than others. In such case, Kalman filter is not a good choice. The particle filter be a better solution. But particle filter gets exponentially worse if a model has many state variables. Yet a particle filter can handle almost any kind of model by discretising the underlying problem into separate particles. Each particle is one possible state of the model. A sufficiently large number of particles can handle any kind of probability distribution.

In this paper, we used SVM along with Hungarian method and particle filter to get trajectories of movers. Thus this paper would be considered as an incremental improvement of Galip et al. [50,52] and Sharif et al. [65]. Figure 2 compares various flowcharts. The usage of SVM along with Hungarian method and particle filter to get the trajectories of movers from laser scanned datasets be the cardinal contribution of this paper. To get most qualified data, four laser scanners were employed. Upon combining the obtained data from all laser scanners background subtraction was applied to get the moving points. As background points were removed, the processing time for foreground points was reduced.

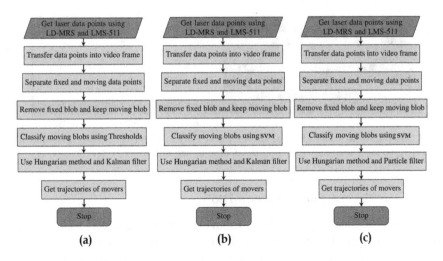

Fig. 2. Comparison of flow diagrams of Galip et al. [50], Sharif et al. [65], and our proposed method as marked in (a), (b), and (c), respectively.

Our proposed approach was tested against the same laser scanned datasets, which were collected by the usage of both single and combined laser scanners [50,52,65]. On the same dataset, the proposed approach of this paper reported the best minimization of error rates.

This paper is designed as follows. Section 2 shows our implementation steps; Sect. 3 reports experimental results and errors; Sect. 4 concludes the paper.

2   Implementation Steps

2.1   Data Collection from LD-MRS and LMS-511

The laser scanners provide objects information such as distance and angle between device and echo-pulse width. They scan an area in two dimension by sending beams and then each beam hits objects e.g., vehicles, pedestrian legs, trees, walls, and etc. They return distances with angles that the laser beams hit. Laser beam cannot be seen with human eyes. The LD-MRS has 110° scanning range. It has 4 layers to scan with various heights. The maximum distance that the device can recognize is 250 m. Angular resolution can be 0.125°, 0.25° or 0.5°. The LMS511/581/531 (e.g., Fig. 3(a)) can function with an infrared-light laser diode [66]. Connection between laser scanner and computer is provided by Ethernet cable. Data are captured by SOPAS Engineering Tool, which is a program developed by SICK AG (Aktiengesellschaft). There are more than one laser scanners, thus those coordinates of points should be changed by taking a laser scanner as reference. Afterwards, those distances are converted into X-Y coordinates as plotted in Fig. 3(c) (after scanning a real world video frame e.g., Fig. 3(b)) with blue in color as well as their timestamps using MATLAB.

Fig. 3. (a) points to LMS-511. (b) shows a real world video frame. Blue dots and lines of (c) denote laser scanner data points. (Color figure online)

2.2 Extraction of Each Mover's Blob

During scanning, the position data of moving objects (e.g., feet, legs, etc.) and motionless objects (e.g., buildings, walls, trees, and etc.) are collected. To separate them, in each sampling angle of range scanning, a histogram is generated with range values from all range frames being examined. A peak value above some threshold is estimated, which tells that an object is continuously measured at the identical direction, i.e., a static object. Background image is consisted of the peak values at all sampling angles. By estimating the difference between range images to background image, we can get movers as depicted in Fig. 4(a) with red color. After suppression of noise, we can obtain the blob of each mover. Afterwards, images are converted into black and white pixels as sampled in Fig. 4(b). Such binary images are very suitable for the input of SVM.

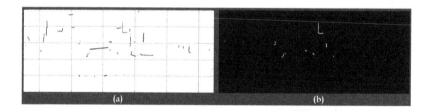

Fig. 4. (a) points the detection of moving and fixed blobs as marked red and blue. (b) hints the estimation of movers on deleting fixed and noisy blobs. (Color figure online)

2.3 SVM to Recognize Movers

The SVM is an approach to construct learning machine that minimizes the generalization error. It is based on very plain and intuitive ideas. It finds an optimal separating hyperplane between data points of various classes in a possibly high dimensional space. The elements of the input data that define boundaries are called support vectors. The genuine support vectors are the points that form the decision boundary between two classes. Normally, non-linear boundary gives

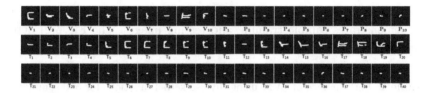

Fig. 5. First row demos the sample training inputs of vehicles (V_1 to V_{10}) and pedestrians (P_1 to P_{10}). Second and third rows contain the sample test inputs of vehicles (T_1 to T_{20}) and pedestrians (T_{21} to T_{40}), respectively.

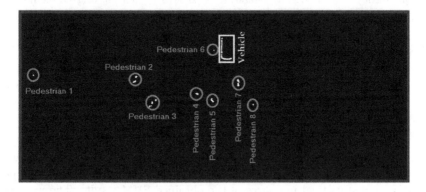

Fig. 6. Classification result of the movers in Fig. 4(b) using SVM.

good result. Through the usage of a kernel function, the non-linear boundary problem is implicitly mapped to a higher dimensional space in which hyper planes are sufficient to define the boundaries. Prominent kernel functions are linear, quadratic, polynomial, Gaussian, and multilayer perceptron. Linear kernel function is a dot product. Polynomial kernel function is used with support vector machines to allow learning of non-linear models. Multilayer perceptron kernel function is a variant of the perceptron [67] learning algorithm. Gaussian radial basis kernel function is widely used in SVM classification. However, their performance is problem dependent. If one kernel is not appropriate for an existing problem, we need to tune the other kernel. An optimization method is looked at carefully to identify support vectors s_i, weights α_i, and bias ξ that are used to classify vectors v_{new} according to the following well-known equation:

$$\Psi = \sum_i \alpha_i \kappa(s_i, v_{new}) + \xi \tag{1}$$

where κ is a kernel function. In the case of a linear kernel, κ is a dot product. If $\Psi \geq 0$, then v_{new} is classified as a member of the first group (e.g., pedestrian), otherwise it is classified as a member of the second group (e.g., vehicle). The Fig. 5 demonstrates sample training and testing images. The Fig. 6(e) depicts sample of recognized movers.

Table 2. Performance of SVM using diverse kernel functions for 550 samples.

Kernel functions	Sensitivity	Specificity	Accuracy	T_{PR}	F_{PR}	AUC
Linear	0.9806	0.7603	0.8636	0.9806	0.2397	0.8704
Quadratic	0.9729	0.8014	0.8818	0.9729	0.1986	0.8871
Polynomial	0.9729	0.8151	0.8891	0.9729	0.1849	0.8940
Gaussian	0.9806	0.7740	0.8709	0.9806	0.2260	0.8773
Multilayer	0.9729	0.8014	0.8818	0.9729	0.1986	0.8871

2.4   Performance of SVM

Table 2 delineates the performance of SVM using various kernel functions with 550 samples. To get a wider knowledge of efficacy for our method, we performed several statistical measures of the obtained SVM results. The measures include: $T_P \Rightarrow$ true positive, $T_N \Rightarrow$ true negative, $F_N \Rightarrow$ false negative, $F_P \Rightarrow$ false positive, $T_P/(T_P + F_N) \Rightarrow$ sensitivity, $T_N/(T_N + F_P) \Rightarrow$ specificity, $(T_N + T_P)/(T_N + T_P + F_N + F_P) \Rightarrow$ accuracy, $T_{PR} = T_P/(T_P + F_N) \Rightarrow$ true positive rate, $F_{PR} = F_P/(F_P + T_N) \Rightarrow$ false positive rate, and AUC $\Rightarrow$ area under ROC (receiver operating characteristic) curve using trapezoidal numerical integration method [68]. Sensitivity or true positive rate or recall rate measures the percentage of actual positives which are correctly identified as such condition. It is complementary to the false negative rate. Specificity or true negative rate measures the percentage of negatives which are correctly identified as such condition. It is complementary to the false positive rate. AUC values will always satisfy the inequality of $0 \leq AUC \leq 1$. Larger AUC values indicate better classifier performance [69]. However, we measured the aforementioned statistics for miscellaneous kernel functions. For instance, using polynomial kernel function the following information can be got for 550 samples: $T_P = 251$, $T_N = 238$, $F_N = 7$, and $F_P = 54$. Similarly, the corresponding values of other kernel functions can be obtained. Their comparative performance is listed in Table 2. The best sensitivity was resulted by both Linear and Gaussian kernels. As Gaussian kernel is often called as mapping to infinity dimensions, its capacity is reliable. But its performance would be increased or decreased by setting better or bad parameters, respectively. The polynomial kernel functioned $AUC = 0.8940$, which is slightly better than multilayer perceptron or quadratic kernels. But its performance would not be the same for other datasets. More tests with new datasets and the effect of cache memories [70] are left as future works.

2.5 Trajectories of Movers

If there exist a number of movers in one frame and another number of movers in the next frame, how can we match them? Bipartite graph matching gives one of the best solutions for this problem [71]. A matching in bipartite graph is always excellent as all the vertices are matched. To compute a bipartite graph is easy. We are more interested in the assignment problem, which finds a minimum weight matching in a weighted bipartite graph. For numerical optimization, we can use Hungarian method [72,73]), which is a combinatorial optimization algorithm that gives solution to the bipartite graph matching problem in polynomial time. Although a larger data arrays would carry sizable storage overhead, it more than makes up for this with its comparative speed. Yet false trajectory of any mover can be resulted by using Hungarian method solely. The true trajectory of the mover can be resulted by using both Hungarian method and particle filter. The particle filter is a recursive process of prediction and update. It became an established technique to solve state space models. The Monte Carlo techniques behind particle filters existed since the 1950s [74] but those methods were overlooked due to the lack of computational power mainly. The particle filter computes the posterior recursively using Bayes filter. It works online to approximate the marginal distribution of the latent process as observations become available. Importance sampling is used at each time point to approximate the distribution with a set of discrete values, called particles, each with a corresponding weight. Importance sampling forms the basis for the sequential Monte Carlo methods used in particle filtering to solve recursion equation. Locations of particles, where weights have large values, are deemed to be the most locations of the movers. There are many papers and books (e.g., [75,76]) which provide detailed reviews of particle filters and their applications. However, we can use a combined tracking algorithm of Hungarian method and particle filter to get trajectory of each SVM recognized mover. The Fig. 7 depicts the tracking results of the movers recognized by polynomial kernel function and tracked by Hungarian method along with particle filter.

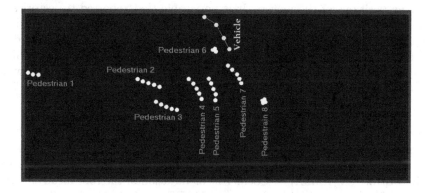

Fig. 7. Sample result of trajectories for movers in Fig. 6.

3   Experimental Results

3.1   Dataset and Parameters

To conduct our experiment, a total of 550 ground truth images were employed. Those images were obtained by the usage of both LMS-511 and LD-MRS. A total of 258 pedestrians and 292 vehicles were leveled. Randomly 25 pedestrians and 25 vehicles were selected for training and the rests for testing purposes. Polynomial kernel with order 3, Gaussian radial basis function kernel with a scaling factor of 1, and multilayer perceptron kernel with scale [1 1] were considered.

3.2   Functional and Nonfunctional Requirements

Functional requirements of our approach include: (i) It should produce the correct results; (ii) It should provide trajectories of pedestrians and vehicles; (iii) It may track other objects (e.g., aeroplanes, fishes [77], birds [71], and etc.); (iv) It may not track small insects or so on. Nonfunctional requirements include reliability, usability, maintainability, and supportability.

3.3   Accuracy of the Trajectories of Movers

In general, average quality of trajectories in Fig. 7 obtained by Hungarian method with particle filter is better than that of Galip et al. [50] or Sharif et al. [65]. Basically, Galip et al. [50] hinted a technique of how the type of blobs can be specified based on the right threshold values of the variables (e.g., speed, area, and frames). They assumed that those variables were interpreted according to the detection area and datasets. All blobs were classified as vehicle, pedestrian, and noise based on threshold values of area, velocity, and life-time. Sharif et al. [65] improved the proposed algorithm of Galip et al. [50] by removing estimation of thresholds with the help of SVM, Hungarian algorithm, and Kalman filter. Our current approach also removed the usage of thresholds concept of Galip et al. [50] by using SVM kernels to recognize movers. To remove the shortcomings of Kalman filter, the particle filter and Hungarian algorithm were used to estimate next true positions of the movers. It is noticeable that reported trajectories of movers using SVM with Hungarian method and particle filter are more accurate than those of SVM with Hungarian method and Kalman filter as implemented by Sharif et al. [65] or thresholds method with Hungarian method and Kalman filter as implemented by Galip et al. [50]. The numerical error study in the following subsection puts valid points to this observation.

3.4   Comparative Study of Errors

To come into possession of the knowledge of efficacy for our particle filter based approach, we performed several statistical measures, e.g., RMSE $\Rightarrow$ Root Mean Squared Error, CV(RMSE) $\Rightarrow$ Coefficient of variation of the root mean squared error, MAE $\Rightarrow$ Mean Absolute Error, and MAPE $\Rightarrow$ Mean Absolute Percentage Error. Their formulae are formulated in Eqs. 2 and 3 as:

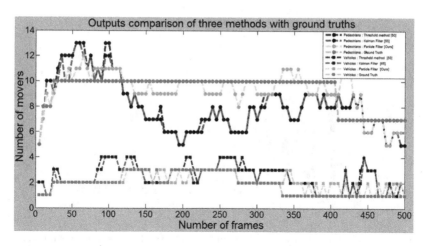

Fig. 8. Comparative study of ground truths and the outputs from three approaches to track movers using the same laser scanned dataset.

$$RMSE = \sqrt{\frac{\sum_{i=1}^{100}(G(i) - A(i))^2}{100}}; \quad CV(RMSE) = \frac{RMSE}{\frac{1}{100}\sum_{i=1}^{100}G(i)} \qquad (2)$$

$$MAE = \frac{1}{100}\sum_{i=1}^{100}|G(i) - A(i)|; \quad MAPE = \frac{1}{100}\sum_{i=1}^{100}\frac{|G(i) - A(i)|}{G(i)} \qquad (3)$$

where G, A, and i represent ground truth, algorithmic detection, and number of frame, respectively. Different statistical measures of data in Fig. 8 were listed in Table 3 as well as Fig. 9. These recorded results demonstrate that SVM and Hungarian method with particle filter outperform both the threshold based method of Galip et al. [50] and the Kalman filter based approach of Sharif et al. [65]. The methods of both Galip et al. [50] and Sharif et al. [65] reported identical errors for pedestrians' case. However, our particle filter implementation demonstrated much reduced error in both pedestrians (e.g., RMSE more than 50% less) and vehicles (e.g., RMSE more than 40% less). The qualities of our movers' trajectories are the best among those methods. In concise and succinct, the detailed error results suggest that our approach can robustly and efficiently provide the trajectories of movers from the laser scanned data points.

Table 3. Statistical measures deeming data in Fig. 8.

Movers	Three methods and their error estimations									
	Threshold method [50]				Kalman filter [65]				Particle filter [**Ours**]			
	RMSE	CV (RMSE)	MAE	MAPE	RMSE	CV (RMSE)	MAE	MAPE	RMSE	CV (RMSE)	MAE	MAPE
Pedestrians	2.3937	0.2568	2.0700	21.72%	2.3937	0.2568	2.0700	21.72%	1.1489	0.1233	0.8200	09.54%
Vehicles	1.0100	0.5316	0.7000	47.17%	0.7565	0.3915	0.5300	37.19%	0.5657	0.2977	0.2800	23.67%

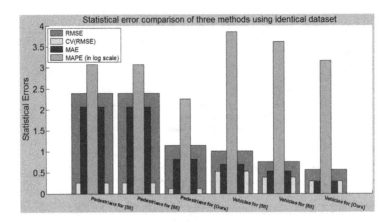

Fig. 9. Comparative error study of three methods to track movers using same dataset.

3.5 Our Finding

To track any object from laser scanned dataset, SVM and Hungarian method with either Kalman filter or particle filter can be used efficiently. But our finding on the same laser scanned dataset shows that the combined algorithm of SVM, Hungarian method, and particle filter works better than that of SVM with Hungarian method and Kalman filter or its alternative (e.g., instead of SVM - a threshold based method which uses Hungarian method and Kalman filter).

4 Conclusion

We evinced an efficient approach to get trajectories of movers from laser scanned datasets. Laser scanned data points from each scan were considered as a video frame. Blobs were extracted and then SVM with Hungarian method and particle filter were applied to get complete trajectories of movers. The results of SVM and Hungarian method with particle filter performed better than those of both threshold based approach with Hungarian method using Kalman filter and SVM with Hungarian method using Kalman filter by deeming same laser scanned dataset. Future study would decrease the error rates a bit further.

References

1. Sharif, M.H., Djeraba, C.: PedVed: pseudo euclidian distances for video events detection. In: Bebis, G., et al. (eds.) ISVC 2009. LNCS, vol. 5876, pp. 674–685. Springer, Heidelberg (2009). https://doi.org/10.1007/978-3-642-10520-3_64
2. Sharif, M.H.U., Uyaver, S., Sharif, M.H.: Ordinary video events detection. In: CompIMAGE, pp. 19–24 (2012)
3. Ihaddadene, N., Sharif, M.H., Djeraba, C.: Crowd behaviour monitoring. In: International Conference on Multimedia, pp. 1013–1014 (2008)

4. Mahmoudi, S.A., Sharif, M.H., Ihaddadene, N., Djeraba, C.: Abnormal event detection in real time video. In: International Workshop on Multimodal Interactions Analysis of Users in a Controlled Environment, ICMI, pp. 1–4 (2008)
5. Sharif, M.H., Djeraba, C.: A simple method for eccentric event espial using mahalanobis metric. In: Bayro-Corrochano, E., Eklundh, J.-O. (eds.) CIARP 2009. LNCS, vol. 5856, pp. 417–424. Springer, Heidelberg (2009). https://doi.org/10.1007/978-3-642-10268-4_48
6. Sharif, M.H., Djeraba, C.: Exceptional motion frames detection by means of spatiotemporal region of interest features. In: ICIP, pp. 981–984 (2009)
7. Sharif, M.H., Uyaver, S., Djeraba, C.: Crowd behavior surveillance using Bhattacharyya distance metric. In: Barneva, R.P., Brimkov, V.E., Hauptman, H.A., Natal Jorge, R.M., Tavares, J.M.R.S. (eds.) CompIMAGE 2010. LNCS, vol. 6026, pp. 311–323. Springer, Heidelberg (2010). https://doi.org/10.1007/978-3-642-12712-0_28
8. Sharif, M.H., Ihaddadene, N., Djeraba, C.: Finding and indexing of eccentric events in video emanates. J. Multimedia 5(1), 22–35 (2010)
9. Sharif, M.H., Djeraba, C.: An entropy approach for abnormal activities detection in video streams. Pattern Recogn. 45(7), 2543–2561 (2012)
10. Surmann, H., Nuchter, A., Hertzberg, J.: An autonomous mobile robot with a 3D laser range finder for 3D exploration and digitalization of indoor environments. Robot. Auton. Syst. 45(3), 181–198 (2003)
11. Wang, C.C., Thorpe, C., Suppe, A.: Ladar-based detection and tracking of moving objects from a ground vehicle at high speeds. In: Intelligent Vehicles Symposium, pp. 416–421 (2003)
12. Mendes, A., Nunes, U.: Situation-based multi-target detection and tracking with laser scanner in outdoor semi-structured environment. In: IEEE/RSJ International Conference on Intelligent Robots and Systems (IROS), pp. 88–93 (2004)
13. Vosselman, G., Gorte, B.G., Sithole, G., Rabbani, T.: Recognising structure in laser scanner point clouds. Int. Arch. photogramm. Remote Sens. Spat. Inf. Sci. 46(8), 33–38 (2004)
14. Nakamura, K., Zhao, H., Shibasaki, R., Sakamoto, K., Ooga, T., Suzukawa, N.: Tracking pedestrians by using multiple laser range scanners. In: International Society for Photogrammetry and Remote Sensing (ISPRS) Congress, vol. 35, B4, pp. 1260–1265 (2004)
15. Topp, E., Christensen, H.: Tracking for following and passing persons. In: IEEE/RSJ IROS, pp. 2321–2327 (2005)
16. Xavier, J., Pacheco, M., Castro, D., Ruano, A., Nunes, U.: Fast line, arc/circle and leg detection from laser scan data in a player driver. In: ICRA, pp. 3930–3935 (2005)
17. Zhao, H., Shibasaki, R.: A novel system for tracking pedestrians using multiple single-row laser-range scanners. IEEE Trans. Syst. Man Cybern. Part A Syst. Hum. 35(2), 283–291 (2005)
18. Cui, J., Zha, H., Zhao, H., Shibasaki, R.: Robust tracking of multiple people in crowds using laser range scanners. In: ICPR, pp. 857–860 (2006)
19. Zhao, H., Shao, X., Katabira, K., Shibasaki, R.: Joint tracking and classification of moving objects at intersection using a single-row laser range scanner. In: Intelligent Transportation Systems Conference (ITSC), pp. 287–294 (2006)
20. Serment, L.E.N., Mertz, C., Hebert, M.: Predictive mover detection and tracking in cluttered environments. In: Army Science Conference (ASC) (2006)
21. Arras, K., Mozos, O., Burgard, W.: Using boosted features for the detection of people in 2D range data. In: ICRA, pp. 3402–3407 (2007)

22. Shao, X., Zhao, H., Nakamura, K., Katabira, K., Shibasaki, R., Nakagawa, Y.: Detection and tracking of multiple pedestrians by using laser range scanners. In: IEEE/RSJ IROS, pp. 2174–2179 (2007)

23. Cui, J., Zha, H., Zhao, H., Shibasaki, R.: Laser-based detection and tracking of multiple people in crowds. CVIU **106**(2–3), 300–312 (2007)

24. Zhao, H., Chiba, M., Shibasaki, R., Shao, X., Cui, J., Zha, H.: A laser-scanner-based approach toward driving safety and traffic data collection. Trans. Intell. Transp. **10**(3), 534–546 (2009)

25. Arras, K., Grzonka, S., Luber, M., Burgard, W.: Efficient people tracking in laser range data using a multi-hypothesis leg-tracker with adaptive occlusion probabilities. In: ICRA, pp. 1710–1715 (2008)

26. Song, X., Cui, J., Wang, X., Zhao, H., Zha, H.: Tracking interacting targets with laser scanner via on-line supervised learning. In: ICRA, pp. 2271–2276 (2008)

27. Vu, T.D., Aycard, O.: Laser-based detection and tracking moving objects using data-driven Markov chain Monte Carlo. In: ICRA, pp. 3800–3806 (2009)

28. Gate, G., Nashashibi, F.: Fast algorithm for pedestrian and group of pedestrians detection using a laser scanner. In: Intelligent Vehicles Symposium, pp. 1322–1327 (2009)

29. Gidel, S., Blanc, C., Chateau, T., Checchin, P., Trassoudaine, L.: A method based on multilayer laser scanner to detect and track pedestrians in urban environment. In: Intelligent Vehicles Symposium, pp. 157–162 (2009)

30. Mozos, O., Kurazume, R., Hasegawa, T.: Multi-part people detection using 2D range data. Int. J. Soc. Robot. **2**(1), 31–40 (2010)

31. Musleh, B., Garcia, F., Otamendi, J., Armingol, J.M., de la Escalera, A.: Identifying and tracking pedestrians based on sensor fusion and motion stability predictions. Sensors **10**(9), 8028–8053 (2010)

32. Gidel, S., Checchin, P., Blanc, C., Chateau, T., Trassoudaine, L.: Pedestrian detection and tracking in an urban environment using a multilayer laser scanner. Trans. Intell. Transp. **11**(3), 579–588 (2010)

33. Shao, X., Zhao, H., Shibasaki, R., Shi, Y., Sakamoto, K.: 3D crowd surveillance and analysis using laser range scanners. In: IEEE/RSJ IROS, pp. 2036–2043 (2011)

34. Fu, G., Corradi, P., Menciassi, A., Dario, P.: An integrated triangulation laser scanner for obstacle detection of miniature mobile robots in indoor environment. IEEE/ASME Trans. Mechatron. **16**(4), 778–783 (2011)

35. Song, X., Shao, X., Shibasaki, R., Zhao, H., Cui, J., Zha, H.: A novel laser-based system: fully online detection of abnormal activity via an unsupervised method. In: ICRA, pp. 1317–1322 (2011)

36. Zhao, H., Wang, C., Yao, W., Davoine, F., Cui, J., Zha, H.: Omni-directional detection and tracking of on-road vehicles using multiple horizontal laser scanners. In: Intelligent Vehicles Symposium, pp. 57–62 (2012)

37. Garcia, F., et al.: Environment perception based on LIDAR sensors for real road applications. Robotica **30**(2), 185–193 (2012)

38. Song, X., Shao, X., Zhang, Q., Shibasaki, R., Zhao, H., Zha, H.: Laser-based intelligent surveillance and abnormality detection in extremely crowded scenarios. In: ICRA, pp. 2170–2176 (2012)

39. Fotiadis, E.P., Garzon, M., Barrientos, A.: Human detection from a mobile robot using fusion of laser and vision information. Sensors **13**(9), 11603–11635 (2013)

40. Song, X., Shao, X., Zhang, Q., Shibasaki, R., Zhao, H., Zha, H.: A novel dynamic model for multiple pedestrians tracking in extremely crowded scenarios. Inf. Fus. **14**, 301–310 (2013)

41. Wada, Y., Higuchi, T., Yamaguchi, H., Higashino, T.: Accurate positioning of mobile phones in a crowd using laser range scanners. In: International Conference on Wireless and Mobile Computing, Networking and Communications, pp. 430–435 (2013)

42. Akamatsu, S., Shimaji, N., Tomizawa, T.: Development of a person counting system using a 3D laser scanner. In: ROBIO, pp. 1983–1988 (2014)

43. Adiaviakoye, L., Patrick, P., Marc, B., Auberlet, J.M.: Tracking of multiple people in crowds using laser range scanners. In: International Conference on Intelligent Sensors, Sensor Networks and Information Processing (ISSNIP), pp. 1–6 (2014)

44. Kim, B., Choi, B., Yoo, M., Kim, H., Kim, E.: Robust object segmentation using a multi-layer laser scanner. Sensors **14**(11), 20400–20418 (2014)

45. Kaneko, H., Osaragi, T.: Method for detecting sitting-and-moving behaviors and face-to-face communication using laser scanners. Procedia Environ. Sci. **22**, 313–324 (2014)

46. Leigh, A., Pineau, J., Olmedo, N., Zhang, H.: Person tracking and following with 2D laser scanners. In: ICRA, pp. 726–733 (2015)

47. Kim, S., Kim, H., Yoo, W., Huh, K.: Sensor fusion algorithm design in detecting vehicles using laser scanner and stereo vision. Trans. Intell. Transp. **17**(14), 1072–1084 (2015)

48. Shalal, N., Low, T., McCarthy, C., Hancock, N.: Orchard mapping and mobile robot localisation using on-board camera and laser scanner data fusion-Part B: mapping and localisation. Comput. Electron. Agric. **119**, 267–278 (2015)

49. Hashimoto, M., Tsuji, A., Nishio, A., Takahashi, K.: Laser-based tracking of groups of people with sudden changes in motion. In: IEEE ICIT, pp. 315–320 (2015)

50. Galip, F., et al.: A novel approach to obtain trajectories of targets from laser scanned datasets. In: International Conference on Computer and Information Technology (ICCIT), pp. 231–236 (2015)

51. Weinrich, C., Wengefeld, T., Volkhardt, M., Scheidig, A., Gross, H.-M.: Generic distance-invariant features for detecting people with walking aid in 2D laser range data. In: Menegatti, E., Michael, N., Berns, K., Yamaguchi, H. (eds.) Intelligent Autonomous Systems 13. AISC, vol. 302, pp. 735–747. Springer, Cham (2016). https://doi.org/10.1007/978-3-319-08338-4_53

52. Galip, F., Sharif, M.H., Caputcu, M., Uyaver, S.: Recognition of object from laser scanned data points using SVM. In: ICMIP, pp. 231–236 (2015)

53. Kim, S., Kim, H., Yoo, W., Huh, K.: Sensor fusion algorithm design in detecting vehicles using laser scanner and stereo vision. IEEE Trans. Intell. Transp. Syst. **17**(4), 1072–1084 (2016)

54. Tsugita, R., Nishino, N., Chugo, D., Muramatsu, S., Yokota, S., Hashimoto, H.: Pedestrian detection and tracking of a mobile robot with multiple 2D laser range scanners. In: International Conference on HSI, pp. 412–417 (2016)

55. Zou, C., He, B., Zhang, L., Zhang, J.: Dynamic objects detection and tracking for a laser scanner and camera system. In: ROBIO, pp. 350–354 (2017)

56. Liu, K., Wang, W.: Pedestrian detection on the slope using multi-layer laser scanner. In: International Conference on Information Fusion (FUSION), pp. 1–7 (2017)

57. Zhang, X., Xu, W., Dong, C., Dolan, J.M.: Efficient L-shape fitting for vehicle detection using laser scanners. In: Intelligent Vehicles Symposium, pp. 54–59 (2017)

58. Ishi, Y., Kawakami, T., Yoshihisa, T., Teranishi, Y., Shimojo, S.: A system design for detecting moving objects in capturing video images using laser range scanners. In: Barolli, L., Enokido, T., Takizawa, M. (eds.) NBiS 2017. LNDECT, vol. 7, pp. 1027–1036. Springer, Cham (2018). https://doi.org/10.1007/978-3-319-65521-5_94

59. Zou, C., He, B., Zhang, L., Zhang, J.: Static map reconstruction and dynamic object tracking for a camera and laser scanner system. IET Comput. Vis. **12**(4), 384–392 (2018)
60. Kim, D., Jo, K., Lee, M., Sunwoo, M.: L-shape model switching-based precise motion tracking of moving vehicles using laser scanners. IEEE Trans. Intell. Transp. Syst. **19**(2), 598–612 (2018)
61. Gizlenmistir, Y.: Production of airborne laser scanner skilled advanced unmanned air vehicle and the potential of preliminary data. In: Signal Processing and Communications Applications Conference, Izmir, Turkey, pp. 1–4 (2018)
62. Zeng, J., Che, J., Xing, C., Zhang, L.-J.: A two-stage Bi-LSTM model for chinese company name recognition. In: Aiello, M., Yang, Y., Zou, Y., Zhang, L.-J. (eds.) AIMS 2018. LNCS, vol. 10970, pp. 3–15. Springer, Cham (2018). https://doi.org/10.1007/978-3-319-94361-9_1
63. Halmheu, R., Otto, B., Hegel, J.: Layout optimization of a system for successive laser scanner detection and control of mobile robots. Robot. Auton. Syst. **101**, 103–113 (2018)
64. Urano, K., Hiroi, K., Kato, S., Komagata, N., Kawaguchi, N.: Road surface condition inspection using a laser scanner mounted on an autonomous driving car. In: International Conference on Pervasive Computing and Communications Workshops, pp. 826–831 (2019)
65. Sharif, M.H., Shehu, H., Galip, F., Ince, I.F., Kusetogullari, H.: Object tracking from laser scanned dataset. Int. J. Comput. Sci. Eng. Tech. **3**(6), 19–27 (2019)
66. Sick, A.G.: LMS5xx laser measurement sensors : Operating instructions (2015). https://www.sick.com/media/pdf/4/14/514/IM0037514.PDF
67. Aizerman, M.A., Braverman, E.M., Rozoner, L.I.: Theoretical foundations of the potential function method in pattern recognition learning. Autom. Remote Control **25**, 821–837 (1964)
68. Rahman, Q.I., Schmeisser, G.: Characterization of the speed of convergence of the trapezoidal rule. Numer. Math. **57**(1), 123–138 (1990)
69. Sharif, M.H.: An eigenvalue approach to detect flows and events in crowd videos. J. Circuits Syst. Comput. **26**(07), 1750110 (2017)
70. Sharif, M.H.: High-performance mathematical functions for single-core architectures. J. Circuits Syst. Comput. **23**(04), 1450051 (2014)
71. Sharif, M.: A numerical approach for tracking unknown number of individual targets in videos. Digit. Signal Proc. **57**, 106–127 (2016)
72. Kuhn, H.: The Hungarian method for the assignment problem. Naval Res. Logist. **2**, 83–97 (1955)
73. Munkres, J.: Algorithms for the assignment and transportation problems. J. Soc. Ind. Appl. Math. **5**, 32–38 (1957)
74. Hammersley, J.M., Morton, K.W.: Poor man's Monte Carlo. J. Roy. Stat. Soc. **16**(1), 23–38 (1954)
75. Doucet, A., Godsill, S., Andrieu, C.: On sequential Monte Carlo sampling methods for Bayesian filtering. Stat. Comput. **10**(3), 197–208 (2000)
76. Ristic, B., Arulampalam, S., Gordon, N.: Beyond the Kalman filter: Particle filters for tracking applications. Artech House, Norwood (2004)
77. Sharif, M.H., Galip, F., Guler, A., Uyaver, S.: A simple approach to count and track underwater fishes from videos. In: International Conference on Computer and Information Technology (ICCIT), pp. 347–352 (2015)

Video Steganography Using 3D Convolutional Neural Networks

Mahdi Abdolmohammadi[1], Rahil Mahdian Toroghi[1(✉)], and Azam Bastanfard[2]

[1] Iran Broadcasting University (IRIBU), Tehran, Iran
mahdiabdolmohammadi@yahoo.com, mahdian.t.r@gmail.com
[2] Department of Computer Engineering, Karaj Branch,
Islamic Azad University, Tehran, Iran
azambastanfard1396@gmail.com

Abstract. In an steganography we intend to hide information of interest in another data, aiming at secure data transaction, such as hiding an image in another image. The same task could be performed in video steganography. One approach to steganography is through manipulating *least significant bits (LSB)*. Increasing the precision of the approaches in this regard, is still challenging and desired. The attention toward the sequence of video frames is an important issue which affects the accuracy of these methods. In this paper, a 3D convolutional neural network has been employed for the first time, to our knowledge, to perform video steganography. The incentive of exploiting the spatial and temporal features together, pushed us toward using this approach. Implementing the proposed method over the UCF101 dataset, lead to 22.75 bits per pixel improvement and output video frame enhancement level of 1 dB compared to the LSB, on average, respectively.

Keywords: Video steganography · 3D CNN · Spatio-temporal features

1 Introduction

There are techniques such as cryptography, or steganography, in order to prevent the digital multimedia information (e.g., Audio or video files) from illegal copying or unauthorized transactions [7,9].

Cryptography is implemented in an end-to-end fashion, between the transmitter and the receiver, with no capability of further security over data in the middle of this path. On the other hand, in steganography we have the ability to encrypt a data and hide it inside another data hierarchically, such that multiple layers of encryptions makes it difficult for the original information be decrypted through eavesdropping. When there is a video information hidden in a host video file, the process is called **video steganography**. In an ideal steganography the hidden or secret video message has to have no distortion or bad impact on the cover or host video [1,4]. A complete process of hiding and recovering the video message in a host video is depicted in Fig. 1.

C. Djeddi et al. (Eds.): MedPRAI 2019, CCIS 1144, pp. 149–161, 2020.
https://doi.org/10.1007/978-3-030-37548-5_12

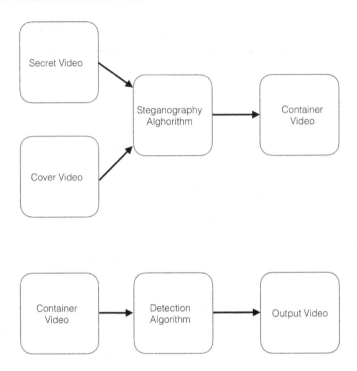

Fig. 1. The general steganography architecture; (Up)-Hiding structure vs. (Down)-Detection (Uncovering) structure

1.1   Background Works on Steganography

The most common techniques of steganography include the Least Significant Bits (LSB) manipulation, in order to hide the information inside the host [2]. A highly undetectable steganography uses weights for local pixels to calculate the distortion and to reduce the cost of distortion along the edges of the image and image textures. Wavelet obtained weights, which are obtained by applying directional filterbanks in order to penalize the distortion of predictable parts of the images, are similar to wavelet coefficients, however they are apt for the placement in an arbitrary region in the image [4].

In JPEG-Steganography the message is hidden in the quantized DCT components. Another method is to use Genetic algorithm along with a two-layered neural network aiming to extract the DCT components again [3,5]. These are conventional methods in this regard. However, the most prevalent method so far, is the LSB method, which tries to posit the message bits in the least significant parts at each byte of the image data. In three-bits and four-bits methods of LSB, the three or four least significant bits of the host are replaced with the three or four most significant bits of the message, respectively. As a consequence, the color bit depth and its quality is degraded. This type of steganography is not sensible by human eyes, since the dynamic of the changes in the image is so small.

The advantage of using the LSB technique is its simplicity, and low possibility of being identified [2]. Contrary to the image steganography, in video-based applications there are more issues to be taken care of. The extraction of the video content, during the movement of the camera and changing of the background images gets more difficult over time. This is one point that has been made the video steganography inefficient thus far, compared to the image steganography. Due to this fact, the extraction of temporal features out of the video, which contain further information about the video, seems very crucial [6]. Employing these temporal and spatial features together, which is contrary to the existed solutions, is the main novelty of this paper.

2 The Proposed Technique

Here, we propose to extract the temporal features as well as the spatial features out of the video frames, and use them in the process of steganography in order to achieve better results. These features are decided to be extracted using a designed 3-dimensional convolutional neural network (3D CNN).

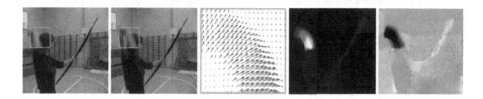

Fig. 2. Temporal features, optical flow and dynamic directions [8]

2.1 3D Convolutional Neural Network

In 3D CNN, a combination of spatial and temporal information are used to learn the movement. As it is shown in Fig. 3, the kernel in 3D CNN is a 3D cube, which considers the local spatial areas in adjacent frames of data. The 3D convolution has the following equation,

$$y_{xyt} = f\left(\sum_{i}\sum_{j}\sum_{k} w_{ijk} v_{(x+i)(y+j)(t+k)} + b\right) \tag{1}$$

where y_{xyt} is the feature-map over x, y and t, f is the activation function, w_{ijk} is a kernel weight, and $v_{(x+i)(y+j)(t+k)}$ is an input value. Therefore, every scalar in a feature-map contains information from different frames within that specific region [6].

Previous layer   Kernel   Feature map

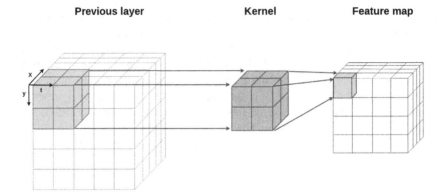

Fig. 3. A Conv3D layer: (left) - previous layer, (middle) - a $(2 \times 2 \times 2)$ kernel, (right) - The feature map (convolution output)layer. (x, y) are the locations; t is the frame-time [6]

2.2 The Proposed Steganography Model

The proposed model consists of three different networks: (1) Preparation network, (2) Hiding network, and (3) Detector network. The block diagrams of how they are bundled in the entire steganography and detection process are depicted in Figs. 4 and 5.

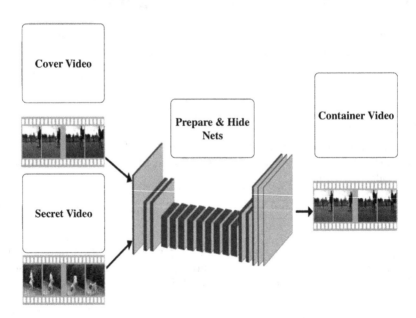

Fig. 4. The preparation, and hiding networks blocks

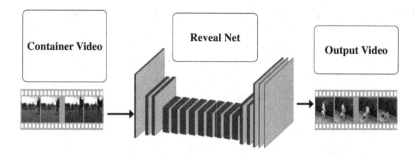

Fig. 5. Detection network block

Preparation Network. As already mentioned, the goal of steganography is to hide the secret video inside a cover video. Therefore, these two videos are to be fed into the preparation network with the same frame numbers and dimensions. Frames are as 3-dimensional matrices, since every colored pixel contains three color depths based upon the red, green, and blue colors. Therefore, one dimension contains three numbers associated to the colors, and two other dimensions contain the $x - y$ dimensions (i.e, the number of pixels in length and width of the frame). However, the network input is four-dimensional, in which the fourth dimension is the number of the input frames given to this network, and are determined based on the number of frames in the video.

Architecturally, the preparation network incorporates two 3D-convolutional layers, followed by a nonlinear ReLU activation function. All the necessary information, including the dimensions of the kernels, stride size and zero-padding status of this network is depicted in Table 1.

The task of the preparation network is to create the feature-map which contains the spatial and temporal information of the video frames. In the preparation network, from both secret and cover video with the input dimension 3, is given to the network and a 64 dimension feature-map is created from each, to be fed to the hiding network. These are concatenated to create a 128-dimension feature-map, half of which belongs to the secret video and half belongs to the cover one. The number of the layers represents the model complexity and has been determined through a trade-off policy between the bias and variance of the true error with respect to the training error, as usually performed in machine learning algorithms.

Hiding Network. In this network, after every convolutional layer, there would be a 3D batch-normalization layer, followed by a nonlinear ReLU activation function, except for the last layer which contains none of the two layers mentioned above, and instead uses a *Tanh* nonlinear activation function. The sixth row in Table 1, denotes a *ConvTransposed3D*, which differs from *Conv3D* in the sense that there is no dimensionality reduction over the frame size or frame number, due to the 3-dimensional kernels.

Table 1. The design **parameters** of the **networks**: rows (1, 2): **Preparation** network, (3–8): **Hiding** network, (9–14: **Detection** network)

Number	Layer	Kernel Size	Stride	Padding	Input depth	Output depth
1	Conv3d	(3, 3, 3)	(1, 1, 1)	(1, 1, 1)	3	64
2	Conv3d	(3, 4, 4)	(1, 2, 2)	(1, 1, 1)	64	64
3	deConv3d	(1, 1, 1)	(1, 1, 1)	(0, 0, 0)	128	64
4	deConv3d	(3, 3, 3)	(1, 1, 1)	(1, 1, 1)	64	64
5	deConv3d	(3, 3, 3)	(1, 1, 1)	(1, 1, 1)	64	32
6	ConvTr3d	(3, 4, 4)	(1, 2, 2)	(1, 1, 1)	32	32
7	deConv3d	(3, 3, 3)	(1, 1, 1)	(1, 1, 1)	32	16
8	deConv3d	(3, 3, 3)	(1, 1, 1)	(1, 1, 1)	16	3
9	Conv3d	(3, 3, 3)	(1, 1, 1)	(1, 1, 1)	3	32
10	Conv3d	(3, 3, 3)	(1, 1, 1)	(1, 1, 1)	32	32
11	Conv3d	(3, 3, 3)	(1, 1, 1)	(1, 1, 1)	32	64
12	deConv3d	(3, 3, 3)	(1, 1, 1)	(1, 1, 1)	64	32
13	deConv3d	(3, 3, 3)	(1, 1, 1)	(1, 1, 1)	32	16
14	deConv3d	(3, 3, 3)	(1, 1, 1)	(1, 1, 1)	16	3

The output of this network is a four-dimensional tensor with the same dimensions and frame numbers as of the input-frame data of the message and the host videos. The output video of this stage is called *container*. This video is pretty much similar to the host video, but also carries the message video in an insensible way. Figure 4, depicts the two networks at the same time.

Detection Network. The secretly merged video is fed to the detection network, in order to extract the spatial and temporal information of the message video out of that, and reconstruct an output with the maximum similarity to the message (secret) video and minimum possible distortion. The practical setting of this network is depicted in Table 1, as well. In this network, all the 3D convolution layers, except for the first and the last ones, are completely the same. Moreover, After every convolution layer, except for the last one, there is a batch normalization and ReLU activation layer. The last layer contains a *Tanh* activation, instead.

3 Experimental Study

The dataset being used in this study is **UCF101**[1], which is commonly used in steganography application. This dataset contains 101 video categories, including 13320 video clips, and one human action in each category. This dataset has been

---

[1] www.crcv.ucf.edu/data/UCF101.

provided by the computer vision research center, and is used as a benchmark for the human action recognition applications. The major human activities included in this dataset, are sport activities, music playing with different instruments, body movements, and human-human interactions. These videos are taken from youtube, and each class contains about 100 videos. Video clips have 30 frames per second, with 320×240 resolution. Videos of each class are grouped into divisions from the main video. Moreover, the videos are divided into training (90% of the data) and testing video datasets. This dataset is prevalently used for training the deep neural networks in related applications, as what it is considered in this study. The only preprocessing performed to this dataset is the conversion into matrices and normalization, as usual.

The conversion of the training data, 16 frames with 8 frames per second taken from each video, has been performed using **FFMPEG** software. This concluded 170496 frames out of 10656 videos from this dataset (i.e., training data part), which has been converted into 64×64 frame-sizes. For more robust and efficient models during training, we learned the three networks using the **jpeg** format, since it has less redundancy compared to **png**, therefore the models are to be trained in more difficult conditions.

During the training, each of the videos are randomly chosen to be a message or a cover video. Training has been performed by 16 frames, however during the test, any frames with any size could be given. The cost function being used as the similarity measure between the message data and the output video, also the container and the cover video is the least square error function.

Training of both networks are performed simultaneous and therefore the cost function to be minimized is as follows:

$$\text{cost} = \alpha \sum_{\substack{i \in M \\ j \in N}} (O_{ij} - S_{ij})^2 + \sum_{\substack{i \in M \\ j \in N}} (Co_{ij} - Cv_{ij})^2 \qquad (2)$$

where α is a trade-off coefficient between the quality of the output video (denoted by O) and the container video which contains a combination of the message or secret video (denoted by S), and the cover video. This parameter has been set to 1.05 during the training, in order to give vantage to the message video quality with respect to the container. Co, and Cv, denote the container video frames, and cover video frames, respectively. M and N are dimensions of the video frames (e.g., 64×64 in our examples).

The learning rate for the training set is fixed, and is equal to 0.0001. The cost function is the summation of two convex functions and therefore is convex, as well. The batch size being used, is 64. The optimizer has been AdamW, with weightdecay rate of 0.0001. Number of epochs has been 120, and the GPU being used has been Tesla K80.

The entire time being spend for the complete hiding and detecting cycle did not take more than two seconds. Therefore, its implementation would be reasonably fast, however still considerably slower than the LSB method.

3.1   Evaluation

The main measure to evaluate the performance of the steganography algorithm, is the peak signal-to-noise- ratio (**PSNR**). further, the empirical evaluation has been performed in this study. Moreover, we need to evaluate the performance of the hiding network and the detection network, in the sense that how much message video is portable inside the cover video, and evaluate the distortions of the output of the detection network with respect to the cover video. For the latter evaluation, there are measures such as **capacity, decoding rate**, and **security** measures which could be used, as well.

Capacity. The difference between the pixels of message video and their corresponding pixels of output video over the total number of frames included in each of them, gives us the rate of differences. The decoding rate would be then,

$$DecodedRate = 1 - \frac{\sum\limits_{i=1}^{N} \sum\limits_{j=1}^{M} |S_{i,j} - O_{i,j}|^2}{N \times M} \tag{3}$$

Based upon the decoding rate, the capacity measure (Bits per Pixel) is then calculated as follows,

$$Capacity = DecodedRate \times 8 \times 3 \quad (bpp) \tag{4}$$

where 8 denotes the color bits and 3 denotes the RGB colors [7].

Cover Changing Rate. This measure shows the changing rate of the output of the detection network, with respect to the cover video, and is calculated as,

$$CoverChangingRate = \frac{\sum\limits_{i=1}^{N} \sum\limits_{j=1}^{M} |C_{i,j} - Co_{i,j}|^2}{N \times M} \tag{5}$$

where $C_{i,j}$, and $Co_{i,j}$ represent the pixels of the frames belonging to the cover video, and the container, respectively [7]. Now, to represent the security and indiscoverability of the message-video from the cover-video the PSNR measure is calculated as follows,

$$PSNR_s = 20 \, log_{10}(\frac{255}{\sqrt{MSE_s}}) \tag{6}$$

$$PSNR_c = 20 \, log_{10}(\frac{255}{\sqrt{MSE_c}}) \tag{7}$$

where MSE_s is the mean of the pixel-wise differences between the output video frame and the associated input message or secret video frame. Accordingly, the MSE_c denotes the pixel-wise differences between the container video frame and the input cover video frame. Further, the $PSNR_s$, and $PSNR_c$ denote the corresponding PSNR values for the associated MSE values.

Secret Video

Output Video

Cover Video

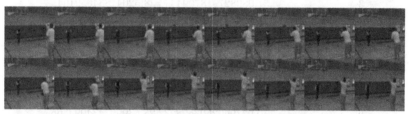

Container Video

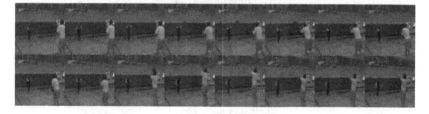

Fig. 6. A complete set of input and output videos, for 3-bits **LSB**-based steganography; Secret video (the top video) has been hidden in the cover video (3rd from top), and the output video (2nd from top) is extracted from the detection algorithm, which uses the container video (the bottom video). 16 video frames has been depicted in this image, for every input and output, started from left-2-right and top-2-bottom.

3.2   Analysis of the Results

The results of the 3D CNN based steganography is comparable with the LSB method, from three aspects [4]. One, is the security aspect which could be evaluated through the *PSNR* measure. The second, are the *capacity*, and *cover changing rate* which could be measured as in Eqs. (4, 3 and 5). The third aspect is resistance against compression. For the latter, the containers̓ video have been compressed using H.264 codec, and the output video has been extracted from this container using the detection network. The third evaluation is not mentioned explicitly in this paper, however it has been consistently more resistive against compression for the 3D CNN compared to the LSB method, just to mention. All the implementations have been performed on UCF101 dataset, in a Python framework. 90% of the dataset has been used for training and the rest for testing. There is a random examples selected from the experimental data, in order to visualize the analytics. For this sample, the incorporated videos associated to the LSB-based and 3D CNN-based steganography are depicted in Figs. 6 and 7.

Table 2. The comparison of PSNRc for the **output** video frames and the **secret** video frames, for both 3-bits LSB, and 3D CNN methods, for all 16 video frames.

Nth frame\PSNR	3DCNN	LSB
1	30.638893736958824	28.532431218967233
2	31.02065124425294	28.552757902583327
3	31.08982791870944	28.52041834659194
4	31.02376684532728	28.507540401530814
5	31.05879710676763	28.53269872176923
6	31.10064115214676	28.565548160749657
7	31.09369269086198	28.504484796713683
8	31.01157853537992	28.526170932969343
9	30.977960260352823	28.539997434993865
10	31.171968439954764	28.54723452497087
11	31.153895336684407	28.537679608483224
12	31.121243878660437	28.55582038919931
13	30.959773410342116	28.570715504585692
14	30.908264076162077	28.545865471504342
15	30.959766630809575	28.51321804934141
16	30.80643406223134	28.54389821293804

The resulting table of PSNR calculations for both the LSB, and 3D CNN methods are also depicted in Tables 2, and 3.

By looking at the test dataset samples individually, we could realize that there are small portion of samples which achieve almost the same PSNRs for both methods, while for most of the data the 3D CNN approach outperforms the LSB method. For those trivial portion, we noticed that the density of the background pixels which are stationary over the course of the video frames are much higher than the other samples. This logically justifies why the results of the two methods are so close, for these cases.

Table 3. The comparison of PSNRs for the **container** video frames and the **cover** video frames, for both 3-bits LSB, and 3D CNN methods, for all 16 video frames.

Nth frame\PSNR	3DCNN	LSB
1	33.501135917989615	32.62392294739592
2	33.569773788969066	32.658270018311285
3	33.92074195021714	32.74147087522151
4	33.894558820066095	32.77190455925922
5	34.04488213106164	32.72442991907823
6	33.87305174507063	32.91058113041708
7	34.003188530161204	33.03540296609264
8	33.981559520818834	32.943362171723415
9	33.949161463811166	32.87528388252188
10	34.066552335925124	32.95417628026732
11	34.14500409198443	32.94829966755184
12	34.08163443165856	32.96692193623409
13	33.65150519284155	32.974580854444724
14	34.01973842099307	33.0068510041905
15	33.79073930152109	32.97037808772147
16	33.86014291343581	33.02172473224963

Table 4. The results of capacity and cover changing rate, for 3D CNN method, for the same test sample of dataset, which was already evaluated, by PSNRs.

Decoded rate	Capacity(bpp)	Cover changing rate
0.956428	22.9542	0.018096

Table 5. The results of capacity and cover changing rate, for LSB method, for the same test sample of dataset, which was already evaluated, by PSNRs.

Capacity(bpp)	Cover changing rate
9	0.018166

The evaluation of methods are further performed from the capacity aspect. For this case, the previously mentioned example of the dataset is selected. The results of the capacity measure, is consistent with the security measure, and the resistance measure, as well these results are depicted in Tables 4, and 5.

Secret Video

Output Video

Cover Video

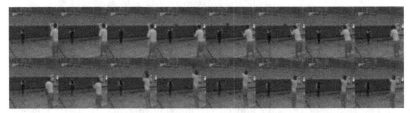

Container Video

Fig. 7. A complete set of input and output videos, for **3D CNN**-based steganography; Secret video (the top video) has been hidden in the cover video (3rd from top), and the output video (2nd from top) is extracted from the detection algorithm, which uses the container video (the bottom video). 16 video frames has been depicted in this image, for every input and output, started from left-2-right and top-2-bottom.

4   Conclusion

In this paper the problem of video steganography has been addressed using a 3-dimensional convolutional neural network (3D CNN). The entire process has been implemented in two phases, using three neural networks. The message or secret video is to be merged with the cover video first in the hiding phase. The output is called a container video. The container is then given to a detection network (again a 3D CNN) to recover the message video, exactly similar to the secret video message, as much as it would be possible. The proposed method has been compared in three different evaluation aspects with the state-of-the-art Least Significant Bits (LSB) technique. These aspects represent the security, the capacity, and the robustness of the algorithms using different measures for each case. Through the experiments, it was clearly shown that the proposed 3D CNN-based method could consistently outperform the LSB method over the UCF101 dataset. It is strongly recommended to use a richer dataset such as **KINETICS-600** dataset, to perform a more improved training of the networks.

References

1. Baluja, S.: Hiding images in plain sight: deep steganography. In: Advances in Neural Information Processing Systems, pp. 2069–2079 (2017)
2. Deshmukh, P., Rahangdale, B.: Hash based least significant bit technique for video steganography. Int. J. Eng. Res. Appl. **4**(1), 44–49 (2014)
3. Goyal, H., Bansal, P.: Video steganography using neural network and genetic algorithm. Int. J. Emerg. Technol. Innov. Eng. **1**(9) (2015)
4. Liu, Y., Liu, S., Wang, Y., Zhao, H., Liu, S.: Video steganography: a review. Neurocomputing **335**, 238–250 (2019)
5. Pathak, N., Disa, R., Saroni, S., Kumar Dash, U., Jyoti, A.: A survey on video steganography using genetic algorithm and artificial neural network, pp. 56–58, June 2016 (2016)
6. Teivas, I.T.: Video event classification using 3D convolutional neural networks (2017)
7. Wu, P., Yang, Y., Li, X.: StegNet: mega image steganography capacity with deep convolutional network. Future Internet **10**(6), 54 (2018)
8. Wu, Z., Yao, T., Fu, Y., Jiang, Y.G.: Deep learning for video classification and captioning. arXiv preprint arXiv:1609.06782 (2016)
9. Zhu, J., Kaplan, R., Johnson, J., Fei-Fei, L.: HiDDeN: hiding data with deep networks. In: Ferrari, V., Hebert, M., Sminchisescu, C., Weiss, Y. (eds.) ECCV 2018. LNCS, vol. 11219, pp. 682–697. Springer, Cham (2018). https://doi.org/10.1007/978-3-030-01267-0_40

DeepRank: Adapting Neural Tensor Networks for Ranking the Recommendations

Raaiha Humayun Kabir[1]([✉]), Bisma Pervaiz[1]([✉]),
Tayyeba Muhammad Khan[1]([✉]), Adnan Ul-Hasan[2], Raheel Nawaz[3],
and Faisal Shafait[1,2]

[1] School of Electrical Engineering and Computer Science,
National University of Sciences and Technology (NUST), Islamabad, Pakistan
{rkabir.bese15seecs,bpervaiz.bese15seecs,tkhan.bese15seecs,
faisal.shafait}@seecs.edu.pk
[2] Deep Learning Laboratory, National Center of Artificial Intelligence,
Islamabad, Pakistan
[3] School of Computing, Mathematics and Digital Technology,
Manchester Metropolitan University, Manchester, UK
R.Nawaz@mmu.ac.uk

Abstract. Online real estate property portals are gaining great attraction from masses due to ease in finding properties for rental or sale/purchase. With a few clicks, a real estate portal can display relevant information to a user by ranking the searched items according to user's specifications. It is highly significant that the ranking results display the most relevant search results to the user. Therefore, an efficient ranking algorithm that takes user's context is crucial for enhancing user experience in finding real estate properties online. This paper proposes an expressive Neural Tensor Network to rank the properties when searched for based on the similarity between the two property entities. Previous similarity techniques do not take into account the numerous complex features used to define a property. We showed that the performance can be enhanced if the property entities are represented as an average of their constituting features before finding the similarity between them. The proposed method takes into account each feature dynamically and ranks properties according to similarity with an accuracy of 86.6%.

Keywords: Neural Tensor Networks · Similarity · Recommender system · Real estate · Ranking

1 Introduction

The purpose of recommendation systems is to filter information in such a way that it is presented to the querying user in an order according to his/her preference. Many well-known recommendation systems today like Amazon, Netflix

© Springer Nature Switzerland AG 2020
C. Djeddi et al. (Eds.): MedPRAI 2019, CCIS 1144, pp. 162–176, 2020.
https://doi.org/10.1007/978-3-030-37548-5_13

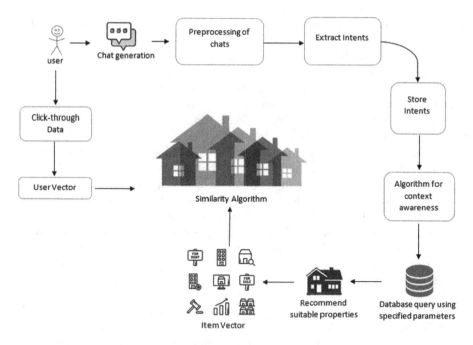

Fig. 1. Visual representation of the system used to store context and preferences, to recommend properties and to display ranked recommendations.

and YouTube take input from the user and show the results to the querying user based on that input. However, they do not take into account that user preferences cannot be correctly judged by a single query. Recommendations generated based on a single input from the user are hence not very reliable.

In this paper, we aim to improve the recommendations generated by taking into account a user's context. The user's context is defined by their browsing data on a particular website and the chat history retrieved from the Chatbot, which is the end product where recommendations are to be shown. The data of a user's browsing history will help to rank the recommendations fetched based on the user's query.

We used real estate data set for our research where when a user wants a property with certain specifications, similar properties from the database are ranked using the browsing data of that user. Data from the real estate domain is very complex as a single property can have multiple features that describe it fully. Moreover, many personal variables can influence a person's choice regarding a property. For example, one person might be looking for a house near to a certain school for his/her convenience whereas another person might want an apartment with 4 bedrooms. Hence determining what each user may like becomes a difficult task because of personal variants and because of how vast the property types can be. We chose this domain to solve the problem mentioned above so that users can be shown the properties most important to them during a particular period.

Figure 1 is a simplified version of the model we used to rank the recommendations. A user will generate certain chats by conversing with the chatbot (a platform where a user can input their preferences like the number of rooms, size of the house, etc.) and their preferences will be saved. The chats will be preprocessed to extract the intents, which will be stored in the database to improve the Chatbot's conversation. The chatbot will generate certain recommendations for the user. These recommendations will be ranked using the user's context. Recommendations will be ranked based on what the user's visited pages (on the same website) contain, and by finding out the similarity between the generated recommendations and the visited properties. The similarity model is based on Neural Tensor Networks which instead of predicting the relations [17] is used to rank the recommendations. To make this possible we have represented each property as an entity (a description of the property's feature). To rank different properties we calculate a similarity score of two properties. Property with the highest score gets the highest rank.

The first contribution of this paper is the adaptation of the Neural Tensor Network (NTN), to find out the similarity between two entities and then rank them, instead of using it to model relational information. We modified the Neural Tensor Networks so that instead of determining the relationship between two properties, it could calculate the similarity score by assessing commonalities between two properties.

The second contribution is that since the property entities can be displayed as the average of each of the word/feature vector in the property, it can be scaled up to a great amount to incorporate a million features, which can further increase the strength of the model resulting in better output.

The third contribution is of maintaining context. The results are ranked according to the similarity scores between the recommended properties and the ones visited by the user previously. It can automatically prioritize the features of a property that are important for the user in a particular period. Hence, it takes into account both the user's manually entered preferences and inferred preferences.

2 Related Work

A lot of work has been done on finding good recommendations for a user who is querying the system. Several recommendation systems have applications related to e-commerce. Online shopping sites like Alibaba, Amazon, and eBay recommend to the user their desired product. We will discuss some of the existing work in the field of recommendation systems done by these organizations.

Lee et al. [1,6,9] provided us with deep insights into how a user's context can be defined and what are the problems associated with these systems. When building a context-aware system for users performance has to maintained since multiple users may be accessing the service simultaneously. Privacy protection of the user's data is another problem that should be taken care of since context-aware systems monitor users activities.

In Shawar et al. [14] the chatbot described is designed to generate a recommendation for hotels. They were able to answer queries of the user using RBM and clarifying the knowledge by asking more questions from the user but another problem emerged in this approach, that was related to context maintenance. Every time the user left the conversation their previous history would be lost.

Fuzzy et al. [4] used a Hybrid Content-Based Fuzzy Conformal Recommender System for finding items online without the hassle to go through piles of data available online. However, they have not used the user's context hence the recommendations are not highly personalized.

The technique used by Qadir et al. [12] provides the aggregated score of the driver to the requesting passenger in case of carpooling services because of the conflicting needs of the driver and the passenger. However, the preferences of the passengers, like the gender of the driver has not been taken into account and the priority to each ride request is assigned based on spatial closeness to the current location of the vehicle.

Anwaar et al. [3] tackled collaborative filtering cold start cases of user rating records but other methods of feedback are not discussed. Ying et al. [18] talked about collaborative deep ranking using the Bayesian framework model but, the only scenario with sparse implicit feedback is discussed. Liu et al. [11] however, showed the comparison between ranking based recommender systems and rating-based recommender systems and also showed the effectiveness of ranking based recommender systems. Guan et al. [8] talked about ranking the recommendations of tags on social networks; they have achieved this ranking using a graph-based algorithm that takes into account a user's interests. However, the algorithm only uses keywords for generating the result and the rest of the information is ignored.

Singhal et al. [16] talked about the latest deep learning techniques used in current recommendation systems. This helped us to obtain a summary of the work that has been done up till now for recommendation systems using deep learning in different domains. It explains the results of using deep learning in recommender systems across different domains and whether using deep learning in recommender systems has shown any noteworthy improvement over the conventional systems for generating recommendations.

Feng et al. [7] introduced a new personalized ranking metric to make the point-of-interest recommendations for social networks. This was useful to us since we also had to find a suitable metric to check our ranked recommendations.

The most relevant approach is described in Socher et al. [17]. They introduce Neural Tensor Networks which are essentially neural networks but instead each layer is replaced by many tensor layers. Using these Neural Tensor Networks, they showed how two unknown entities can be related by finding the relationship between them. Before this paper, the entities were represented as single entity vector but with Neural Tensor Networks, the entities can be represented as the average of the words in it and hence the performance increases. The cost function uses triplets in the form of *(Entity 1, Relationship, Entity 2)*; if the two entities have the correct relationship between them, their confidence score is higher than when either of the two entities is replaced by a random entity. The algorithm in this paper has been used to find a relation between two entities; it handles multiple relations between entities but has not been adapted to find out the similarity between multiple entity pairs, and then ranking all the entity pairs on the basis of how similar are the two entities in a particular pair, mainly in the domain of real estate recommendations.

With the help of Neural Tensor Networks, not only can we solve the problem of ranking complex domain entities, but it can also enhance the deep learning modern recommendation systems [16] to elevate user experience.

3   Methodology

This section describes the proposed methodology in detail. In the subsequent subsections, we first discuss the distance model that has been traditionally used to find the similarity between the two entities. Then we introduce how we adapted the Neural Tensor Networks (NTN) to work on complex real estate data. The NTN evaluates the property entities and finds out the similarity score to rank the properties based on the user's context.

3.1   The Distance Model

The distance-based model calculates the distance between two entities and based on a threshold it defines whether two entities are similar or not. We initially used the distance model approach to rank the recommendations provided to the user by the chatbot. The problem with using the distance model is that it does not take into account the user's context in any way. This approach only calculates the distance between the user's preferences vector and the properties recommended by the bot. Hence, the distance model is unable to use the context to infer the user's current priorities. Therefore, the process of ranking the recommended properties according to the user's context is not possible with the distance model.

3.2   Neural Tensor Networks (NTN)

We use Neural Tensor Networks (NTN) for ranking different properties based on the property's features and the user's context. The NTN is used to calculate the similarity between two properties, by finding the common features amongst them and then evaluating their score. For example, we fetch 4 properties *(B, C, D, E)* from the database that are similar to property *A*; the NTN will calculate the similarity between the properties. Assuming that the similarity score for *"PropertyA similar PropertyD"* is higher than *"PropertyA similar PropertyB"*, then we can conclude that *D* will precede *B* in the ranking list. Hence the result is a ranked list of property recommendations that can be displayed. To use Neural Tensor Networks, we need to define a relationship between the two

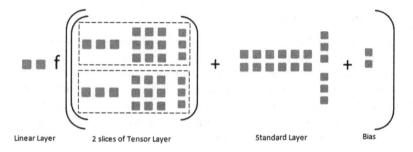

Fig. 2. Representation of a Neural Tensor Layer, for visualizing Eq. (1), used to compute similarity.

entities in question. The only relation useful for this purpose was of "similar" to find out whether two entities are similar to each other or not. Figure 2 is a visual representation of the neural tensor layer that is used to find the similarity between two property entities. The diagram contains two slices of tensor layers.

As described in [17], Neural Tensor Networks are used because they replace each linear layer of a neural network with a bi-linear tensor layer and hence can relate two vectors across multiple dimensions. The relation we use is similarity; therefore, we can compute the similarity score between two entities by:

$$g(e1, S, e2) = u_S^T f(e_1^T W_S^{[1:k]} e2 + V_S \begin{vmatrix} e1 \\ e2 \end{vmatrix} + b_S) \tag{1}$$

This equation from [17] was used to determine how similar two properties are to each other in terms of their features. The function $f = tanh$ applies a standard non-linearity on each element. A tensor is represented by $W_S^{[1:k]}$ whereas its product is represented as $e_1^T W_S^{[1:k]} e2$ which produces a vector that belongs to $\mathbb{R}^k$ and every entry is computed by one slice of tensor $1:k$.

$$e_1^T W_S^{[1:k]} e_2 \tag{2}$$

Equation (2) presents the bilinear tensor product. Each slice of the tensor is used to determine the similarity between two entities. The model, for example, will learn that two types of properties are similar if their price is within each other's range, or their size is within the same range. Hence the tensor layers help to recognize how close each feature of the property is and whether both are similar or not. The activation function used for training is $tanh$, which acts as a scaled sigmoid function. It is nonlinear in nature, so it can easily be used to stack layers. Its range is bound to $(-1, 1)$ hence, it prevents the problem of activation's blowing up. The gradient of $tanh$ is stronger than sigmoid that means that the derivatives are steeper.

3.3   Minimizing the Cost

The cost function used to minimize the cost is the Tensor Net cost function. The main idea behind it is to replace one entity in each training line with a random entity so that the score of the correct sample can be greater as compared to the one where one entity was randomly replaced. This helps the model to learn the pattern and determine the similarity between two entities. The cost function is as stated below and its validity has been proved by Socher et al. [17] and is also described with detail. The NTN parameters used [17] are

$$\Omega = u, W, V, b, E \tag{3}$$

$$J(\Omega) = \Sigma_{i=1}^{N}\Sigma_{c=1}^{C}max(0, 1 - g(T^{(i)}) + g(T_c^{(i)})) + \lambda \parallel \Omega \parallel_2^2 \tag{4}$$

In the above equation, N is the number of triplets used in training. The score of a correctly identified triplet is greater than the incorrect one up to a margin of 1. We take C incorrect samples for each correct triplet and use L2 regularization of all the parameters, weighted by λ.

4   Experimentation

Experiments were done on the real estate data, by finding out which properties were similar to each other and then ranking them based on a particular user's context

4.1   Dataset

The real estate data consists of original properties in Pakistan that have been obtained from the real estate website[1] in Pakistan. Our data consists of properties that are available on the website, browsing history of a user on website and chats generated by the user when he/she converses with the chatbot to describe his/her preferences.

Each property is identified by a property identifier and similarly. Each user also has a user identifier. We have limited the property type to houses for this research work, but it can easily be extended to other property types like shops and commercial offices. Areas of barren land with no construction were not made a part of this research. Similarly, we restricted the data of the properties by passing it through a city filter so, our database only consists of properties in Islamabad, Pakistan. For each user, their chat history and preferences given to the chatbot are recorded in the database alongside the properties that were recommended to the user as a result of some previous conversations with the bot. In addition to this data, the click-through data, which consists of the user's clicking on properties of interest, is also maintained in the database. The click-through data of a user is managed unless new data is generated as a result of the user's activity.

---

[1] www.aarz.pk.

The data set has been divided into three parts; the training data set, development data set (validation data set) and testing data set. The training data set includes only positive examples (properties similar to each other); with a total of 103,100 properties, of which 50% is obtained from the original data set of actual properties in Islamabad, and 50% of which is synthetically generated by changing the values of the features to generate properties that can serve as an example of similar properties for the training the model. The development data set contains both positive and negative examples (properties that are not similar to each other) with a label of 1 for the positive examples and a −1 for the negative example. The development data set has 4,000 properties in total where each positive example has its counterexample. Thus, there were 2,000 positive and 2,000 negative examples. The testing data set contains 608 properties with positive and negative examples. Furthermore, all of the properties to be tested were extracted from the original data set.

4.2   Data Representation

The data is represented in the form of triplets. Each triplet has two entities and a relation. In our model, we used a single relation that is of similarity and the entities represent the two properties under consideration.
General representation of a triplet is:

`Entity1 Relation Entity2`

Representation specific to our use case is:

`PropertyA Similar PropertyB`

Each property consists of its features. The general representation of a property is:

`City Sector Size Bedrooms Bathrooms Kitchen PowerRoom`

`Price PropertyType Purpose`

For example, if there is an apartment in the database that is situated in Sector G-10 Islamabad, has 3 bedrooms, 2 bathrooms, 1 kitchen, available for rent at Rs. 50,000 per month, it will be represented as:

`Islamabad G − 10 0 3 2 1 0 50000 Apartment Rent`

4.3   Features of Properties

A real estate can either be land or a built unit, so we extracted features for both of these types, and concluded that the features of a plot are a subset of the features of a house. The features that were extracted are tabulated in Table 1.

Due to the data availability issue, there was no data available for many of the features from each category listed in Table 1, in several of the properties. Hence,

Table 1. Features that define the properties.

Land features	House specific features	Surrounding environment features
City	Bedrooms	Adjacent to water
Locality (Area)	Bathrooms	Sidewalks or walking paths
Area (Size)	Kitchen	Distance from airport
Price	Power Room	Distance from park
Property type	Storey	Distance from Mosque
Purpose (buy or rent)	Taxes	Distance from local commute
	Garage/parking	Distance from market
	Basement	Kid friendly environment
	Basement Bathroom	Dog friendly environment
	Basement ceiling height	
	Basement kitchen	
	Basketball court	
	Bedrooms on basement	
	Bedrooms on main level	
	Central heating/cooling system	
	Furnished	
	Fence Yard	
	Grill	
	Guestroom	
	Home theatre	
	Library	
	Pool	
	Rec room	
	Security system	

we selected only those features for which there was complete and consistent data available. The features with the missing data could not be assigned a weight in the training, therefore excluding them was inevitable to prevent the distortion of the results. The model and the similarity algorithm can further be improved by obtaining data for all features listed above, which can then also be used to cater to diverse groups of people with diverse needs.

The features that were used are listed below:

1. City
2. Locality (Sector)
3. Area (Size)

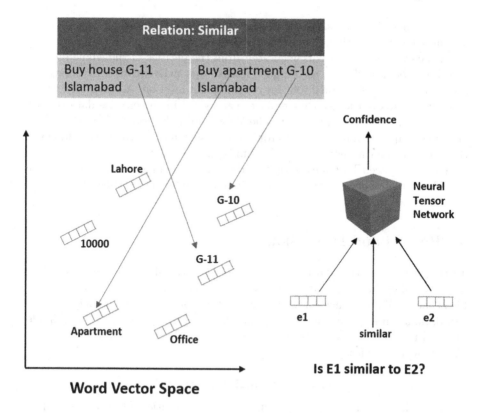

Fig. 3. Word2Vec mapping giving an overview of how entities in database are represented in the word vector space and how neural networks are used to find the confidence score.

4. Price
5. Property type
6. Purpose (buy or rent)
7. Bedrooms
8. Bathrooms
9. Kitchen
10. Power Room

4.4 Inputs for Similarity Classification

The inputs required for testing include property entities, word embeddings, development set and the test data itself. While testing, the threshold is calculated at run-time for each sample in the test file. This threshold is later used to check if the predicted value is either above or below the threshold so that the label of 0 or 1 can be assigned accordingly. The entities that have been labeled as 1 or are above the threshold are then collected and are arranged in descending order of similarity scores. The best match properties, according to preferences and user history are then displayed to the user.

A separate set of words is generated from the entities in the whole data set. Words can be described as the unique "words" that make up an entity along with a special unique ID assigned to it for referencing it later on. Additionally, we also generated a tree structure that replaces each word in the entities data set with its relevant ID from the words set. The algorithm makes words from the entities and then maps them to a word-vector space as shown in Fig. 3. This is done with the *word2vec* neural network [17]. It simply groups the vectors of similar words in a vector space. This means that it detects the similarities mathematically. *word2vec* creates vectors that are distributed numerical representations of the word features.

5   Results and Discussion

Testing was done on the data with original properties only, excluding all synthetic data. We labeled the test data manually with labels 1 for positive samples and -1 for negative. We used accuracy to measure the working of our model on unseen test data; accuracy was defined as the number of correct labels predicted divided by total test samples. Initially, we tested the model by giving the properties in the following format:

`Property1 similar Property1`

meaning the model had to determine if the two entities on either side of the similar relation are the same, then the accuracy should be 100%. For 20,000 similarity relations in the test file, in the above format, the expected results were obtained (100%). Hence this ensured that the model was at least recognizing two same properties.

In the next phase, we had to test how our model performed when the two properties are not the same. We manually determined if two properties are similar or not by assessing whether the features of the two properties are similar to each other. For example, if there is a house in the sector G-10, Islamabad with a price of Rs. 50,0000 with a size of 20 Marlas, it would be similar to a house in the neighboring sectors of G-10 (like G-11 or F-10) with a price range close to Rs. 50,0000 (within the range Rs. 40–60,0000) and a size of around 20 Marlas. Following this method, we built the whole test data to determine whether our model is predicting correct similarity relation on the original data set.

On the 20,000 lines of test data, the accuracy was 86.6%. Our confidence in this accuracy is high since our test data included very different samples of similarity.

Figure 4 shows a particular use case where the algorithm performs well and displays the ranked results. Suppose a user converses with the chatbot to find a suitable home for themselves. We can see from the diagram that the user's context contains information about certain properties that they visited for the past few days before conversing with the chatbot. The user then asks the bot for

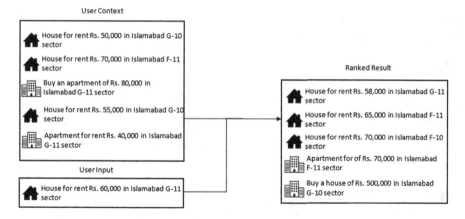

Fig. 4. Example of a positive use case. The model successfully ranks the recommendations based on the user's context.

a recommendation close to a house for rent of around Rs. 60,000 in the sector G-11, Islamabad. The output that the user receives from the chatbot has a certain pattern to it based on the user's context. Our model inferred from the user's context that they are more interested in renting a house, within a range of Rs. 50,000 to 70,000 in Islamabad, but the sector can vary to some extent and is not entirely fixed. Hence the recommendations are generated from the database according to the user's query and are then ranked based on the priorities inferred from the user's context. So it can be observed that the top three properties displayed are the ones with the option of renting a house specifically, within an acceptable price range in Islamabad. Whereas the last two recommendations are not fulfilling the user's request based on their context (i.e. are either not houses or are not available for rent) and have been placed lower in the list.

Figure 5 is an example of a negative use case where our model is unable to rank the recommendations on the user's context. We can observe from the context that the user has visited many different properties online before conversing with the chatbot. The context contains properties from different cities of Pakistan, with different types of properties (house or apartments), with prices that are varying a lot. The user then requests a house for rent of Rs. 60,000 in the sector G-11, Islamabad. The chatbot does retrieve some properties of Islamabad, but the results displayed have not been successfully ranked. The results displayed are although according to the query of the user, for example, there are properties in Islamabad within an appropriate price range and an acceptable location; however, the model was unable to infer any priorities from the user's context. One plausible reason for such failure is the random search pattern of the user such that our model could not determine what the user was looking for.

Finally, given the right context, the model achieved what it was intended to. It mostly predicts the similarity between properties correctly. The real-world testing data in our system is the user's past visited properties on the website

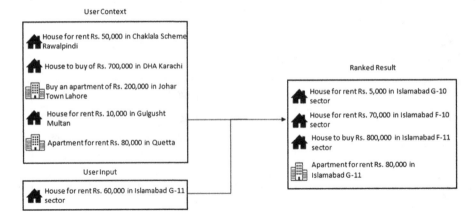

Fig. 5. Example of a negative use case where the model was unable to rank the recommendations. User's context in this example is not clear; it contains properties where none of the features are similar.

and, the properties recommended to them by the chatbot. The chatbot checks the similarity of each property in the recommended list with each property in the user's context. It then uses the predicted output (raw score) to sort them in descending order. From that list eventually, the ranked list of recommendations is displayed to the user.

6   Conclusion and Outlook

The main problem that we addressed was to generate recommendations that are personalized for each user based on their previous activity on the system. The use of Neural Tensor Networks to identify the similarity between two properties has proved to be very useful and efficient. Now, when the user is browsing on the website, their activity can be recorded and maintained that can be translated into their context. A user's preferences are used to fetch the properties from the database and then the similarity between the user's context and properties fetched is tested. Thus, the problem of exclusion of relevant context has been addressed since now a user's context is also used to rank and recommend properties.

In the future, this work can be extended by getting complete data of the features that were missing; training the model on those added features and then testing it again. Our work was limited to the city of Islamabad in Pakistan, and only for houses; this can be extended for all cities of the country. If the data for many diverse features can be obtained, the model can be trained to cater to many cities of Pakistan and can also be applied generally for any place in the world with even more accuracy.

Another suggestion for the extension that would make the results more accurate and stronger is to incorporate the user's browsing history related to similar websites (more real estate websites instead of a single site as in this paper) to gain more insight about the interests of the user [1,15]. For example, if a user has visited 3 other real estate websites and has viewed some properties, a more comprehensive context can be built and the user's current priorities can be inferred with more accuracy due to more history.

Moreover, the algorithm does not perform well when a user visits the website for the very first time and converses with the bot, as there is no previous history regarding the user. Hence, there is no (or very little) context, which the algorithm needs to extract the priorities of the user. This means that less accurate or no priorities can be inferred resulting in the algorithm recommending unranked properties based only on the features of the property that the user entered at the beginning of the conversation with the bot. One solution to this problem is to use the existing techniques of collaborative filtering [2,5,10,13] to find out similarities between different users of the website. To implement collaborative filtering for cold start cases, some personal data like each user's likes, dislikes, the location where they currently reside in, and other such useful information has to be collected from each user when they visit the website. Then if a new user with no history wants ranked recommendations, their priorities can be inferred by finding out the similarity of this user with other users of the website. If the new user has some commonalities with another user, his priorities can be inferred from the other user because they had the same taste or requirements, hence their context would be relatively similar. The recommended properties can then be ranked based on these inferred priorities for the new user.

Another use of the collected personal information is that the user profiles can be more comprehensive and have details related to their hobbies, interests, and background so that a general idea of the user's context can also be incorporated while generating ranked recommendations for the user. For example, people with big families will be interested in bigger homes that fit the needs of their families or people with children might prefer houses that have parks or recreational areas near them.

Acknowledgment. This research was partly supported by HEC Grant TDF-029 and National Center for Artificial Intelligence (NCAI).

References

1. Abowd, G.D., Dey, A.K., Brown, P.J., Davies, N., Smith, M., Steggles, P.: Towards a better understanding of context and context-awareness. In: Gellersen, H.-W. (ed.) HUC 1999. LNCS, vol. 1707, pp. 304–307. Springer, Heidelberg (1999). https://doi.org/10.1007/3-540-48157-5_29

2. Ahn, J.H.: A new similarity measure for collaborative filtering to alleviate the new user cold-starting problem. Inf. Sci. **178**(1), 37–51 (2008)

3. Anwar, F., Iltaf, N., Afzal, H., Nawaz, R.: HRS-CE: a hybrid framework to integrate content embeddings in recommender systems for cold start items. J. Comput. Sci. **29**, 9–18 (2018)

4. Ayyaz, S., Qamar, U., Nawaz, R.: HCF-CRS: a hybrid content based fuzzy conformal recommender system for providing recommendations with confidence. PLoS One **13**(2018). https://doi.org/10.1371/journal.pone.0204849

5. Bobadilla, J., Ortega, F., Hernando, A., Bernal, J.: A collaborative filtering approach to mitigate the new user cold start problem. Knowl.-Based Syst. **26**, 225–238 (2012)

6. Dey, A.K.: Understanding and using context. Pers. Ubiquitous Comput. **5**(1), 4–7 (2001)

7. Feng, S., Li, X., Zeng, Y., Cong, G., Chee, Y.M., Yuan, Q.: Personalized ranking metric embedding for next new POI recommendation. In: IJCAI, pp. 2069–2075. AAAI Press (2015)

8. Guan, Z., Bu, J., Mei, Q., Chen, C., Wang, C.: Personalized tag recommendation using graph-based ranking on multi-type interrelated objects. In: SIGIR, pp. 540–547. ACM (2009)

9. Lee, S., Park, S., Lee, S.: A study on issues in context-aware systems based on a survey and service scenarios. In: SNPD, pp. 8–13. IEEE Computer Society (2009)

10. Lian, D., et al.: Content-aware collaborative filtering for location recommendation based on human mobility data. In: ICDM, pp. 261–270. IEEE Computer Society (2015)

11. Liu, Y., Yang, J.: Improving ranking-based recommendation by social information and negative similarity. Procedia Comput. Sci. **55**, 732–740 (2015). ITQM

12. Qadir, H., Khalid, O., Khan, M.U.S., Khan, U.A., Nawaz, R.: An optimal ride sharing recommendation framework for carpooling services. IEEE Access **6**, 62296–62313 (2018)

13. Sedhain, S., Sanner, S., Braziunas, D., Xie, L., Christensen, J.: Social collaborative filtering for cold-start recommendations. In: RecSys, pp. 345–348. ACM (2014)

14. Shawar, B.A., Atwell, E.: Chatbots: are they really useful? LDV Forum **22**(1), 29–49 (2007)

15. Shen, X., Tan, B., Zhai, C.: Context-sensitive information retrieval using implicit feedback. In: SIGIR, pp. 43–50. ACM (2005)

16. Singhal, A., Sinha, P., Pant, R.: Use of deep learning in modern recommendation system: a summary of recent works. CoRR abs/1712.07525 (2017)

17. Socher, R., Chen, D., Manning, C.D., Ng, Y.-T.A.: Reasoning with neural tensor networks for knowledge base completion. In: Advances in Neural Information Processing Systems 26: 27th Annual Conference on Neural Information Processing Systems 2013. Proceedings of a meeting held Lake Tahoe, Nevada, United States, 5–8 December 2013, pp. 926–934 (2013)

18. Ying, H., Chen, L., Xiong, Y., Wu, J.: Collaborative deep ranking: a hybrid pairwise recommendation algorithm with implicit feedback. In: Bailey, J., Khan, L., Washio, T., Dobbie, G., Huang, J.Z., Wang, R. (eds.) PAKDD 2016. LNCS (LNAI), vol. 9652, pp. 555–567. Springer, Cham (2016). https://doi.org/10.1007/978-3-319-31750-2_44

An Intelligent Context Aware Recommender System for Real-Estate

Faiza Rehman[1], Hira Masood[1], Adnan Ul-Hasan[2(✉)], Raheel Nawaz[3],
and Faisal Shafait[1,2]

[1] School of Electrical Engineering and Computer Science,
National University of Sciences and Technology (NUST), Islamabad, Pakistan
faisal.shafait@seecs.edu.pk

[2] Deep Learning Lab, National Center for Artificial Intelligence, Islamabad, Pakistan
adnan.ulhasan@gamil.com

[3] School of Computing, Mathematics and Digital Technology,
Manchester Metropolitan University, Manchester, UK
R.Nawaz@mmu.ac.uk

Abstract. Finding products and items in large online space that meet user needs is difficult. Time spent searching before finding a relevant item can be a significant time sink for users. As with other economic branches, growing Internet usage also changed user behavior in the real-estate market. Advancements in virtual reality offer virtual tours and interactive map and floor plans which make an online rental websites very popular among users. With the abundance of information, recommender systems become more important than ever to give the user relevant property suggestions and reduce search time. A sophisticated recommender in this domain can help reduce the need of a real-estate agent. Session-based user behavior and lack of user profiles leads to the use of traditional recommendation methods. In this research, we propose an approach for real-estate recommendation based on Gated Orthogonal Recurrent Unit (GORU) and Weighted Cosine Similarity. GORU captures the user search context and weighted cosine similarity improves the rank of pertinent property. We have used the data of an online public real estate web portal (AARZ.PK). The data represents the original behavior of the user on an online portal. We have used Recall, User coverage and Mean Reciprocal Rank (MRR) metrics for the evaluation of our system against other state-of-the-art techniques. The proposed solution outperforms various baselines and state-of-the-art RNN based solutions.

Keywords: Recommender systems · Deep learning · Real estate · GORU · RNN

1 Introduction

The recommender system falls in the information retrieval domain. The main purpose of the recommendation system is to improve the consumer experience

© Springer Nature Switzerland AG 2020
C. Djeddi et al. (Eds.): MedPRAI 2019, CCIS 1144, pp. 177–191, 2020.
https://doi.org/10.1007/978-3-030-37548-5_14

and provide users with relevant items. Recommender system is a software utility that provides suggestions for the item to be used by the user [17]. Relying on these suggestions, users make various decisions including which movie to watch, which song to hear, which news to read, which house to purchase, etc. These systems have proved to be helpful when a user deals with an overwhelming amount of information searching online through pervasive large item space. The online product catalogs evolve continuously to include high-value products such as apartments and computers; hence, the task of locating the desired choice among a large set of options is intimidating for an average customer [3].

Like many other fields, the internet has also reshaped the behavior of a consumer and a supplier in the real estate domain. It is very difficult for both the supplier and customer to survey the real estate market physically, whereas an online real-estate portal provides an abundance of information with just a few clicks. Advancements in virtual reality provide the facility of a virtual tour. The introduction of interactive maps and floor plans makes online real estate portal users first choice for property search. By integrating a sophisticated recommender system, online search time can be reduced and reduce the need for a real-estate agent in property transactions. The importance of the real estate market is demonstrated by the fact that it tends to have a big impact on the economy of any country. In the US, the real estate industry accounted for $3,372,634 million or 17.3% of the gross state product in 2017.

Despite the importance of a recommender system in real estate domain, it has been given relatively little attention in the research community. Most of the literature in our research comes from generic recommender system techniques. Most research in recommender system focused on models where user's proper identifiers and profiles are available. In this setting matrix factorization based approaches and the neighborhood model dominated the literature [7]. However, in real systems the website rarely saves a users identifier. Even if tracking is possible, the users rarely visit the rental portal for the same purpose; instead they usually exhibit session based behavior. Lack of user profiles with session based behavior leads to the use of relatively simple methods that do not take into account the user profile, i.e., item to item similarity. These methods only take into account user's last click, ignoring the context of user search.

In this work, we propose a deep learning based recommender system specifically for the real estate domain for efficient online searching. The proposed approach recommends properties based upon user search context instead of just last clicked item. Section 2 overviews the related work on recommender systems. Section 3 describes the details of our methodology. Section 4 outlines the experimental details including the features used, experimental setups, results, and comparison with the baseline methods. Section 5 concludes the paper and provides points for future research.

2 Related Work

Despite the existence of many years of research, recommender systems in real-estate have remained little focused on in the research sphere. One of the first approaches which highlights the application of a recommender system in real estate was proposed by Shearin et al. [18]. The proposed system attempted to reproduce suggestions similar to a human real estate agent. The system was based upon an interactive learning procedure which was not further particularize in this study. It was based upon extensive user feedback, gathering user views about various aspects and attributes of properties. The information gathered through questionnaires was used to set the standard filter on the database and make a recommendation about relevant properties.

Graaff et al. [5] proposed a geosocial recommender system that used data from different data sources. The system was able to make recommendations about local businesses. It used data mainly from social media. The proposed approach applied a profile matching mechanism. The profile matching was based upon collaborative filtering to make suggestions. The authors claimed that the concept of a geoprofile could be shifted to the real estate domain. However, this approach was dependent on social media data to make suggestions.

Yuan et al. [22] proposed an approach to improve the efficiency and affordability of an online housing search. They proposed a user-oriented recommender system for real-estate portal using ontology and case-based reasoning relied which relied upon user search behavior. They aimed to find the semantic construction of housing unit information and designed all the sub-modules for building a recommender system. They used questionnaires and user search behavior for semantic relationship construction. The extracted ontology contained information about the knowledge collected in the user study and real estate domains. Finally it used case representation and case indexes to find the similarity between search queries and user cases.

A simulation-based recommender study using real estate data was published by Chulyadyo et al. [12]. They proposed a personalized Probabilistic Relational Model (PRM) based on users' preferences in decision making. They also demonstrated that the same PRM could be used to achieve content-based, collaborative filtering and hybrid approaches.

The first ever machine learning based approach in real-estate recommender systems was proposed by Knoll et al. [14]. In their research, they used MLP to make recommendations. The proposed solution makes recommendations based upon the ratings given by the user to a specific property. The MLP takes user id and property features as input and predicts a rating for the property that the user has not already rated. They also showed the various possibilities of embedding recommenders in the real-estate portal during the user search journey. The algorithm required explicit feedback from the user to make it work, and for every recommendation, the algorithm had to predict a rating for all the properties available in the system.

2.1 Recurrent Neural Network for Recommendation

RNN is a deep model that works particularly well when dealing with sequential or temporal data. RNNs have been successfully used in image and video captioning, time series prediction, and natural language processing. Long short-term memory

(LSTM) [11] are a type of RNN that work particularly well. It includes additional gates that control the hidden state of the RNN. This helps with the vanishing gradient problem*(add a fa line or two about it) that comes up in standard RNN.

Gated Recurrent Unit (GRU) [4] is comparatively simpler thn LSTM. Recently, URNN and GORU have been proposed which help in reducing the gradient explosion problem. In this work, we have used GORU [13] for real-estate recommendation problem. GORU combines the ability of unitary RNN to remember the long-term dependencies with gated RNN's ability to forget irrelevant information.

RNNs were first used to model session data in [9]. This GRU based recurrent neural network is trained with the pairwise ranking loss function Top1. This network takes clicked item IDs as input and provides a recommendation after each click. Parallel RNNs were also used to incorporate item features, i.e., textual description and a thumbnail image of the item to make recommendations [10]. This technique provides a better recommendation compared to plain RNNs but has the drawback of increased training time.

In [19] the author used data augmentation technique to improve the performance of RNN in session-based recommendation. This technique has the drawback of increased training time because in this work a single session is split into sub-sessions. RNNs have also been used in user-item collaborative filtering [6,21] where results are not up to par and hardly outperform matrix factorization method. In [16] authors proposed hierarchical RNN (HRNN) to make recommendations in the scenario when information about the user's previous session is available.

In [15] the authors proposed a recommender system for Carpooling services which allows the drivers to share rides with other passengers. This reduces the passengers' fares and time, as well as traffic congestion and increases income for drivers. Another recommender system for movie recommendations was proposed in [2] which used the content based filtering approach with fuzzy logic and conformal prediction algorithm.

The goal of our study is to use novel sequence model GORU and URNN [1] for recommendation. Results show that GORU based models train faster with fewer epochs and hidden units. At the same time it performs better in terms of different measures as compared to GRU and URNN. It also outperforms other state of the art session based recommendation techniques by a significant margin.

3   Methodology

Our proposed system consist of two main modules. The first is a candidate generation module which is based upon deep learning (i.e. Gated Orthogonal Recurrent Unit) and the second is a ranking module. The candidate generation module generates properties based upon the user search context. The ranking module takes candidate properties as input and, using weighted cosine similarity, improves the rank of the most relevant property. Figure 1 depicts the proposed solution.

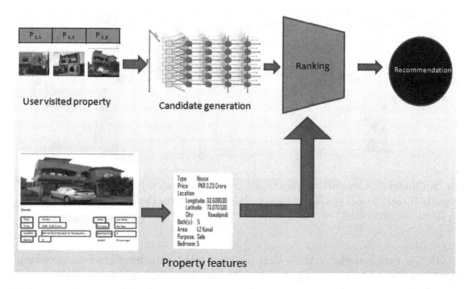

Fig. 1. An illustration of the proposed approach, *Candidate generation* module based upon deep learning takes one hot-encoding of property-ID and generate candidate properties, *Ranking* module takes candidate properties and apply Weighted Cosine Similarity between last click property and candidate properties.

3.1   Candidate Generation Using GORU

This module is based on the RNN-based Gated Orthogonal Recurrent Unit (GORU). GORU models user's search behavior on the online real estate portal. For our study we used data from an a online real-estate portal. Our model takes in a 1 of N representation of user searched property ID and outputs the probability of the next possible items.

In our setup, we use a ranking loss function TOP1. For training, we use sequences of user clicked property IDs generated in session during searching online real estate website and model user search behavior. This module serves as a unit to generate the property IDs that are most likely to be the user most relevant property. Properties with a high probability serve as the candidates. Figure 2 shows the process of candidate generation.

Gated Orthogonal Recurrent Unit. Recurrent neural network has been devised to model sequential data. The hidden state h_t of RNN makes them different from a feed-forward neural network.

$$h_t = g(W x_t + U h_{t-1}) \tag{1}$$

Where g is the activation function. x_t is the input at time step t, h_{t-1} is previous hidden state.

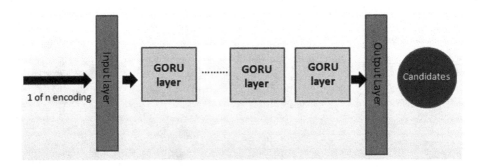

Fig. 2. Candidate Generation using GORU,*Input layer* takes 1 of N encoding of visited property ID and pass it to *GORU layers*, *Output layer* gives the probability corresponding to all the properties

GRU is gated model of RNN that deals with the vanishing gradient problem. Gates controls the changes of the hidden state The hidden state in GRU is the linear interpolation of previously hidden state and candidate hidden state.

$$h_t = (1 - z_t)h_{t-1} + z_t\hat{h}_t \tag{2}$$

where z is the update gate computed as

$$z_t = \sigma(W_z x_t + U_z h_{t-1}) \tag{3}$$

where σ is the activation function. The candidate hidden state $\hat{h}_t$ is computed in a similar manner

$$\hat{h}_t = tanh(W x_t + U(r_t \odot h_{t-1})) \tag{4}$$

and finally, the reset gate rt is given by

$$r_t = \sigma(W_r x_t + U_r h_{t-1}) \tag{5}$$

A complex-valued matrix O is unitary when it satisfies $OO^T = I$ where I is the identity matrix. And real-valued unitary matrix is called orthogonal. Any vector multiplied by orthogonal matrix satisfies $OO^T = I$. A complex-valued matrix U is unitary when it satisfies $OO^T = I$.

$$||Ox|| = ||x|| \tag{6}$$

Due to the above property, the U matrix is able to preserve the norm of matrix passing through it and allows the gradient to propagate for a longer time. In our scenario, to use GORU we change the hidden state matrix in orthogonal matrix and activation function to modRELU given as

$$h_t = z_t \odot h_{t-1} + (1 - z_t) \odot \hat{h}_t \tag{7}$$

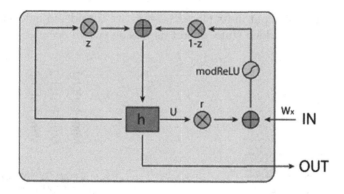

Fig. 3. An illustration of GORU [13], h is the hidden state. z and r are update and reset gate, here U is the orthogonal matrix. Here activation function in $modRELU$

$$\hat{h}_t = modReLU(W_x x_t + r_t \odot (Oh_{t-1}) + b_h) \tag{8}$$

where $\hat{h}_t$ is candidate hidden state.

Figure 3 represents the working of GORU. We use 1-of-n encoding with session parallel mini-batches. We also tried other sequence learning algorithms i.e. GRU, URNN and LSTM. Results show that GORU outperforms the others. We also tried different loss functions, TOP1 and BPR show competitive results and outperform the others.

1 of N Encoding. The input of the network is the current state of the session while the output is the item of the next event in the session. For input, we use a 1 of N encoding representation of the item. The length of the input vector equals the number of items and only the coordinate corresponding to the current item is one, the others are zeros. We also experimented with adding an additional embedding layer, but the 1-of-N encoding always outperforms.

Session Parallel Mini Batches. RNNs mostly use in-sequence mini-batches for natural language processing tasks. For example, it is common practice to use a sliding window over sentences and place these windowed segments adjoining each other to form mini-batches. This strategy does not suit our task, because (1) The length of sessions can be very diverse, even more than that of sentences: some sessions consist of only 2 events, while others may contain hundreds of events. (2) Our goal is to capture how a session progress over time, so breaking it down into segments would make no sense.

For this purpose, we use session-parallel mini-batches, depicted in Fig. 4. First, we create an order for the sessions Then, we put the first occurrence of the first X sessions to form the input of the first mini-batch (the required output is the second occurrence of our active sessions). The second mini-batch consists of the second occurrence and so on. If any of the sessions terminate than the next available session is put in its place. Sessions are considered independent, so we reset the suitable hidden state when this session switch occurs.

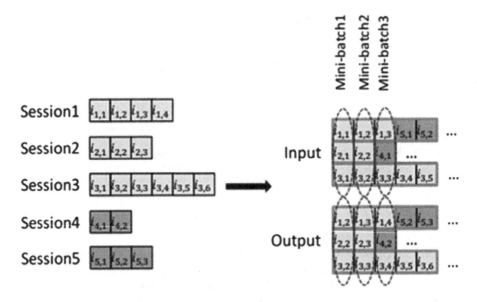

Fig. 4. Session Parallel Mini Batches

Ranking Loss Function. The key to recommender systems is the relevance-based ranking of recommended items. Although this task can also be considered a classification task, learning-to-rank approaches generally outperform other approaches. Ranking can be point-wise, pairwise and list-wise.

Point-wise ranking independently estimates the score or the rank of items, and the loss is defined in such a way that the rank of relevant items is low. The *pairwise* ranking compares the score or the rank of pairs of a positive and a negative item and the loss is defined so that the rank of the relevant or positive item should be lower than that of the negative item. *List-wise* ranking uses the scores and ranks of all items and compares them to the perfect ordering. As this last method requires sorting, it is computationally expensive and not often used. In our case, we use a pair-wise loss function named TOP1 proposed by Hidasi et al. [9] specifically for recommendation tasks. It is the regularized approximation of the relative rank of the pertinent property. The relative rank of the pertinent property is given by $L_s = \frac{1}{N_S} \cdot \sum_{j=1}^{N_S} I\{\hat{r}_{s,j} > \hat{r}_{s,i}\}$. $I\{.\}$ is approximated with a sigmoid function. Optimizing for this would modify parameters such that the score for i would be high. But in some cases, certain relevant items also act as a negative example and the score tends to become increasingly higher. To circumvent this, we want to impose the scores of the negative sample to be near zero. Which is the organic expectation towards the scores of negative items, Thus regularization term has added to the function. This regularization term must be in the same range as the relative rank and acts similarly to it. Finally, the loss function is as follows: $L_s = \frac{1}{N_S} \cdot \sum_{j=1}^{N_S} \sigma \{\hat{r}_{s,j} > \hat{r}_{s,i}\} + \sigma \hat{r}^2_{s,j}$

3.2   Ranking

In this module, we took generated candidates as inputs and measured the similarity of all candidate to a user's last clicked item. The similarity measure we use in our study is weighted cosine similarity. In Tonara et al. [20]'s survey, they identify 7 major deciding factors in real estate sales and purchase. These criteria are price, number of rooms, number of bathrooms, location, building area, land area, and house certificate. As on the portal websites, the information about the house certificate is not available, we excluded this and we identified two further deciding factors, Property type (i.e. house, plot, flat etc) and property purpose (i.e. whether it is available for rent or sale). The location is subdivided into City, longitude, and latitude. Each property is represented as an array of attributes. We used min-max normalization for features normalization.

$$P1 = (\text{PropertyType}, \text{PropertyPurpose}, \text{City}, \text{Longitude},$$
$$\text{Latitude}, \text{Area}, \text{NumRooms}, \text{NumBaths}) \tag{9}$$

Assign weights according to the relative importance of features.

$$P1 = (w_1 \times \text{PropertyType}, w_2 \times \text{PropertyPurpose}, w_3 \times \text{City}, w_4 \times \text{Longitude},$$
$$w_5 \times \text{Latitude}, w_6 \times \text{Area}, w_7 \times \text{NumRooms}, w_8 \times \text{NumBaths}) \tag{10}$$

For some candidate property C:

$$C1 = (\text{PropertyType}, \text{PropertyPurpose}, \text{City}, \text{Longitude},$$
$$\text{Latitude}, \text{Area}, \text{NumRooms}, \text{NumBaths}) \tag{11}$$

Assign weights according to the relative importance of features.

$$C1 = (w_1 \times \text{PropertyType}, w_2 \times \text{PropertyPurpose}, w_3 \times \text{City}, w_4 \times \text{Longitude},$$
$$w_5 \times \text{Latitude}, w_6 \times \text{Area}, w_7 \times \text{NumRooms}, w_8 \times \text{NumBaths}) \tag{12}$$

$$\cos(\mathbf{P1}, \mathbf{C1}) = \frac{\mathbf{P1C1}}{\|\mathbf{P1}\|\|\mathbf{C1}\|} = \frac{\sum_{i=1}^{n} \mathbf{P1}_i \mathbf{C1}_i}{\sqrt{\sum_{i=1}^{n} (\mathbf{P1}_i)^2} \sqrt{\sum_{i=1}^{n} (\mathbf{C1}_i)^2}} \tag{13}$$

The cosine similarity measure is used to find the similarity between generated candidates and last clicked property. Candidate properties with high similarity values are used as recommendations. The result shows that this module improves the ranking of the relevant property.

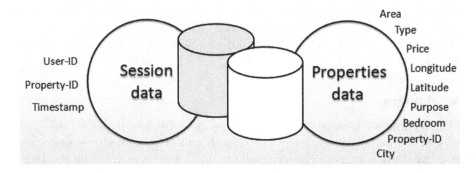

User-ID
Property-ID
Timestamp

Area
Type
Price
Longitude
Latitude
Purpose
Bedroom
Property-ID
City

Fig. 5. *Session data* contains information about user behavior in session. *Property data* contain information about the particular real estate property.

4   Experimental Evaluation

To thoroughly evaluate our algorithm, we have performed a number of experiments. This section describes the data-set used and the protocol followed,as well as outlining the key results obtained.

4.1   Data Description

We have obtained the data of an online real-estate portal. It consists of two types of data, the Google analytics data of the online portal, which contains session-based user data and user browsing history, (this session based data grabs the user behavior in the form of click stream)and the property attributes stored in the database of the online portal.

Figure 5 shows the data we have used in our research study. The session based data demonstrates the user's session based behavior. Property data contains information about property attributes that the users are concerned about while purchasing property. These include primary attributes such as the number of rooms, area, and the location of the property, as well as derived attributes such as distance to school, distance to shopping center, etc. These attributes are fundamental to establishing similarity between properties and identifying a particular user's interest.

The following table (Table 1) shows session data that we have used for model training and testing purpose.

4.2   Baselines

The following are the most used approaches in session-based recommendation systems.

POP: Popularity predictor that always recommends the most popular item. Although this approach is quite simple, it is widely used in practical systems and in certain domains it acts as a strong baseline.

Table 1. The specification of the data set used in our study

Data	Number of events	Number of session
Train data	26,121	6,390
Test data	8,238	2,608

S-POP: Recommend most popular item in the current session. In our setting, we choose most popular item in the current batch.

KNN: It is a item to item collaborative filtering approach in which an item similar to the current items is recommended. Cosine similarity measure is used to find the similarity between the item's session vectors.

BPR-MF: BPR-MF is a matrix factorization method. To make it work in a session based setting, we used the same approach as described in [9].

GRU4rec: It is the first system that applies RNN in recommender system [9]. In this system, GRU has been used to generate the recommendations. This paper serves as the basis for our candidate generation module as well.

RNN with TOP-K Gain: This applies RNN with a new rank function [8]. They introduced a new class of loss functions that, together with an improved sampling strategy, provide top-k gains for RNNs.

4.3 Evaluation Metrics

Recall: Recall is also known as the sensitivity. It is the fraction of relevant items retrieved through the recommender over the total number of relevant items.

$$\text{Recall} = \frac{\text{relevant\_items} \cap \text{recommended\_items}}{\text{relevant\_items}} \tag{14}$$

MRR: In information retrieval and recommender systems the rank of the relevant item is also important, i.e., at what rank the system is retrieving the relevant item. Mean reciprocal rank (MRR) is the average of the inverse of the rank given to the first relevant item.

$$MRR = \frac{1}{S} \sum_{i=1}^{S} \frac{1}{rank_i} \tag{15}$$

Here $rank_i$ is the rank given to the first recommended relevant item. S is the number of sessions.

User_coverage: User coverage is the fraction of number of users getting a correct recommendation over total number of users getting recommendations.

$$\text{User\_coverage} = \frac{U_r}{U} \tag{16}$$

Here U_r is the number of user getting relevant recommendations. U is the total number of users. In our scenario the number of users is the same as the number of sessions.

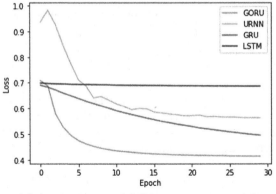

(a) A comparison of different *sequence models*

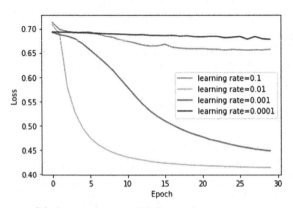

(b) A comparison of different *learning rates*

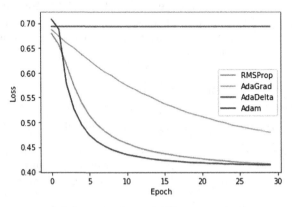

(c) A comparison of different *optimizers*

Fig. 6. Loss vs Epoch graphs for different parameters

Table 2. A comparison of the proposed method with different baseline methods. The results show a clear superiority of the presented method as it significantly outperforms the baseline methods on all evaluation metrics.

Method	User-coverage	Recall @20	MRR@ 20
POP	0.9	0.7	0.1
S-POP	31.6	35.8	26.2
KNN	40.9	35.4	14.2
BPR-MF	29.4	32.0	25.2
GRU4rec [9]	34.6	30.9	17.3
TOP-K Gain [8]	43.1	37.5	19.1
Hybrid GORU	**58.5**	**59.9**	**29.3**

4.4 Results and Discussion

We optimized the hyperparameters by running multiple experiments and randomly selecting parameter points. Then the parameters were further optimized by tuning each parameter separately. The optimization was done on a separate validation set, then evaluated on test data. We have experimented with different sequence models i.e. LSTM, GRU, URNN, and GORU. For our experiments, we have used GeForce Titan X GPU. However, even it can be trained in a reasonable time even on a CPU.

Figure 6(a) shows the loss vs epoch graph for different sequence models. Note that GORU shows faster convergence than the other sequence models, as well as achieving the lowest loss after 20 epochs. The loss function of GRU showed a steady decline but the convergance was slow. Therefore, we chose GORU as the model of choice in our study. Figure 6(b) shows the effect of using different learning rates when training GORU. According to the results, a learning rate of 0.01 performs the best. It is interesting to note that both a high learning rate of 0.1 and a low learning rate of 0.0001 resulted in poor convergence. We also tried different optimizers i.e. RMSprop, Adagrad, Adadelta and Adam. Figure 6(c) shows the convergence for different optimizers. In our case Adam performed better than others, while AdaDelta could not converge. We have experimented with different loss function i.e. TOP1, BPR, TOP1-MAX, CCE, Blackout. In terms of evaluation metrics TOP1 and BPR both give competitive results. Blackout performed the worst but at the same time increases the diversity factor.

Our proposed Hybrid GORU approach outperforms various baselines including RNN based solutions. Table 2 shows the results of the best performing network. Error analysis shows that this network performs particularly well for long sessions and the items that have higher support count i.e. the properties that are most visited. The GORU based approach has a significant gain over previous approaches included GRU based approaches. By increasing the number of hidden units within a single layer, results can be further improved with respect to all the evaluation metrics whereas adding layers decreases the performance of the network. In terms of the loss function, BPR and TOP1 both give competitive results and outperforming other loss function i.e. CCE and Blackout [6].

The proposed approach is popularity based, therefore it doesn't work well for rarely visited items. Moreover, the database of real estate portals tends to update frequently. This change requires the retraining of model frequently to integrate new properties in the recommendation.

5 Conclusion

The personalized real estate recommender system can help the user to find the relevant property in significantly less search time. Although our ranking module requires manually static weights, it can be used to incorporate the business needs e.g. increase diversity in the recommendations, prioritize the candidate properties whose advertisements have been submitted earlier than others. Our work can serve as a basis to explore the real estate domain further with deep learning techniques.

Advanced features in online real-estate portals i.e. virtual tours, interactive maps, 3d tours etc. attract increasingly large numbers of visitors. To accommodate this large amount of online visitors, implementation of this recommender system for distributed platforms would be an effort worth making both for its academic value and market potential.

Acknowledgment. This research was partly supported by HEC Grant TDF-029.

References

1. Arjovsky, M., Shah, A., Bengio, Y.: Unitary evolution recurrent neural networks. In: International Conference on Machine Learning, pp. 1120–1128 (2016)
2. Ayyaz, S., Qamar, U., Nawaz, R.: HCF-CRS: a hybrid content based fuzzy conformal recommender system for providing recommendations with confidence. PLOS One **13**(10), 1–30 (2018). https://doi.org/10.1371/journal.pone.0204849
3. Chen, L., Pu, P.: Preference-based organization interfaces: aiding user critiques in recommender systems. In: Conati, C., McCoy, K., Paliouras, G. (eds.) UM 2007. LNCS (LNAI), vol. 4511, pp. 77–86. Springer, Heidelberg (2007). https://doi.org/10.1007/978-3-540-73078-1_11
4. Chung, J., Gulcehre, C., Cho, K., Bengio, Y.: Empirical evaluation of gated recurrent neural networks on sequence modeling. arXiv preprint arXiv:1412.3555 (2014)
5. De Graaff, V., van Keulen, M., de By, R.A.: Towards geosocial recommender systems. In: Proceedings of the 4th International Workshop on Web Intelligence & Communities, p. 8. ACM (2012)
6. Devooght, R., Bersini, H.: Collaborative filtering with recurrent neural networks. CoRR abs/1608.07400 (2016)
7. Anwaar, F., Iltaf, N., Afzal, H., Nawaz, R.: HRS-CE: a hybrid framework to integrate content embeddings in recommender systems for cold start items. J. Comput. Sci. **29**, 9–18 (2018)
8. Hidasi, B., Karatzoglou, A.: Recurrent neural networks with top-k gains for session-based recommendations. In: CIKM (2018)

9. Hidasi, B., Karatzoglou, A., Baltrunas, L., Tikk, D.: Session-based recommendations with recurrent neural networks. arXiv preprint arXiv:1511.06939 (2015)
10. Hidasi, B., Quadrana, M., Karatzoglou, A., Tikk, D.: Parallel recurrent neural network architectures for feature-rich session-based recommendations. In: Proceedings of the 10th ACM Conference on Recommender Systems, pp. 241–248. ACM (2016)
11. Hochreiter, S., Schmidhuber, J.: Long short-term memory. Neural Comput. 9(8), 1735–1780 (1997)
12. Hodoň, M., Eichler, G., Erfurth, C., Fahrnberger, G. (eds.): I4CS 2018. CCIS, vol. 863. Springer, Cham (2018). https://doi.org/10.1007/978-3-319-93408-2
13. Jing, L., et al.: Gated orthogonal recurrent units: on learning to forget. Neural Comput. 31(4), 765–783 (2019)
14. Knoll, J., Groß, R., Schwanke, A., Rinn, B., Schreyer, M.: Applying recommender approaches to the real estate e-commerce market. In: Hodoň, M., Eichler, G., Erfurth, C., Fahrnberger, G. (eds.) I4CS 2018. CCIS, vol. 863, pp. 111–126. Springer, Cham (2018). https://doi.org/10.1007/978-3-319-93408-2_9
15. Qadir, H., Khalid, O., Khan, M.U.S., Khan, A.U.R., Nawaz, R.: An optimal ride sharing recommendation framework for carpooling services. IEEE Access 6, 62296–62313 (2018). https://doi.org/10.1109/ACCESS.2018.2876595
16. Quadrana, M., Karatzoglou, A., Hidasi, B., Cremonesi, P.: Personalizing session-based recommendations with hierarchical recurrent neural networks. In: Proceedings of the Eleventh ACM Conference on Recommender Systems, pp. 130–137. ACM (2017)
17. Ricci, F., Rokach, L., Shapira, B.: Introduction to recommender systems handbook. In: Ricci, F., Rokach, L., Shapira, B., Kantor, P.B. (eds.) Recommender Systems Handbook, pp. 1–35. Springer, Boston, MA (2011). https://doi.org/10.1007/978-0-387-85820-3_1
18. Shearin, S., Lieberman, H.: Intelligent profiling by example. In: Proceedings of the 6th International Conference on Intelligent User Interfaces, pp. 145–151. ACM (2001)
19. Tan, Y.K., Xu, X., Liu, Y.: Improved recurrent neural networks for session-based recommendations. In: DLRS@RecSys (2016)
20. Tonara, D.B., Widyawono, A.A., Ciputra, U.: Recommender system in property business a case study from Surabaya, Indonesia. SPECIAL ISSUE-Int. J. Comput. Internet Manag. 23(May), 30–31 (2013)
21. Wu, C.Y., Ahmed, A., Beutel, A., Smola, A.J., Jing, H.: Recurrent recommender networks. In: Proceedings of the tenth ACM International Conference on Web Search and Data Mining, pp. 495–503. ACM (2017)
22. Yuan, X., Lee, J.H., Kim, S.J., Kim, Y.H.: Toward a user-oriented recommendation system for real estate websites. Inf. Syst. 38(2), 231–243 (2013)

Integration of Fuzzy Clustering into the Case Base Reasoning for the Prediction of Response to Immunotherapy Treatment

Fatima Saadi[1]([✉]), Baghdad Atmani[1]([✉]), and Fouad Henni[2]([✉])

[1] Laboratoire d'Informatique d'Oran (LIO), University Oran 1, Oran, Algeria
saadi_fatima@hotmail.fr, baghdad.atmani@gmail.com
[2] Laboratoire d'Informatique d'Oran (LIO), University of Mostaganem (FSEI),
Mostaganem, Algeria
fouad.henni@univ-mosta.dz

Abstract. The functioning of the medical diagnostic process is very similar to the pattern of the case-based reasoning cycle (CBR). This resemblance has prompted several research groups to build on the CBR, which is a paradigm of problem solving based on past experiences, in the design of medical decision support systems. In this article, we propose a medical decision support system specifically in dermatology based on fuzzy logic to predict the response of a patient with plantar and common warts to immunotherapy treatment. The aim of this work is to improve the retrieval step, which is a very important phase in the CBR cycle, by incorporating segmentation techniques "fuzzy clustering". The proposed approach is composed of two parts; the part of the clustering by the Fuzzy C-Means algorithm and the part of case-based reasoning realized by the JColibri platform. The use of the FCM is to reduce the search space and solve the problem of rapid retrieval of similar cases.

Keywords: Case based reasoning · Datamining · Fuzzy clustering · Decision support · Immunotherapy · jCOLIBRI · Warts disease

1 Introduction

Clinicians or physicians have experience gained through many years of practice. For example, when an experienced clinician faces a new problem (symptoms that are unfamiliar), he/she could begin to analyze the whole situation and try to diagnose based on knowledge, but also by taking advantage of previous situations already diagnosed correctly. This task may take a long time and may lead to not finding a good diagnosis. Previous situations represent a huge help in the daily work of health practitioners. The similarity between the reasoning used in medical diagnosis and case-based reasoning has resulted in several projects that address a variety of medical applications using the CBR for the design of medical decision support systems [1].

The induction of reasoning from cases by physicians is often approximate rather than exact. Fuzzy logic is a mathematical theory whose main objective is the modeling of vague and uncertain notions of natural language. For this purpose, it should exploit the fuzzy reasoning based on cases for medical surveillance support.

C. Djeddi et al. (Eds.): MedPRAI 2019, CCIS 1144, pp. 192–206, 2020.
https://doi.org/10.1007/978-3-030-37548-5_15

In this article, we propose a medical decision support system in dermatology based on fuzzy logic to predict the response of the patient with plantar and common warts to immunotherapy treatment. The objective of this work is to improve the retrieval step using a technique of partitioning "fuzzy Clustering". We opted for the fuzzy c-means (FCM) algorithm. The proposed approach offers the possibility of looking for cases based on past experiences by limiting the search to the most relevant cases resulting from clustering.

The CBR process goes through four stages (Retrieve-Reuse-Revise-Retain) [1]. We are interested in the retrieval phase because of its significant impact on the performance of any case-based reasoning system. This step consists of searching, among the memorized cases, those who have the problem part similar to the new situation to be diagnosed. The step of remembering is based on the calculation of similarity between two problems. In our approach the similarity calculus will be carried out by the method of the k nearest neighbors.

Improving the retrieval stage will save time, which is one of the most important factors in the medical field [1].

To implement our approach, we customized the jCOLIBRI 2.1 case-based reasoning platform [2] according to the characteristics of the application domain.

The article is organized as follows. In Sect. 2, we explain some proposed approaches that use the CBR and Datamining in medical field. In Sect. 3, we explain the principle of the FCM method and we set an example afterwards. In Sect. 4, we present our main contribution and explain the proposed approach. Then in Sect. 5, we give a presentation of experimentation, interpretation and evaluation of results. Finally, Sect. 6 is devoted to the conclusion and some perspectives of this work.

2 State of the Art

Nowadays, many works have directly addressed the use of CBR and datamining techniques for the analysis and prediction of data in the medical field [3]. We quote below some works:

Ramos-Gonz et al. [4] proposed a new CBR framework for the classification of lung cancer subtypes based on microchips. The proposed system is based on the selection of attributes to reduce the number of genes that the system must take into account to evaluate and predict the class of a new case, this system remembers similar cases by the KNN method.

Nasiri et al. [5] proposed a system called DePicT (Diagnosis and Prediction of Diseases using Image Classification and Text Information from Patient Health Records) for diagnosis and medical recommendation. This system uses case-based reasoning by analyzing the image and text of the patient's records. DePicT can find a solution concerning the description of the patient's problem even with partially missing information.

Saraivaa et al. [6] presented a medical decision support system based on case-based reasoning (CBR) and rule-based reasoning (RBR) for the diagnosis of cancer. The system uses as entry the symptoms, signs and personal information of patients. They used rules to define the importance of the latter according to the characteristics of the patient. The exit of the system presents the probability that the patient reaches a type of cancer.

Saadi et al. [1] proposed a medical decision support system to predict the response of patients with plantar and common warts to the immunotherapy treatment. The objective of this work is to improve the retrieval step through the integration of a datamining technique (decision tree) as a discriminating tool that eliminates less pertinent attributes and reduces the number of attributes used in the calculation of similarity in order to accelerate the recuperation of similar cases.

Blanco et al. [7] proposed an approach applied to the area of diagnosis and health published. This approach aims to improve the adaptation phase using association rules to reduce the number of cases and facilitate adaptation rules.

Nilashi et al. [8] developed a case-based reasoning system for breast cancer classification using two techniques of datamining: optimizing expectations (EM) to group data into similar groups, then classification and regression trees (CART) to generate the fuzzy rules used for the classification of breast cancer.

Remembering cases must face a certain degree of vagueness and uncertainty that are almost always encountered while dealing with complex applications of the real world [9]. Banerjeea et al. [10] proposed a decision support system based on CBR for classifying the most common abnormalities in retina images occur due to age related macular degeneration and diabetic retinopathy. The process integrates two methods of datamining: fuzzy C-Means (FCM) is applied to retinal images for partitioning, and decision trees for combining contextual information with images obtained from a database.

Ekong et al. [11] proposed a decision support system based on case-based reasoning, neural networks and fuzzy logic for the diagnosis of depression disorders. Neural networks are used to manage non-linear, noisy or incomplete data. The integration of fuzzy logic into this system provides a means of dealing with inaccuracies and uncertainties in medical data.

Begum et al. [12] presented a case-based reasoning system (CBR) that offers the ability to classify healthy and stressed people based on the fusion of sensor signals. They used fuzzy logic for similarity calculation.

Khelassi et al. [13] developed a decision support system that uses a cognitive amalgam to derive from distributed and heterogeneous knowledge bases. The latter is constructed in a combination of case-based reasoning, distributed reasoning based on rules and fuzzy sets. The objective of this system is to meet the needs of medical applications and improve their efficiency and transparency.

Jagannathan et al. [14] presented a decision support system for radiation therapy treatment planning for brain cancer using case-based reasoning. This system relies on a new measure of similarity that takes into account the no-linear effect of individual case attributes on the similarity measure. The similarity measure uses fuzzy sets.

Benamina et al. [9] developed a fuzzy CBR system for diabetes diagnosis that integrates fuzzy decision tree in the case-based reasoning to improve the response time and accuracy of recovery of similar cases.

3   The Fuzzy C-Means Algorithm (FCM)

Bezdek introduced the Fuzzy C_Means (FCM) classification method in 1981, based on the K-means classification method [16]. FCM has a wide range of applications such as agricultural engineering, astronomy, chemistry, geology, image analysis, medical diagnosis, shape analysis and target recognition [15]. It is an unsupervised clustering technique that groups a set of data in n clusters based on the distance between the data points, and each of these points in the dataset belongs to each cluster with a degree of belonging.

To describe a method for determining the fuzzy membership degree matrix $\underset{\sim}{U}$ that makes it possible to group a collection of "n" sets of data into "c" clusters, we define an objective function J_m:

$$J_m\left(\underset{\sim}{U}, v\right) = \sum_{j=1}^{m} \sum_{i=1}^{c} (\mu_{ik})^{m'} (d_{ik})^2 \tag{1}$$

Where

$$d_{ik} = d(x_k - V_i) = \left[\sum_{j=1}^{m} (x_{kj} - v_{ij})^2\right]^{1/2} \tag{2}$$

μ_{ik} is the membership of the kth data point in the ith class.
d_{ik} is the Euclidean distance between the ith cluster center and the kth data set (data point in $m\psi$ space).
m' is a weighting parameter where $m' \in [1, \infty)$. This parameter controls the amount of fuzziness in the classification process and is discussed shortly [16].
V_i is the ith cluster center, which is described by m features (m coordinates).

Each of the cluster coordinates can be calculated as follows:

$$v_{ij} = \frac{\sum_{k=1}^{n} \mu_{ik}^{m'} \cdot x_{ki}}{\sum_{k=1}^{n} \mu_{ik}^{m'}} \tag{3}$$

Where $j\psi$ is a variable on the feature space, that is $j = 1, 2, \ldots, m$.

An effective algorithm for fuzzy classification, called iterative optimization, was proposed by Bezdek (1981). The steps in this algorithm are as follows [16]:

1. Fix c ($2 \le$ c < n) and select a value for parameter m'. Initialize the partition matrix $\underset{\sim}{U}^{(0)}$. Each step in this algorithm will be labeled r, where r = 0, 1, 2, ...

2. Calculate the $c\psi$ centers $\left\{V_i^{(r)}\right\}$ for each step.

3. Update the partition matrix for the rth step $\underset{\sim}{U}^{(r)}$ as follows:

$$\mu_{ik}^{(r+1)} = \left[\sum_{j=1}^{m}\left(\frac{d_{ik}^{(r)}}{d_{jk}^{(r)}}\right)^{2/(m'-1)}\right]^{-1} \qquad for\ I_k = \phi \qquad (4)$$

Or

$$\mu_{ik}^{(r+1)} = 0,\ for\ all\ class\ i\ where\ i \in \underset{\sim k}{I} \qquad (5)$$

Where

$$I_k = \left\{i|2 \leq c < n; d_{jk}^{(r)} = 0\right\} \qquad (6)$$

And

$$\underset{\sim k}{I} = \{1, 2, \ldots, c\} - \underset{\sim k}{I} \qquad (7)$$

And

$$\sum_{i \in I_k} \mu_{ik}^{(r+1)} = 1 \qquad (8)$$

4. If $\left\|\underset{\sim}{U}^{(r+1)} - \underset{\sim}{U}^r\right\| \leq \varepsilon_L$, stop; otherwise set r = r + 1 and return to step 2.

To illustrate the principle of C_Means in our case study we begin with an example of two variables with four individuals and two clusters from the data set "Immunotherapy" which was extracted from UCI Machine Learning [17].

$$x_{ki} = \left\{\begin{array}{cc} 22 & 2.25 \\ 15 & 3.0 \\ 16 & 10.5 \\ 27 & 4.5 \end{array}\right\}$$

Assuming a weighting factor of $m' = 2$ and a criterion for convergence of $\varepsilon_L = 0,01$, that is,

$$\max_{i,k}\left\|\mu^{(r+1)} - \mu^r\right\| \leq 0.01$$

To begin, the initial fuzzy partition is:

$$\underset{\sim}{U}^{(0)} = \begin{bmatrix} 1 & 1 & 1 & 0 \\ 0 & 0 & 0 & 1 \end{bmatrix}$$

Next is the calculation of the initial centers using Eq. (3), where $m' = 2$:

$$v_{ij} = \frac{\sum_{k=1}^{n} (\mu_{ik})^2 . x_{ki}}{\sum_{k=1}^{n} (\mu_{ik})^2}$$

Where for c = 1,

$$v_{1j} = \frac{\mu_1^2 x_{1j} + \mu_2^2 x_{2j} + \mu_3^2 x_{3j} + \mu_4^2 x_{4j}}{\mu_1^2 + \mu_2^2 + \mu_3^2 + \mu_4^2}$$

$$= \frac{(1)x_{1j} + (1)x_{2j} + (1)x_{3j} + (0)x_{4j}}{1+1+1+0} = \frac{x_{1j} + x_{2j} + x_{3j}}{1^2 + 1^2 + 1^2 + 0}$$

$$V_1 = \{17.66, 5.26\} \begin{cases} v_{11} = \frac{22+15+16}{3} = 17.66 \\ v_{12} = \frac{2.25+3.0+10.5}{3} = 5.25 \end{cases}$$

And for c = 2,

$$v_{2j} = \frac{x_{4j}}{0+0+0+1} \qquad since \ x_{21} = x_{22} = x_{32} = 0$$

$$V_2 = \{27, 4.5\} \begin{cases} v_{21} = \frac{27}{1} = 27 \\ v_{22} = \frac{4.5}{1} = 4.5 \end{cases}$$

Now the distance measures (distances of each data point from each cluster center) are found using Eq. (2):

$$d_{11} = \sqrt{(22 - 17.66)^2 + (2.25 - 5.26)^2} = 5.27 \quad d_{21} = \sqrt{(22 - 27)^2 + (2.25 - 4.5)^2} = 5.48$$

$$d_{12} = \sqrt{(15 - 17.66)^2 + (3 - 5.26)^2} = 3.48 \quad d_{22} = \sqrt{(15 - 27)^2 + (3 - 4.5)^2} = 12.09$$

$$d_{13} = \sqrt{(16 - 17.66)^2 + (10.5 - 5.26)^2} = 5.50 \quad d_{23} = \sqrt{(16 - 27)^2 + (10.5 - 4.5)^2} = 12.52$$

$$d_{14} = \sqrt{(27 - 17.66)^2 + (4.5 - 5.26)^2} = 9.36 \quad d_{24} = \sqrt{(27 - 27)^2 + (4.5 - 4.5)^2} = 0.0$$

With the distance measures, we can now update $\underset{\sim}{U}$ using Eqs. (6) and (8) (for $m' = 2$), that is,

$$\mu_{jk}^{(r+1)} = \left[\sum_{j=1}^{c} \left(\frac{d_{ik}^{(r)}}{d_{jk}^{(r)}} \right)^2 \right]^{-1}$$

And we get

$$\mu_{11} = \left[\sum_{j=1}^{c}\left(\frac{d_{11}}{d_{j1}}\right)^2\right]^{-1} = \left[\left(\frac{d_{11}}{d_{11}}\right)^2 + \left(\frac{d_{11}}{d_{21}}\right)^2\right]^{-1} = \left[\left(\frac{5.27}{5.27}\right)^2 + \left(\frac{5.27}{5.48}\right)^2\right]^{-1} = 0.51$$

$$\mu_{12} = \left[\left(\frac{d_{12}}{d_{12}}\right)^2 + \left(\frac{d_{12}}{d_{22}}\right)^2\right]^{-1} = \left[1 + \left(\frac{3.48}{12.09}\right)^2\right]^{-1} = 0.92$$

$$\mu_{13} = \left[\left(\frac{d_{13}}{d_{13}}\right)^2 + \left(\frac{d_{13}}{d_{23}}\right)^2\right]^{-1} = \left[1 + \left(\frac{5.50}{12.52}\right)^2\right]^{-1} = 0.83$$

$$\mu_{14} = \left[\left(\frac{d_{14}}{d_{14}}\right)^2 + \left(\frac{d_{14}}{d_{24}}\right)^2\right]^{-1} = \left[1 + \left(\frac{9.36}{0}\right)^2\right]^{-1} = 0.0$$

The new membership functions form an updated fuzzy partition, which is given as:

$$\underset{\sim}{U}^{(1)} = \begin{bmatrix} 0.51 & 0.92 & 0.83 & 0.0 \\ 0.49 & 0.08 & 0.17 & 1.0 \end{bmatrix}$$

To determine whether we have achieved convergence, we choose a matrix norm $\|$ such as the maximum absolute value of pairwise comparisons of each of the values in $\underset{\sim}{U}^{(0)}$ and $\underset{\sim}{U}^{(1)}$; for example:

$$\max_{i,k}\|\mu^{(1)} - \mu^{(0)}\| = 1.75 > 0.01.$$

This result suggests that our convergence criteria has not yet been satisfied, so we need another iteration of the method.

For the next iteration, we proceed by again calculating cluster centers, but now using values from the latest fuzzy partition, $\underset{\sim}{U}^{(1)}$;

For c = 1,

$$= \frac{(0.51)x_{1j} + (0.92)x_{2j} + (0.83)x_{3j} + (0)x_{4j}}{0.51 + 0.92 + 0.83 + 0} = \frac{x_{1j} + x_{2j} + x_{3j}}{0.51^2 + 0.92^2 + 0.83^2 + 0}$$

$$V_1 = \{16.96, 5.58\}\begin{cases} v_{11} = \frac{0.51(22) + 0.92(15) + 0.83(16)}{2.28} = 16.96 \\ v_{12} = \frac{0.51(2.25) + 0.92(3.0) + 0.83(10.5)}{2.28} = 5.58 \end{cases}$$

For c = 2:

$$= \frac{(0.49)x_{1j} + (0.08)x_{2j} + (0.17)x_{3j} + (1)x_{4j}}{0.49 + 0.08 + 0.17 + 1} = \frac{x_{1j} + x_{2j} + x_{3j} + x_{4j}}{0.49^2 + 0.08^2 + 0.17^2 + 1^2}$$

$$V_2 = \{24.03, 4.36\} \begin{cases} v_{21} = \frac{0.49(22) + 0.08(15) + 0.17(16) + 1(27)}{1.71} = 24.03 \\ v_{22} = \frac{0.49(2.25) + 0.08(3.0) + 0.17(10.5) + 1(4.5)}{1.71} = 4.36 \end{cases}$$

The new membership function is as follows:

$$\underset{\sim}{U}^{(2)} = \begin{bmatrix} 0.06 & 0.82 & 0.85 & 0.12 \\ 0.93 & 0.18 & 0.15 & 0.88 \end{bmatrix}$$

Now using the values of $\underset{\sim}{U}^{(2)}$;

For c = 1:

$$= \frac{(0.06)x_{1j} + (0.82)x_{2j} + (0.85)x_{3j} + (0.12)x_{4j}}{0.06 + 0.82 + 0.85 + 0.12} = \frac{x_{1j} + x_{2j} + x_{3j} + x_{4j}}{0.06^2 + 0.82^2 + 0.85^2 + 0.12^2}$$

$$V_1 = \{16.96, 5.58\} \begin{cases} v_{11} = \frac{0.06(22) + 0.82(15) + 0.85(16) + 0.12(27)}{1.86} \approx 16.96 \\ v_{12} = \frac{0.06(2.25) + 0.82(3.0) + 0.85(10.5) + 0.12(4.5)}{1.86} \approx 5.58 \end{cases}$$

For c = 2:

$$= \frac{(0.93)x_{1j} + (0.18)x_{2j} + (0.15)x_{3j} + (0.88)x_{4j}}{0.93 + 0.18 + 0.15 + 0.88} = \frac{x_{1j} + x_{2j} + x_{3j} + x_{4j}}{0.93^2 + 0.18^2 + 0.15^2 + 0.88^2}$$

$$V_2 = \{24.03, 4.36\} \begin{cases} v_{21} = \frac{0.93(22) + 0.18(15) + 0.15(16) + 0.88(27)}{2.14} \approx 24.03 \\ v_{22} = \frac{0.93(2.25) + 0.18(3.0) + 0.15(10.5) + 0.88(4.5)}{2.14} \approx 4.36 \end{cases}$$

We see that these two cluster centers are identical to those from the first step, at least to within the stated accuracy of (0.01); hence, the final partition matrix will be unchanged, to an accuracy of two digits, from that obtained in the previous iteration.

4 Contribution

The objective of the proposed approach is to predict the response of the patient with plantar and common warts to immunotherapy treatment. The architecture of the proposed approach is shown in Fig. 1. It is composed of two complementary parts; the fuzzy clustering part and the case-based reasoning part using the JColibri platform.

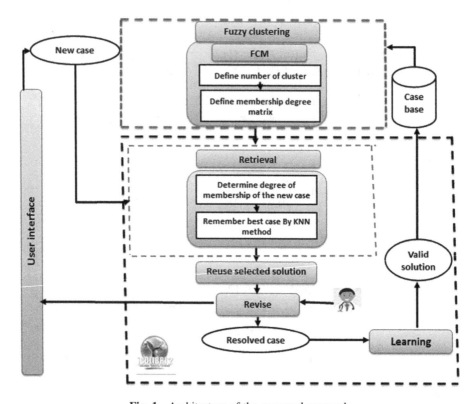

Fig. 1. Architecture of the proposed approach

The dataset was extracted from the UCI Machine Learning Repository [17]. Data was collected in the dermatology clinic of Ghaem Hospital in Mashhad (Iran) between January 2013 and February 2015, from 90 patients with plantar and common warts who have referred to the dermatology clinic [1]. These two types of warts are the most common [18]. The dataset consists of seven features gathered when the immunotherapy method was applied. These features are depicted in Table 1. These features, as important factors for treatment, were selected based on the physician's opinion [18]. The class attribute in these datasets is the Response to Treatment feature.

- Fuzzy Clustering

Clustering techniques can be used to reduce the search space and facilitate search in the case base. In previous work [19], we proposed an approach guided by CBR and clustering using the k-means method.

The K-means algorithm necessarily assigns a point to one of the classes giving them the same credibility. But this is highly questionable for some individuals where the attachment to one class rather than another holds very little in the calculation of distances to centers of gravity. To solve this problem, we opted for fuzzy clustering (Fuzzy C-means FCM) which introduces an indicator of membership degree to classes.

Table 1. Features employed in the immunotherapy [19]

Feature name	Semantic	Value
X1: Sex	Gender	41 Man 49 Woman
X2: Age	Age (year)	15–56
X3: Time	Time elapsed before treatment (months)	0–12
X4: Number of warts	The number of warts	1–19
X5: Type	Type of warts	Common (47) Plantar (22) Both (21)
X6: Area	Surface area of biggest wart (mm^2)	6–900
X7: Induration diameter	Induration diameter of the initial test (mm)	5–70
Y: Result of treatment	Response to treatment	Success or Failure

In fuzzy clustering, each point has a probability of belonging to each cluster, rather than belonging completely to a single cluster, as is the case in traditional k-means.

In [19], we have partitioned the case base "immunotherapy" by the k-means method into six clusters (the choice of the cluster number is done by the elbow method). We obtain as a result a boolean matrix of 0 and 1. The 1 indicates the presence of cases in the cluster and the 0 indicates the absence of this case in the cluster.

We then apply the FCM method on our case base; we give it as an input parameter the matrix deduced from the k-means method as membership degree matrix instead of using random values.

The output of this step gives us a membership degree matrix of each case in each cluster.

- Case based reasoning using jCOLIBRI

When a new case arrives, the system restarts the FCM method to calculate its degree of membership in each cluster.

The retrieval step is done in the jCOLIBRI platform; similar cases are selected based on the similarity calculation. We used the KNN method to calculate the similarity.

We take from the resulting matrix of the FCM (membership degree matrix) the two clusters to which the new case has a high degree of membership and that is the advantage over the K-means. It is up to say instead of searching in one and only one cluster, with FCM we search in more than one cluster and that gives us a high percentage to find the case similar to the new problem.

- Similar cases will be adapted to the new problem to predict the result of the treatment.
- The revision consists in validating the solution adapted by the expert who is the doctor.

- If the generated solution does not exist in the case base and is considered a success in the revision step, this new case is added to the case base which allows the system to learn.

5   Implementation and Experimentation

To study the effectiveness of our approach, we have developed a medical decision support system based on CBR, as mentioned above. In this study, we used the immunotherapy dataset available on the official website of the UCI (Machine Learning repository). Each case is described by 8 attributes where each case consists of a problem part and a solution part. The problem part is described by a set of relevant attributes that we call descriptors. The solution part represents the result of the treatment (0 to say failure, 1 to say success) (Fig. 2).

```
<?xml version="1.0"?>
<!DOCTYPE hibernate-mapping PUBLIC "-//Hibernate/Hibernate Mapping DTD//EN" "http://hibernate.sourceforge.net/hibernate-mapping-3.0.dtd">
<hibernate-mapping default-lazy="false">
<class name="jcolibri.test.test1.ImmunoDescription" table="Immunotherapy">

    <id name="Id" column="Id">
      <generator class="native"/>
    </id>
    <property name="Sexe" column="Sexe"/>
    <property name="Age" column="Age"/>
    <property name="Time" column="Time"/>
    <property name="Number_of_Warts" column="Number_of_Warts"/>
    <property name="Type" column="Type"/>
    <property name="Area" column="Area"/>
    <property name="Induration_diameter" column="Induration_diameter"/>
    <property name="num_c" column="num_c"/>

</class>
</hibernate-mapping>                             Problem part of the case
<?xml version="1.0"?>
<!DOCTYPE hibernate-mapping PUBLIC "-//Hibernate/Hibernate Mapping DTD//EN" "http://hibernate.sourceforge.net/hibernate-mapping-3.0.dtd">
<hibernate-mapping default-lazy="false">
<class name="jcolibri.test.test1.ImmunoSolution" table="Immunotherapy">

    <id name="Id" column="Id">
      <generator class="native"/>
    </id>
    <property name="Result_of_Treatment" column="Result_of_Treatment"/>

</class>
</hibernate-mapping>
                                                Solution part of the case
```

Fig. 2. XML representation of cases.

The data collected were reported in a table to form a data file in CSV (Comma Separated Values) format. Since jCOLIBRI uses ".txt" files to generate the basis of the system case, it was necessary to add a feature (to jCOLIBRI) that allows to filter the data from a ".csv"file format.

After its launching, the system loads functions of the case base and configuration is started. At the same time, the system executes the FCM method and partitions the case base into six clusters in order to generate the membership degree matrix of each case in each cluster.

Once the loading is completed, the system is in the form of a simple interface which makes it possible to launch a request. This request obviously represents the case of a new patient with either plantar or common warts or both.

In addition, we provide the opportunity for the physician to define the number of cases to remember. This last option is used to modify the "Cycle" function of the jCOLIBRI main interface "StandardCBRApplication" by adding a parameter to allow the doctor to choose the number of cases to remember to give an effective decision [19].

The system goes to the retrieval stage and re-executes the FCM algorithm to generate the two clusters to which the new case has a membership high degree and searches in these two clusters for the best similar case instead of searching throughout the case base. At the end of this phase the system displays to the user the best cases resulting from the retrieval. These cases are displayed in descending order of similarity. The user can consult the cases one by one and then choose the case that he/she thinks most appropriate. After this choice, the user can make changes (adjustments) to the proposed solution. This solution with the query represents a case that the system has just solved (Fig. 3).

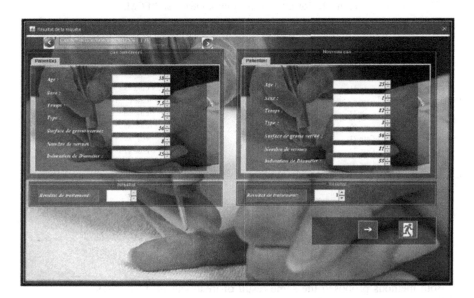

Fig. 3. Result interface

Once the solution is adjusted by the doctor, the system gives the possibility to retain this new case and integrates it into the case base (learning), or leave it in a temporary case base that we have added to our application where the user may decide to get extra time before deciding on the retention of this new case. Subsequently, the user can from time to time, consult the temporary case base to complete cases and/or decide to retain a few cases.

To evaluate the effectiveness of our approach, we found it interesting to compare it with the results obtained in [19]. For this, we evaluated the FCM method and the k-means method on the same case base to make a comparison between these two methods. The purpose of these methods is to find a solution to the target case.

We propose a set of target cases (cases that belong to our case base) on which we apply clustering with both methods and recall by K-NN (K = 3).

Table 2. shows the results obtained by the two methods:

The K-means method will provide the best cluster, the three best similar cases with the degrees of similarity and response to treatment.

The FCM method will provide the two best clusters with the membership degree of the new case to these clusters, the three best similar cases with the degrees of similarity and response to treatment.

Table 2. Results obtained by k-means and FCM.

New case	K-means				FCM				
	No. cluster	No. Similar case	Similarity degree	Response to treatment	No. cluster	Membership degree	No. similar case	Similarity degree	Response to treatment
Case no. 10	1	Case 23	0.32	Failure	5	0.28	Case 10	0.0	Failure
		Case 90	0.40	Success	2	0.25	Case 17	0.29	Success
		Case 11	0.41	Success			Case 45	0.37	Success
Case no. 6	2	Case 6	1	Success	4	0.29	Case 6	0.0	Success
		Case 72	0.20	Success	3	0.25	Case 66	0.22	Success
		Case 66	0.22	Success			Case 36	0.23	Failure
Case no. 81	2	Case 21	0.34	Success	4	0.32	Case 81	0.0	Success
		Case 32	0.40	Success	3	0.23	Case 71	0.33	Success
		Case 6	0.47	Success			Case 42	0.34	Success
Case no. 32	1	Case 61	0.51	Success	4	0.28	Case 32	0.0	Success
		Case 63	0.58	Success	3	0.26	Case 4	0.25	Failure
		Case 74	0.59	Success			Case 6	0.27	Success
Case no. 89	3	Case 10	0.42	Failure	5	0.26	Case 89	0.0	Failure
		Case 27	0.45	Success	2	0.26	Case 21	0.25	Failure
		Case 18	0.45	Success			Case 59	0.27	Success

Both methods proposed the same result of treatment in most cases.

The k-means method failed to find the cluster that contains the best case therefore it could not give the exact similar case, unlike the c-means method which managed to find the best similar case with a total similarity (similarity degree = 0).

6   Conclusion

In this paper we proposed an approach based on case-based reasoning (CBR) and fuzzy clustering (FCM) for medical decision support in dermatology.

Our proposition consists in the integration of FCM into the CBR cycle to reduce the search space and speed up the search for a similar case.

We applied our approach on a real case base which concerns the diagnosis of plantar and common warts disease. The purpose of this approach is to provide help to physicians to predict the response of immunotherapy treatment to patients with wart disease.

Experimentation has shown that our approach based on fuzzy clustering (C-Means) has made it possible to answer the problem of rapid recall of similar cases.

As a future projection of this work, it would be interesting to use treatment plans in the solution part of the source cases to apply our clustering-based fuzzy retrieval on these plans, to inform the patient not only of the diagnosis with a certain degree and to propose him a general plan to follow, but also to offer him/her a suitable adapted plan for his own case, that is to say a fuzzy adaptation application on treatment plans.

References

1. Saadi, F., Atmani, B., Henni, F.: Integration of datamining techniques into the CBR cycle to predict the result of immunotherapy treatment. In: 2019 International Conference on Computer and Information Sciences (ICCIS), pp. 1–5. IEEE, April 2019
2. Bello-Tomás, J.J., González-Calero, P.A., Díaz-Agudo, B.: JColibri: an object-oriented framework for building CBR systems. In: Funk, P., González Calero, P.A. (eds.) ECCBR 2004. LNCS (LNAI), vol. 3155, pp. 32–46. Springer, Heidelberg (2004). https://doi.org/10.1007/978-3-540-28631-8_4
3. Choudhury, N., Begum, S.A.: A survey on case-based reasoning in medicine. Int. J. Adv. Comput. Sci. Appl. 7(8), 136–144 (2016)
4. Ramos-González, J., López-Sánchez, D., Castellanos-Garzón, J.A., de Paz, J.F., Corchado, J.M.: A CBR framework with gradient boosting based feature selection for lung cancer subtype classification. Comput. Biol. Med. 86, 98–106 (2017)
5. Nasiri, S., Zenkert, J., Fathi, M.: A medical case-based reasoning approach using image classification and text information for recommendation. In: Rojas, I., Joya, G., Catala, A. (eds.) IWANN 2015. LNCS, vol. 9095, pp. 43–55. Springer, Cham (2015). https://doi.org/10.1007/978-3-319-19222-2_4
6. Saraiva, R.M., Bezerra, J., Perkusich, M., de Almeida, H.O., de Siebra, C.: A hybrid approach using case-based reasoning and rule-based reasoning to support cancer diagnosis: a pilot study. In: MedInfo, pp. 862–866 (2015)
7. Blanco, X., Rodríguez, S., Corchado, J.M., Zato, C.: Case-based reasoning applied to medical diagnosis and treatment. In: Omatu, S., Neves, J., Rodriguez, J.M.C., Paz Santana, J. F., Gonzalez, S.R. (eds.) Distributed Computing and Artificial Intelligence. AISC, vol. 217, pp. 137–146. Springer, Cham (2013). https://doi.org/10.1007/978-3-319-00551-5_17
8. Nilashi, M., Ibrahim, O., Ahmadi, H., Shahmoradi, L.: A knowledge-based system for breast cancer classification using fuzzy logic method. Telemat. Inform. 34(4), 133–144 (2017)
9. Benamina, M., Atmani, B., Benbelkacem, S.: Diabetes diagnosis by case-based reasoning and fuzzy logic. IJIMAI 5(3), 72–80 (2018)
10. Banerjee, S., Chowdhury, A.R.: Case based reasoning in the detection of retinal abnormalities using decision trees. Procedia Comput. Sci. 46, 402–408 (2015)
11. Ekong, V.E., Inyang, U.G., Onibere, E.A.: Intelligent decision support system for depression diagnosis based on neuro-fuzzy-CBR hybrid. Mod. Appl. Sci. 6(7), 79 (2012)
12. Begum, S., Ahmed, M.U., Barua, S.: Multi-scale entropy analysis and case-based reasoning to classify physiological sensor signals, edited by Lamontagne, L., Recio-Garcia, J.A., p. 129 (2012)

13. Khelassi, A., CHIKH, M.A.: Cognitive Amalgam with a Fuzzy sets and case based reasoning for accurate cardiac arrhythmias diagnosis, edited by Lamontagne, L., Recio-Garcıa, J.A., p. 69 (2012)

14. Jagannathan, R., Petrovic, S., McKenna, A., Newton, L.: A fuzzy non-linear similarity measure for case-based reasoning systems for radiotherapy treatment planning. In: Papadopoulos, H., Andreou, A.S., Bramer, M. (eds.) AIAI 2010. IAICT, vol. 339, pp. 112–119. Springer, Heidelberg (2010). https://doi.org/10.1007/978-3-642-16239-8_17

15. Yong, Y., Chongxun, Z., Pan, L.: A novel fuzzy c-means clustering algorithm for image thresholding. Measur. Sci. Rev. **4**(1), 11–19 (2004)

16. Ross, T.J.: Fuzzy Logic with Engineering Applications, vol. 2. Wiley, New York (2004)

17. UCI Machine Learning Repository Homepage. https://archive.ics.uci.edu/ml/datasets/Immuno therapy+Dataset. Accessed 28 June 2019

18. Khozeimeh, F., Alizadehsani, R., Roshanzamir, M., Khosravi, A., Layegh, P., Nahavandi, S.: An expert system for selecting wart treatment method. Comput. Biol. Med. **81**, 167–175 (2017)

19. Saadi, F., Atmani, B., Henni, F.: A medical decision making support system for the prediction of response to immunotherapy treatment. In: 2019 International Conference on Computing (ICC2019) (June, 2019, submitted)

Music Generation Using an Interactive Evolutionary Algorithm

Majid Farzaneh and Rahil Mahdian Toroghi$^{(\boxtimes)}$

Iran Broadcasting University (IRIBU), Tehran, Iran
Majid.Farzaneh91@gmail.com, mahdian@iribu.ac.ir

Abstract. Music generation with the aid of computers has been recently grabbed the attention of many scientists in the area of artificial intelligence. Deep learning techniques have evolved sequence production methods for this purpose. Yet, a challenging problem is how to evaluate a music generated by a machine. In this paper, a methodology has been developed based upon an interactive evolutionary optimization method, with which the scoring of the generated musics are primarily performed by human expertise, during the training. This music quality scoring is modeled using a BiLSTM recurrent neural network. Moreover, the innovative generated music through a Genetic algorithm, will then be evaluated using this BiLSTM network. The results of this mechanism clearly show that the proposed method is able to create pleasurable melodies with desired styles and pieces. This method is also quite fast, compared to the state-of-the-art data-oriented evolutionary systems.

Keywords: Music generation · Evolutionary algorithm · BiLSTM neural network

1 Introduction

Music is a ubiquitous, undeniable, and perhaps the most influential part of a media content. It can easily facilitate, transferring of the emotion and concepts in an artistic, and delicate way. This motivates the music accompaniment with all media types and human-oriented places, such as movies, theaters, games, shops, and so on in order to bring human pleasure.

For a machine to create an automatic enjoyable music it should imitate the rules, know-how and subtleties embedded in a pleasurable music or a famous masterpiece of an artist. This could be extracted from a rich database of artistic musics being played by famous musicians, and then being learned to the machine.

There are several methods introduced so far in order to generate musical melodies automatically, such as Hidden Markov Models [2,5,7,20,23–25], models based on artificial neural networks [3,4,8,10,18,22,27,31], models based on the evolutionary and population-based optimization algorithms [11,14,26,30], and models based on local search algorithms [6,9]. Recently, the sequential deep neural networks especially Long Short-Term Memory (LSTM) neural networks

© Springer Nature Switzerland AG 2020
C. Djeddi et al. (Eds.): MedPRAI 2019, CCIS 1144, pp. 207–217, 2020.
https://doi.org/10.1007/978-3-030-37548-5_16

has become prevalently used and achieved successful results generating time series sequences [1, 19, 21].

Music generation can be viewed from different aspects. One can focus on melody generation, while other can work specifically on harmony and rhythm. In terms of data, the music generation methods could also be divided into note-based and signal-based methods. In former, the machine should learn music from the music sheets, while in latter the musical audio signals are learned. Music generation can also be discussed in terms of the difficulty of performing [20, 29], and the narrative [12].

The major questions in this regard are; what kind of music do we prefer to be generated by machine? Do we need new styles to be created, or we want the machine to resort and imitate the existed musics? How the quality of the generated music could be evaluated by machine? Are we able to generate new musics analogous to the manuscripts of a famous musician by machine, and how this similarity could be certified?

In this study, our assumption is that human will judge about the quality of generated musics, and will give them scores. Thereafter, the human scoring will be modeled using a Bi-directional Long-Short-Term Memory (BiLSTM) neural network. This neural network based system will supersede the human scoring system, and will perform as a standard evaluator of the musics generated by optimization-based models. The proposed music generation system of our paper is based on Genetic algorithm, which performs as a note-based method to create melodies.

The novelty of this paper is two-fold. First, the interaction between human and machine in order to generate new meaningful and pleasurable music, and second is introducing a new scoring model in order to evaluate the generated melodies.

The rest of the paper is arranged as follows. Next section belongs to the literature. In section III, the proposed method has been represented in three phases. Then, the experimental results have been provided and analyzed. The paper is then terminated by our conclusion in section V, followed by the cited references.

2   Related Works

The proposed method uses an evolutionary regime to generate melodies. Evolutionary algorithms have been used vastly in the literature for music generation and many other problems. In [28], authors have combined genetic algorithm with genetic programming to create an interactive evolutionary computation system. This system works for the precise composition of rhythms. However, it requires a human agent to listen to the generated rhythms along the way, and therefore is very time-consuming. In [15], authors introduced an interactive music composition system which is driven by the feature evolution. In this work, particle swarm optimization and genetic algorithm have been used to examine the convergence behavior of a two-level technique in an objective manner. In [17], the presented system uses hill climbing method to create short melodies. In this work, the authors use a grammar-based evaluation, and similarity incorporate preexisted melodies to evolve them.

In [13], an evolutionary-based algorithm has been proposed which represents musical pieces as a set of constraints which change over time, and form the musical contexts which allow composing, reusing and reshaping musical fragments. The system implements a multi-objective optimization which aims for statistical measures and structural features of evolved models. In [16], a data-based melody generation system has been introduced which uses a multi-objective evolutionary computation. In this work, the authors use several evaluation methods simultaneously to calculate the fitness of each generated melody by Non-dominated Sorting Genetic Algorithm II (NSGA-II).

According to the related works, most of the proposed interactive systems, are permanently interactive, and a human must supervise the system all the time. In this paper, we have modeled the human scoring using an LSTM neural network. So, after the system has trained, the proposed system can generate melody, independently.

3   The Proposed Music Generation System

The proposed method consists of three major phases. First, a Genetic algorithm (GA) is used to generate a vast spectrum of melodies, from bad ones up to pleasurable ones. The bad melodies, are the ones that are made randomly, when GA starts. In the second phase, the outputs of GA are given to the humans to be scored from zero to 100. Then, these generated and scored melodies are trained by a BiLSTM neural network. This network, when trained by a sufficient amount of musical data and associated scores, would perform as a performance evaluator of the GA music generator system. At the end, the GA musics which can maximize the BiLSTM output as the objective function are played, as the generated pleasurable musics.

3.1   Phase I. Generating Training Melodies

As already mentioned, this interval involves with providing the necessary training data (i.e. melodies) for the next phase. Genetic algorithm has been chosen for this task. The reason is that, GA can generate a population of melodies (chromosomes) randomly, with vast spectrum of qualities. These melodies are generated in the form of ABC notations[1], and then at each iteration, the best melodies among the population are selected based on their similarity to the human made melodies, which are taken from the manuscripts of the most famous musicians. Therefore, a dataset of melodies has to be used as part of the fitness function. Then, the number of 2-gram, 3-gram, and 4-gram structures in generated

---

[1] For more information, please refer to www.abcnotation.com.

melodies are computed, which also exist in the dataset. Then, the fitness function is calculated as,

$$\text{Fitness}(C_i) = N_2 + 10\,N_3 + 100\,N_4 \tag{1}$$

where C_i is the ith chromosome, and N_2, N_3, and N_4 are the number of Bi-grams, Tri-grams, and 4-grams, respectively.

If we set the database for a specific genre, the generated musics will be very much similar to that specific genre, as well. To make this stronger, we calculate the probability of each character (i.e., the characters in ABC notation regime which are going to be played) in the dataset as in the following equation,

$$P(character_i) = \frac{N_i}{N_{total}} \tag{2}$$

where N_i is the number of occurrences of the character$_i$, in the entire dataset, and N_{total} is the total number of characters in the dataset. Hereafter, whenever GA generates new melodies, it makes characters occur according to these probabilities. For example, if note G repeated 100 times in database, and there are 5000 characters overall in the database, the probability of character G will be 0.02 and if GA goes to generate 100 characters for a random melody, 2 characters among those 100 should be G. Therefore, we lead GA make melodies more like the dataset.

The crossover and mutation are applied, then on selected chromosomes (melodies) at each iteration. The **crossover** is applied as follows,

> **for** $i = 0$ to D **do**
>   **if** $rand \geq 0.5$ **then**
> $child(i) = best1(i)$
>   **else**
> $child(i) = best2(i)$
>   **end if**
> **end for**

where D is the chromosome length, $rand$ is a uniform random number between 0 to 1, $best1$ and $best2$ are the selected chromosomes and $child$ is a new chromosome after crossover.

The **mutation** is applied, as follows,

> **for** $i = 0$ to D **do**
>   **if** $rand \geq 0.1$ **then**
> $child(i) = best1(i)$
>   **else**
> $child(i) = random_m elody(i)$
>   **end if**
> **end for**

During GA generation, we save all the generated melodies for the scoring purposes and making the training data for the second phase.

The music generation system tries to produce similar to the melodies. The execution time of music generation is high, since it should compare every generated melody with a large dataset note-by-note, and three times. What we desire is to generate new melodies which are pleasurable for the audience, furthermore to be similar to the existing melodies. To achieve this, we need another phase to be implemented.

3.2 Phase II. LSTM-Based Evaluation Model

To simulate the human scoring mechanism, a BiLSTM neural network has been used. The reason is that the melodies are somewhat a reasonable and sensible sequence of the musical notes being chained to represent a meaningful and pleasurable sensing atmosphere to the audience. This sequence justifies using of recurrent neural networks. LSTM neural network is a solution to that. Bidirectional LSTM (aka BiLSTM) is an LSTM whose parameters represent the forward and backward correlations of the adjacent notes or frames of the musical signal, both.

For a generated music to be qualified as pleasurable, a high score should be assigned to it by human assessment. This score could be within 0 to 100 boundary values. Therefore, we have used the melodies as input to the BiLSTM network and the average of the scores as the output of it. This GA based generated melodies would never be obtainable again, since they are directly used as the training data for the network. The BiLSTM, after being sufficiently trained would be a qualified evaluation system for the quality and pleasurability of the generated musical melodies.

3.3 Phase III. The Proposed Music Generation System

This phase is the same as the first one, except that the objective function being used is different. The flowchart of the proposed music generation system is depicted in Fig. 1.

4 Experimental Results

The proposed architecture, shown in Fig. 1, has been implemented in MATLAB framework. For the phase I, the **Campin** dataset[2] which contains 200 different European melodies in ABC notation has been used. Figure 2 shows the note probabilities in this dataset.

As already mentioned, the GA algorithm in phase I and III are almost the same, except for the performance function they are going to optimize which is different. The initial settings of the genetic algorithms in these two phases are depicted in Table 1. The experimental settings associated to the BiLSTM neural network, are as follows:

- The BiLSTM hidden layer size, is 50
- Number of epochs for the training phase is 5000
- The cost function being used in BiLSTM training, is the mean square of error (mse)
- Melody size for both phases (I and III) contain 30 notes.

---

[2] http://abcnotation.com/tunes.

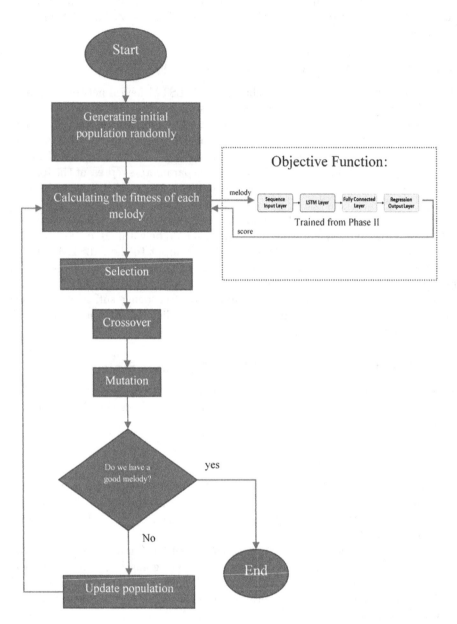

Fig. 1. The entire proposed music generation system. The GA algorithm performs as the generator system, both for training the evaluator system, and for the final generation system. Using the automatic evaluator, the produced melodies are chosen among the most pleasurable ones created from the GA population.

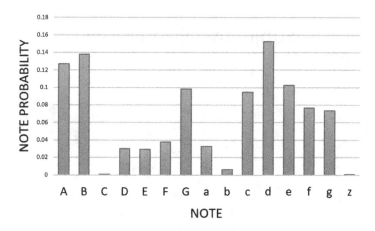

Fig. 2. Notes vs. their probability of occurrence in Campin (European melodies) dataset. Notes are represented in ABC notation standard.

During the human evaluation, we generated 6 melodies through phase I, and 6 melodies through phase III, and then we asked from 20 audiences to give these melodies their scores within 0 to 100. These 12 melodies are available on YouTube [3]. Figure 3 shows the mean of the scores taken from these 20 audiences and the standard deviation of the scores for each melody.

Even though, the genetic algorithms of phase I, and phase III are pretty similar, the execution time of these two phases differ drastically. For the training phase, the execution time is quite dependent on the number of notes it is going to generate, whereas in generation phase (Phase III) the execution time is almost independent of the number of notes it is going to generate and it remains constant. Figure clearly shows this property. This could be explained due to the heavy search the algorithm is going to do note-by-note during the training phase, as explained before (Fig. 4).

Table 1. The initial setting values

Parameter	Phase I	Phase III
Maximum iteration	2000	500
Population size	20	20
Crossover rate	0.5	0.5
Mutation rate	0.1	0.1
Fitness function	Similarity to Campin dataset	BiLSTM neural network

---

[3] https://www.youtube.com/watch?v=Ci6DHEwAYcQ&feature=youtu.be.

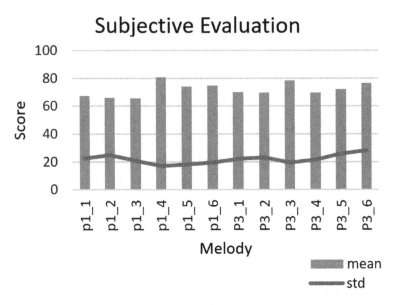

Fig. 3. Subjective evaluation of the pleasurability of the melodies, scored by 20 listeners

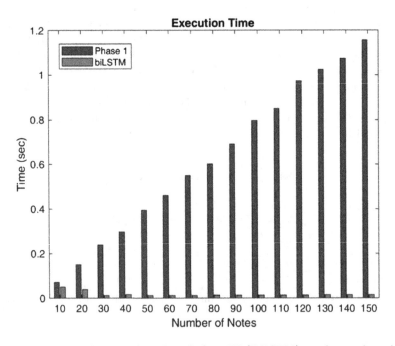

Fig. 4. The execution time at phase I, and phase III (BiLSTM) vs. the number of notes

5 Conclusion

In this paper, the problem of automatic music generation based on interactive (human and machine) evolutionary optimization (here Genetic Algorithm) has been proposed. The goal of the architecture is to enable a machine to generate melodies which are pleasurable, and meaningful. Initially, the evaluation of what machine generates is performed by the listeners, however when a BiLSTM neural network learns how the human evaluates the pleasurable property of the melodies, it supersedes the human and does the task independently. Finally, the GA algorithm generates a population of melodies, among which those with highest scores (evaluated by the neural network) are chosen to be released. The experiments have been performed on Campin dataset, and the results have been satisfying (pleasurable and consistent) for the audiences in a subjective evaluation study. The generation process has been fairly fast, which makes this method outperform the data-based evolutionary systems.

References

1. Agarwal, S., Saxena, V., Singal, V., Aggarwal, S.: LSTM based music generation with dataset preprocessing and reconstruction techniques. In: 2018 IEEE Symposium Series on Computational Intelligence (SSCI), pp. 455–462. IEEE (2018)
2. Agres, K., Herremans, D., Bigo, L., Conklin, D.: Harmonic structure predicts the enjoyment of uplifting trance music. Front. Psychol. **7**, 1999 (2017)
3. Agres, K.R., DeLong, J.E., Spivey, M.: The sparsity of simple recurrent networks in musical structure learning. In: Proceedings of the Annual Meeting of the Cognitive Science Society, vol. 31 (2009)
4. Boulanger-Lewandowski, N., Bengio, Y., Vincent, P.: Modeling temporal dependencies in high-dimensional sequences: application to polyphonic music generation and transcription. arXiv preprint arXiv:1206.6392 (2012)
5. Brooks, F.P., Hopkins, A., Neumann, P.G., Wright, W.V.: An experiment in musical composition. IRE Trans. Electron. Comput. **3**, 175–182 (1957)
6. Browne, T.M., Fox, C.: Global expectation-violation as fitness function in evolutionary composition. In: Giacobini, M., et al. (eds.) EvoWorkshops 2009. LNCS, vol. 5484, pp. 538–546. Springer, Heidelberg (2009). https://doi.org/10.1007/978-3-642-01129-0_60
7. Davismoon, S., Eccles, J.: Combining musical constraints with Markov transition probabilities to improve the generation of creative musical structures. In: Di Chio, C., et al. (eds.) EvoApplications 2010. LNCS, vol. 6025, pp. 361–370. Springer, Heidelberg (2010). https://doi.org/10.1007/978-3-642-12242-2_37
8. Eck, D., Schmidhuber, J.: A first look at music composition using LSTM recurrent neural networks. Istituto Dalle Molle Di Studi Sull IntelligenzaArtificiale **103**, 48 (2002)
9. Herremans, D.: Morpheus: automatic music generation with recurrent pattern constraints and tension profiles (2016)
10. Herremans, D., Chuan, C.H.: Modeling musical context with word2vec. arXiv preprint arXiv:1706.09088 (2017)
11. Herremans, D., Sörensen, K.: Composing first species counterpoint with a variable neighbourhood search algorithm. J. Math. Arts **6**(4), 169–189 (2012)

12. Herremans, D., Sörensen, K.: Composing fifth species counterpoint music with a variable neighborhood search algorithm. Expert Syst. Appl. **40**(16), 6427–6437 (2013)
13. Hofmann, D.M.: A genetic programming approach to generating musical compositions. In: Johnson, C., Carballal, A., Correia, J. (eds.) EvoMUSART 2015. LNCS, vol. 9027, pp. 89–100. Springer, Cham (2015). https://doi.org/10.1007/978-3-319-16498-4_9
14. Horner, A., Goldberg, D.E.: Genetic algorithms and computer-assisted music composition. In: ICMC 1991, pp. 479–482 (1991)
15. Kaliakatsos-Papakostas, M.A., Floros, A., Vrahatis, M.N.: Interactive music composition driven by feature evolution. SpringerPlus **5**(1), 826 (2016)
16. Ponce de León, P.J., Iñesta, J.M., Calvo-Zaragoza, J., Rizo, D.: Data-based melody generation through multi-objective evolutionary computation. J. Math. Music **10**(2), 173–192 (2016)
17. Loughran, R., McDermott, J., O'Neill, M.: Grammatical music composition with dissimilarity driven hill climbing. In: Johnson, C., Ciesielski, V., Correia, J., Machado, P. (eds.) EvoMUSART 2016. LNCS, vol. 9596, pp. 110–125. Springer, Cham (2016). https://doi.org/10.1007/978-3-319-31008-4_8
18. Makris, D., Kaliakatsos-Papakostas, M., Karydis, I., Kermanidis, K.L.: Combining LSTM and feed forward neural networks for conditional rhythm composition. In: Boracchi, G., Iliadis, L., Jayne, C., Likas, A. (eds.) EANN 2017. CCIS, vol. 744, pp. 570–582. Springer, Cham (2017). https://doi.org/10.1007/978-3-319-65172-9_48
19. Manzelli, R., Thakkar, V., Siahkamari, A., Kulis, B.: An end to end model for automatic music generation: combining deep raw and symbolic audio networks. In: Proceedings of the Musical Metacreation Workshop at 9th International Conference on Computational Creativity, Salamanca, Spain (2018)
20. McVicar, M., Fukayama, S., Goto, M.: AutoLeadGuitar: automatic generation of guitar solo phrases in the tablature space. In: 2014 12th International Conference on Signal Processing (ICSP), pp. 599–604. IEEE (2014)
21. Mishra, A., Tripathi, K., Gupta, L., Singh, K.P.: Long short-term memory recurrent neural network architectures for melody generation. In: Bansal, J.C., Das, K.N., Nagar, A., Deep, K., Ojha, A.K. (eds.) Soft Computing for Problem Solving. AISC, vol. 817, pp. 41–55. Springer, Singapore (2019). https://doi.org/10.1007/978-981-13-1595-4_4
22. Lewis, J.P.: Creation by refinement and the problem of algorithmic music composition. In: Todd, P.M., Loy, G. (eds.) Music and Connectionism, p. 212. MIT Press, Cambridge (1991)
23. Pachet, F., Roy, P., Barbieri, G.: Finite-length Markov processes with constraints. In: Twenty-Second International Joint Conference on Artificial Intelligence (2011)
24. Papadopoulos, A., Roy, P., Pachet, F.: Avoiding plagiarism in Markov sequence generation. In: Twenty-Eighth AAAI Conference on Artificial Intelligence (2014)
25. Pinkerton, R.C.: Information theory and melody. Sci. Am. **194**(2), 77–87 (1956)
26. Scirea, M., Togelius, J., Eklund, P., Risi, S.: Affective evolutionary music composition with metacompose. Genet. Program. Evolvable Mach. **18**(4), 433–465 (2017)
27. Todd, P.M.: A connectionist approach to algorithmic composition. Comput. Music J. **13**(4), 27–43 (1989)
28. Tokui, N., Iba, H., et al.: Music composition with interactive evolutionary computation. In: Proceedings of the Third International Conference on Generative Art, vol. 17, pp. 215–226 (2000)
29. Tuohy, D.R., Potter, W.D.: A genetic algorithm for the automatic generation of playable guitar tablature. In: ICMC, pp. 499–502 (2005)

30. Waschka II, R.: Composing with genetic algorithms: *GenDash*. In: Miranda, E.R., Biles, J.A. (eds.) Evolutionary Computer Music, pp. 117–136. Springer, London (2007). https://doi.org/10.1007/978-1-84628-600-1_6
31. Wu, J., Hu, C., Wang, Y., Hu, X., Zhu, J.: A hierarchical recurrent neural network for symbolic melody generation. arXiv preprint arXiv:1712.05274 (2017)

Author Index

Printed in the United States
By Bookmasters